WITHDRAWN

WITHDRAWN

GREAT AMERICAN RACE DRIVERS

GREAT AMERICAN RACE DRIVERS

by Bill Libby

COWLES BOOK COMPANY, INC.

NEW YORK

For Jo

SBN 402-14191-1
Library of Congress Catalog Card Number 79-104361
Cowles Book Company, Inc.
A subsidiary of Cowles Communications, Inc.
Published simultaneously in Canada by
  General Publishing Company, Ltd.
  30 Lesmill Road, Don Mills, Toronto, Ontario
Printed in the United States of America
First Edition

CONTENTS

ACKNOWLEDGMENTS

This was a complicated venture and the author is indebted to many persons, especially to Ron Buehl and Cowles Book Company for the opportunity to do it; to Bon Tronolone for his assistance in gathering photos; and to the subjects themselves.

The author wishes also to thank the following for their cooperation and help: Al Bloemker, Charlene Ellis, Bud Jones, Donald Davidson, Bob Shafer, Bob Thomas, Ross Russell, Darryl Norenberg, Wally Parks, Bob Russo, Bob Carey, Joe Scalzo, T. Taylor Warren, Carol Aaronson, Chris Economaki, Robert Daley, Collene Campbell, Dennis O'Grady, Dennis Bender, John Meador, William Dredge, Allan Krause, John Fowler, Chuck Barnes, Bill Marvel, Paul Preuss, Dennis Shattuck, Al Silverman, Robert Pope, and others at USAC, NASCAR, and the NHRA; the Indianapolis, Ontario, Milwaukee, and Daytona racetracks; *Sport, Car Life,* and *Stock-Car Racing* magazines; the Ford, Firestone, Goodyear, STP, Fram, Mickey Thompson, and Rapid Pace companies; as well as many others the author may have, but should not have, overlooked, including all of the photographers not named herein who took so many splendid pictures.

ROSTER OF DRIVERS

Below are the drivers profiled, in brief or in detail, and the chapters in which the bulk of their stories appear.

Mario Andretti	13	Fred Lorenzen	6
Art Arfons	9	Rex Mays	3
Buck Baker	4	Tom McEwan	10
Tony Bettenhausen	12	Lou Meyer	3
Craig Breedlove	9	Tommy Milton	2
Jimmy Bryan	12	Ralph Mulford	2
Bob Burman	2	John Mulligan	10
Gordon Collett	10	Jimmy Murphy	2, 14
Earl Cooper	2	Barney Oldfield	2
Ralph De Palma	2, 14	Danny Ongais	10
Tim Flock	4	David Pearson	6
A. J. Foyt	1, 14	Lee Petty	4
Don Garlits	10	Richard Petty	5, 14
Richie Ginther	8	Don Prudhomme	10
Masten Gregory	7	Eddie Rickenbacker	2
Dan Gurney	8, 14	Fireball Roberts	4
Jim Hall	7	Mauri Rose	3
Ray Harroun	2	Eddie Sachs	12, 14
Allen Heath	11	Wilbur Shaw	3
Phil Hill	8	Carroll Shelby	7
Ted Horn	3	Mickey Thompson	9
Jim Hurtubise	11	Curtis Turner	4
Bobby Isaac	6	Bill Vukovich	12
Ned Jarrett	6	Rodger Ward	13
Junior Johnson	4	Joe Weatherly	4
Parnelli Jones	12	Cale Yarborough	6
Frank Lockhart	2	Lee Roy Yarbrough	6

PROLOGUE

The great race driver must be the finest of athletes and the bravest of men. He must be smart, strong, and quick, as well prepared, well conditioned and cool under pressure as most great athletes. And he must perform his profession surrounded by injury and death such as haunt few men in their lives.

The great race driver must be able to handle different kinds of cars, some of them small and light, some of them large and heavy, all high-powered and fragile, over different kinds of tracks. Some tracks are loose dirt, some paved, some high-banked ovals, some winding road courses, some short and some long.

The great driver must take his car to the greatest possible speed it can tolerate and still hold together. He must keep it running and maintain sufficient control to stay on the course, not hit other cars, and pass them in fast, heavy, shifting traffic. He takes his car to the thin edge of disaster and no further. He is playing with inches for perhaps hours, and he has only a fraction of a second in which to make critical decisions. He cannot afford many mistakes and perhaps no serious ones.

There have been many mediocre men throughout the history of racing. Only a few drivers have attained greatness. Almost all drivers have crashed at one time or another. For the most part, only the great ones come back from crashes and carry on as before.

The automobile as we know it is an invention of modern times, yet men have been racing cars since they were first developed more than sixty years ago. In this time, many great race drivers have emerged around the world. A large number have been Americans, and they have raced successfully in the United States and other countries. In this book, we are concerned with the greatest of the American race drivers, wherever they have raced.

Contrary to what one might imagine, there is no special type of person who becomes a race driver. As the reader will learn, drivers come in various forms—large men, small men, bold men, cautious men, rich men, and poor men. Some have been hard, serious, withdrawn men, some soft, playful, extroverted characters. One was the son of an opera singer; another was the son of a woman who grew flowers. Many were the sons of race drivers or mechanics.

From the earliest to the latest, the great race drivers have had one thing in common—a love of auto racing. For one does not do this dangerous thing if he does not want very much to do it. Over the years, the circumstances have changed—the types of cars, the tracks, the speeds—but the spirit that has stirred drivers has remained constant.

Some men have built their own cars and worked on them themselves, but all had help, for it is not possible to win important races without costly and well-built cars provided by owners and sponsors and tended by mechanics. Some drivers have had more help than others, and consequently they have had greater chances to win races and achieve greatness. But in choosing the most outstanding we must be governed primarily by accomplishment, not by what might have been.

Many drivers, though not most, have died while racing. Others have been severely injured. It is the nature of the business, this cruelest of sports. And in telling these stories of the immortals, we have had to tell it as it has been, including the injuries and deaths. We can only try to put this element of racing in a proper perspective, without trying to hide it or place too much emphasis on it.

No man should suggest to another that he become a race driver. Every driver enters the sport of his own free will. Clearly, there must be something quite special in this most dramatic of sports that makes men want to live fast, even at the risk of dying young. Possibly it can be found in the following pages.

Bill Libby
Los Angeles, California

1

THE GREATEST
AMERICAN RACE DRIVER

Anthony Joseph Foyt, Jr., was hooked early on the narcotic of racing.
A. J. was born and raised in Houston, Texas, where his father, a former
race driver and mechanic, ran a garage. When he was three years old his
father gave him a bloodred miniature racer. "I thought that little ol' car
was the most beautiful thing there ever was," A. J. recalls. He took to it
as if he had been born in it. When he was six, he was driving the car in
exhibitions between races at a local track.

When A. J. was eleven, his father and mother took one or two midget
cars they owned to a race out of town and left the other at home. When
they returned that night, they found their backyard torn up and their racer
parked in the garage and scorched by fire. After his parents had gone, A. J.
had run it hard until it caught fire. He had jumped out, extinguished the
fire, put the car away, and gone to bed. His parents went into his room to
look at him, but he pretended to be asleep. They didn't awaken him. In the
morning, they bawled him out and he apologized, but they were sort of
proud of him. And A. J. wasn't really sorry.

At seventeen, he quit school and began to race motorcycles. Then he
raced jalopies, old stock cars, and new stock cars. Later he drove midget
cars and sprint cars, which are versions of Indianapolis championship cars.
He campaigned the dusty, dangerous bush-league tracks of the Southwest,
and wherever he drove he won more than his share of races. He was strong
and skilled, fearless and cocky. He wanted to become a race driver and he
felt sure he would become the greatest.

Every year for five years he managed to scrape up the cash to go to the
Indianapolis 500, the greatest of races. In 1958, when he was twenty-three
years old, he was offered and accepted a chance to drive in the United

States Auto Club circuit, the major leagues of American racing. Primarily, this circuit is made up of around twenty championship trail races each year (that is, races of one hundred miles or more on tracks of a mile or more for Indianapolis-styled cars; it also includes what are called "title tours" in sprint car, midget car, and stock car racing).

Foyt sped swiftly to success. He had grown into a big, handsome kid, a six-foot two-hundred-pounder with dark curly hair. He had married a pretty blonde girl and had begun a family. He was a tough Texan who laughed and loved and brawled his way through life, cursing, arguing with promoters, rivals, and his own crew. He was a very bad loser. But he was a good winner, modest and gracious.

Sometimes it seemed he simply was willing to drive harder and take more chances than others in order to win. It wasn't long before the great drivers recognized Foyt's rare ability. Another great driver, Jimmy Bryan, once said of him, "From the first time I saw him, I could see that he was stronger, smarter, and less scared than most drivers."

Veteran Rodger Ward has said, "He is just willing to put himself in places on racetracks other drivers won't go."

Parnelli Jones has said, "I think I succeeded in racing because I had more determination than most drivers. But Foyt had more than I had, more than anyone else ever had. I would do almost anything to win a race. Foyt would do anything."

Foyt says of himself, "I could never settle for being anything but the best. I could never stand to be second. I always loved racing more than anything else in life, and if I couldn't be the best at it, my life wouldn't mean much to me."

For his first couple of years, he did not race the championship trail continually and won only a few races of consequence. In 1958, he qualified for his first 500. At twenty-five he was the youngest driver in the starting field. He drove through a first-lap accident that crippled seven cars and killed driver Pat O'Connor and drove well until just past the 350-mile mark, when he slid on an oil slick and spun out. He was unable to finish the race.

The following year, he drove the full 500 miles and finished tenth. In 1960, his car gave out at the 235-mile mark. However, in September, he won his first championship race, a 100-miler on the dirt track at Du Quoin, Illinois. He wound up the year by winning four of the last six races on the tour, and won his first national driving title.

In 1961, he won his first 500. He started seventh and took over the lead after Parnelli Jones's engine went sour. For most of the race, he fought veterans Eddie Sachs and Rodger Ward, a former winner. In the late stages, he battled only Sachs. Leading, with only twenty-five miles to go, A. J. ran out of fuel and had to go into the pits to refuel. It seemed that Sachs had beaten him, but then, with only eight miles to go, Sachs had to stop to replace a worn-out tire. Foyt won the dramatic duel by a mere eight seconds.

It was a heartbreaking loss for Sachs, but a stirring triumph for Foyt, who was now on his way to greatness. That year he won three other races on tour and his second straight national championship to become the youngest man ever to win the 500 and the United States crown in the same season.

In 1962, he won three of the first four races on the championship trail, but lost the 500. He was the victim of an incredibly careless act. One of his crew neglected to tighten a wheel after a change during a pit stop. Foyt had just rolled away from the pits and was in the lead when the wheel flew off the car. Somehow he succeeded in executing a safe stop in the infield, emerged from the cockpit in grimy disgust, and stood there cursing his crippled car. Then he ran a mile back to the pits, hoping for a chance to relieve a tired driver and race another car. He simply wanted to continue racing, even with little chance of doing anything worthwhile.

After the Indianapolis accident, he fired most of his pit crew. The season went sour on him. He led many races, but he could not finish many because his cars broke down repeatedly. Late in the season, he fired his chief mechanic, George Bignotti. Then he rehired him. Foyt was always hiring, firing, and rehiring Bignotti. They argued continually. Bignotti said, "Foyt is a brilliant driver and a brilliant mechanic, but you can't drive and be your own chief mechanic. He just can't leave his mechanics alone. He changes things around, then blames me when they don't work."

Some racing people said Foyt pushed his cars beyond their limits. But Foyt replied, "I drive them hard enough to win. I don't ask anything of them they're not supposed to do."

Rodger Ward, who had won the point-rich 500, wound up with enough points to beat out Foyt for the title. Foyt didn't like Ward and he didn't like losing the title. That season and the next, "Tough Tony" changed sponsors three times in search of the support and equipment he felt he needed to win. In 1963, his luck changed and he won five races to regain the national championship, even though his car in the 500 was not sound and he had to struggle to finish third with it.

Foyt did not like to drive races he could not win, though he was willing to keep going to finish as high as he could. Along the way, he tried big-time sports car racing and won the 252-mile Nassau Trophy Race in the Bahamas against an international field of star drivers. He drove as many as forty or fifty races a year in all kinds of cars, whatever he could fit into his schedule. "If there's a race somewhere, I seem to want to be in it," he has admitted.

In 1964, Foyt hit his peak. He set records by winning seven straight championship races and ten in all, including his second 500, to gain an unprecedented fourth national title. The 500 was a hard-earned, if somewhat hollow, triumph. By this time, the electricity of change had been generated at the Speedway. A few years before, drivers had come over from the European Grand Prix circuit to introduce lightweight, rear-engine cars to the American classic, and by 1964 these cars clearly were the fastest there, though not yet the safest. Foyt, who grew up in bulky cars on dirt tracks, was one of the old guard, reluctant to turn from the traditional front-engine heavyweights favored by Speedway veterans.

On the second lap of the 500 that year, rookie Dave McDonald, driving one of the new cars, lost control, crashed, and exploded in flames. Black smoke obscured the track and veteran Eddie Sachs, who was also driving one of the new cars, ploughed into him, forming a funeral pyre. Both men died and several other cars cracked up. The race had to be halted while the track was cleared. During the wait, Foyt sat on the ground alongside his roadster and said, "I never have trusted those funny cars. I dread the day when I'll be driving one."

After the race was resumed, Foyt found he could not keep up with the new-style cars driven by Bobby Marshman and Jim Clark. However, they broke down and Foyt found himself locked in a battle of heavyweights with Parnelli Jones. Then Jones's car exploded during a pit stop and Foyt went on to win his second 500 three miles ahead of the second-place Rodger Ward.

That year, while sitting in a motel coffee shop one morning a few days before a race, Foyt talked about living with death. "It hurts when you lose friends. Hell, we got feelings like anyone else. A good guy goes and you want to park your car and chuck your helmet in the cockpit and walk away from it," he said. "But this is our business. Death and injury are part of the sport. Not as big a part as some want you to believe. But a part. We all live with it. We all know it can happen to us. We accept it because we want to race. We try not to make too many close friends. But you can't live with guys and not make friends."

There were drivers all around him in the coffee shop, laughing, cutting up. One was kidding another about a flip he had taken in a recent race.

Race drivers like to joke with one another about accidents that are not fatal. They take pride in their toughness. They're like children who play a deadly game for a living.

By the end of the 1964 season, Foyt seemed to have just about everything a man could want. Turning thirty, still young and handsome, although his hair was thinning out, he and his lovely wife, Lucy, his teen-age sweetheart, had three healthy children. He had a lavish home in Houston and a plush vacation house on a lake. He owned several cars and boats, as well as an airplane he piloted himself. He had investments in stocks, oil wells, and various other businesses, as well as considerable ready cash. He could afford not to work another day for the rest of his life. While sitting on some old tires in a racetrack infield he pondered his success. "I know the longer I drive, the greater the risks, but I'm no more worried about it than I ever was. Everyone wants me to retire," he said with a smile, "except me."

Then in January, while Foyt was driving a stock car on the Riverside road-racing course near Los Angeles, his brakes failed him. He was running at 140 miles per hour just behind cars driven by Junior Johnson and Marvin Panch. As they entered a turn, the cars in front of Foyt slowed down, but his brakes were dead. He had a fraction of a second to figure out a course of action.

"You don't exactly reason it out," he said later. "Hellamighty, there is no time for debate. If you've been doing this thing awhile, you get the picture right away and react by instinct."

Foyt knew that if he rammed either or both of the cars in front of him, he might survive but they might not. He didn't think he could get around them and stay on the track, but he figured he had to try. "You want to live, but if you live, you have to live with yourself," he explained.

He wrenched his steering wheel hard to the left and cut to the inside, tried to straighten out, hung on the rim of the track for a long moment, then slid off and hurtled down the embankment, bouncing end over end, one hundred feet high, fifty feet high, twenty-five feet high, before settling down in a steaming, crumpled heap at the bottom of the gully. Rescue workers pried him from the bent metal and rushed him to a hospital. He had fractured bones in his back and one heel. Almost all of the skin had been scraped from his body.

Foyt was placed in a cast and lay flat on his back for several weeks. When the cast was cut off, he was strapped into a brace and permitted to walk a little with crutches. Three months after the accident, he limped into Atlanta Raceway to run another stock car race. When he was asked what he was doing there in his condition, he stuffed his hands in a windbreaker, made a sour face, shrugged, and replied with the question, "Where else should I be?" Another driver reported, "He hurts so much he can't sleep nights, but he won't admit it."

One-third of the way through the race, Foyt came charging up on Panch again, when his throttle stuck. A. J. could not slow down. "I thought, uh-oh, here we go again," he recounted later. This time, however, there was room on the high side. Foyt scraped a wall but slid to a safe stop. Disappointed, he walked back to the pits. Then, however, Panch signaled his crew that he was feeling sick and needed relief. Panch was in the lead at the time. Foyt was offered the car and accepted without hesitation. Panch came in, jumped out, and Foyt jumped in and took off. He never surrendered the lead and won the race.

The following month, still hurting and limping, he was back at Indianapolis. This time, he had one of the new cars, a Lotus-Ford. He was practicing one afternoon, when a rear wheel broke off at 160 miles per hour. He slid almost a thousand feet out of control, backed rear end first into an outside wall, then shot across the track front end first into an inside wall. Along the way another wheel broke off, flew up, and rolled across his helmet and shoulders. As the car ploughed to a stop in the infield grass, Foyt jumped out. When the rescue crews reached him, he was circling the car, asking over and over, "Am I all right? Am I all right?"

Finally, calming himself, he crouched by the car and inspected the damage. "When this thing hit the wall the first time, I had my seat belt undone," he said. "I told myself that this thing may catch fire, but it's not going to be Foyt that burns."

Fortunately, the car had not caught fire. Foyt had to go to a medical station to be examined. The doctor was astonished to discover that A. J.'s pulse rate was already back to normal. Foyt said, "Hurry up, doc, I got to go back and get my car fixed up."

Foyt managed to have his car ready in time for the first day of qualifying time trials. Early in the day Scotland's Jim Clark set new record speeds of 160.9 miles per hour for one lap and an average of 160.7 for four laps of the two-and-one-half-mile oval. He was still being applauded as Foyt rolled out for his trial. Foyt promptly surpassed the invader, winning the coveted pole for the first time in his career with new records of 161.9 miles per hour for one lap and 161.2 for four. The spectators cheered him wildly. No one considered Foyt a sentimentalist, so it was surprising when he announced patriotically, "I'm glad to get the record back for America."

He was not able to win the race for America, however. Foyt's car went sour just short of the three-hundred-mile mark and Clark went on to win. Depressed, Foyt admitted, "Maybe it's time to quit." But he did not and went on to win five championship trail races, plus the Firecracker 400 against the South's best stock car drivers for the second straight year. In spite of Foyt's performances, Mario Andretti placed high more consistently and nosed him out for the United States crown.

During the season, Foyt finally fired Bignotti for good and hired Johnny Pouelson, who had been Parnelli Jones's mechanic. Bignotti said, "Foyt may be the greatest driver, but Parnelli's a lot easier to live with." Within a year, Foyt fired Pouelson, too, making himself his own chief mechanic and hiring his father to do much of the work.

But 1966 turned out to be his worst year. At Indianapolis he was involved in a first-lap crash that removed eleven cars from contention. As the cars slid around the track on their bellies with wheels broken off and bounding around, Foyt skidded to stop, climbed a fence in front of the grandstand, and hung there like a monkey while fans laughed at his undignified act. He didn't win a big race all year. Three times in his career he had earned more than $100,000 a year. One year, he had earned $179,000. In 1966, he made only $30,000. And his newest challenger, Mario Andretti, won his second straight United States crown.

Still, Foyt pressed on. He began to build his own cars, which he called Coyotes, and to field his own racing teams with the sort of ample sponsorship support his prestige commanded. As a result, 1967 was a different story. This was the year Andy Granatelli brought a turbine-powered car to Indianapolis with Parnelli Jones as pilot. Foyt knew he could not outrun Jones, so he simply decided to outrun everyone else and hope Jones's turbine would not last. It was a shrewd strategy. Jones led most of the race and was far ahead near the finish. With eight miles to go, a ballbearing broke in the gearbox of his turbine and the car shivered and died. Foyt heard the crowd roar and knew it meant something had happened to Jones. Moments later, he drove past his rival, who was parked in the infield, and took the lead.

"All of a sudden I had a third 500 victory in my hands, as many as any man has ever won," Foyt later recalled. "I had a funny feeling something would happen. It's not like me, but I got cautious all of a sudden."

He swept around the track once, twice. As he drove into the final turn of the final lap, all hell broke loose directly in front of him. Five cars, many laps behind him, but in front of him in the traffic, tangled, and in that instant the track was full of cars skidding out of control. Wheels and metal rained like hailstones out of the skies. The crowd stood erect in shock. Dust obscured the scene and most figured Foyt had crashed just as he was within reach of victory.

But he had not. Responding coolly to the pressure, A. J. had braked sharply, sought holes, and picked his way through the debris. He came out clean on the other side and accelerated down the straightaway to take the checkered flag. Al Unser came in second, and Joe Leonard, in another car built and prepared by the Foyt team, took third place. In "victory lane," Foyt accepted the cheers, the kisses, the trophies, and the laurel wreaths. At the victory banquet, he also accepted the winner's check for $171,527.

In France twelve days later, he co-drove a Ford sports car with Dan Gurney in Europe's most classic auto-racing contest, the 24 Hours of Le Mans. It was his first try at this brutal endurance test. He and Gurney left all opposition far behind. From day to night to day again, they covered more than 3,220 miles at an average speed of more than 135 miles per hour. This was 10 miles per hour faster than anyone ever had negotiated the tortuous road course before. No other man has won both Indy and Le Mans, and to win both in one season was even more remarkable.

Foyt won four other championship trail races that season. But, going into the campaign's last event, a 300-mile race at Riverside, he had only a narrow lead in points over Andretti for the national title. If Andretti placed high, Foyt also had to do well to retain his edge. During the race, A. J. tangled with Al Miller in a turn and spun to a stop in the mud. His car was out of the race. Meanwhile, Andretti was contending for the lead. However, Foyt could yet pick up points by driving relief. He rushed back to the pits to take over his sister car from Jim Hurtubise, but it stalled. Foyt rushed over to Roger McCluskey's pit and signaled his friend. McCluskey came in and turned over his car to A. J. Late in the race, the engine began to come apart, but Foyt nursed it along. He finished fifth. Andretti finished second, falling short by a few points to give Foyt his fifth national title.

In 1968, Foyt dropped out of the 500 at the 215-mile mark when his car's rear end gave way. Still, he won four races on the championship trail that year, though Bobby Unser, who won the 500, took the United States title. However, Foyt captured four races on the stock car tour at

50, 100, 200, and 250 miles to take the USAC crown. Throughout the year, he had won many sprint, midget, and stock car races, though he had not concentrated on any one of these divisions enough to win.

In the last year of the 1960s, his seventeenth year of racing, "Super-Tex," as some called him, captured the pole position at the Indianapolis Speedway for the second time in his career with a speed of more than 170 miles per hour. During the race he fought for the lead for more than half the distance until his engine went sour. Even then, as he fell farther and farther back, he kept going until flagged down in eighth place at the finish.

In the last few miles of the race, he had thrilled the crowd by twice passing the leader, Mario Andretti. Foyt had just wanted to race, even though Andretti was several laps ahead by then. Mario went on to win his third United States crown. Foyt did not win a championship race until September, when for the sixth time he captured the "Hoosier Hundred" on the Indiana State Fairgrounds dirt oval, a race he virtually owns. In 1970, he qualified third fastest for the 500, challenged the leaders for a while, but broke down near the finish. He did, however, win the Riverside 500 stock car classic, in which he had been injured five years earlier.

Perhaps his 1969 performance is an indication that Foyt is on his way out. However, one would be a fool to write him off. He has bounced back too many times before. As mentioned earlier, Foyt is the first man in history to win more than $1 million in racing, and he has become a wealthy man with many successful business ventures. He may want to spend more time with his wife and his three children, who are growing up. Possibly he would like to get out of the sport while he is still safe. He turned thirty-five in 1970, so he is not old as race drivers go. But he has worked hard and risked much for what he has, and he admits that he is tempted by the soft life.

Still, he is a proud man, perhaps disinterested in glory, but aware of his standing and hungry to put records out of reach of other drivers. He ranks as the greatest American race driver of all time, probably the greatest single race driver of any nation. Some drivers have dominated their particular circuits—for example, Richard Petty in southern stock car competition and Juan Manuel Fangio on the worldwide Grand Prix tour—but few have challenged other circuits as successfully as Foyt has. Jim Clark has won two Grand Prix titles and Indy, too, but he has never won as many titles or races as Foyt, who has won at Indy, Daytona, Nassau, and Le Mans.

Even the most critical racing experts would find it hard to diminish

Foyt's achievements. Perhaps it could be said that he fell into all three of his Indianapolis victories and never has dominated one of the classic races all the way as some drivers have. But the fact remains that he has won three times at Indianapolis, plus far more championship races than any other man. Some consider him primarily a dirt track driver. True, most of his championship trail victories have occurred on dirt. Certainly he ranks as the greatest dirt track driver of all time. This makes him something of a dinosaur because the dirt tracks are rapidly disappearing. But this rough form of racing may be the most challenging of all. And Foyt still has won more paved track races on the championship trail than most other drivers. And he has won in both front-engine heavyweights and rear-engine lightweights.

Most of the records available to him are his. He has won more than a hundred big-time races; forty-two championship trail races; five national championships; twenty-six sprint car races, more than any other driver. He has also won close to forty stock car and midget car races. As he turns into the 1970s, Foyt is obviously far ahead of the field.

What is left? A fourth Indianapolis 500 crown, certainly. No man ever has won that many. A Grand Prix victory, possibly, though it is unlikely he will shoot for one. More championship trail victories and another United States crown, perhaps. Before the 1970 season began, Mario Andretti had won thirty races on the tour, and he had a third national title. It seems there is always a young tiger coming along to threaten the king.

More than anything else, however, it appears that A. J. Foyt simply does not want to stop racing. Some drivers are like this, though none as much as Foyt. Some suffer in pursuit of their passion, but Foyt has always enjoyed racing—small races as well as big races, poor races as well as rich ones. He is stimulated by the challenge of competition, often to the point of risking his life unnecessarily.

Once, after he had qualified for the 500 and was waiting for the race to begin a few days later, Foyt entered a small, unimportant race on a dangerously incomplete track for an insignificant purse. In order to win he had to drive through a wild accident. Afterward, Parnelli Jones was asked what he thought Foyt would do if his sponsor asked him to quit running such risks with the Indy jackpot at stake. Jones smiled and said, "I guess ol' A. J. would just tell him to go to hell."

Told this, A. J. grinned and said, "I reckon that's what I would do."

The year Foyt won $170,000 in purses, he entered a Terre Haute sprint car race worth $1,500 to the winner, not a particularly large prize.

A big crowd was on hand, but it rained so hard that the drivers refused to run. The promoter of the event pleaded with Foyt to qualify, hoping that the other drivers would follow suit and that he would not have to refund the fans' money. Foyt agreed, though the muddy track held his speed down. Then the sun appeared and the track dried out. The other drivers decided to qualify. Enjoying improved conditions, they bumped Foyt out of the starting field. Angrily, Foyt paid the last-place qualifier for his position, took the unfamiliar car, and came from far behind to win the race. Later he laughed, "Oh, lordy, but the boys are burned up."

It is competition, not cash, that inspires him. That same year, while warming up for a stock car race in Milwaukee, he blew up his engine in practice. Rather than stay on the sidelines, he took over an unfamiliar last-place car, started last, and won again.

Another year, at Sacramento, near the end of what had been a dismal season for him, with nothing of consequence at stake, Foyt's championship car went sour. He yanked the mechanics away and worked on it under a hot sun until the last possible moment. Then, soiled and sweaty, he jumped in, limped into the field, and drove like a demon into first place. Even when the car began to sputter again, Foyt kept going because he would not quit. He did not win, but came close.

In 1969, when Foyt's championship car broke down before a race on a paved track, he pulled his dirt track car off a truck and ran it in the race. With this type of car, he obviously had no chance of keeping up with the leaders, but he ran as hard as he could all the way and took eighth place, much to the pleasure of the devoted fans who had come just to see him in action.

Odd as it may seem, Foyt once gave a powerful display of his compelling desire to win in a harness horse race, not an auto race. As a stunt, promoters at the Indiana State Fairgrounds staged a race between Foyt and Parnelli Jones. As they went out in the sulkies, or little carriages pulled by harness horses, Foyt said to Jones, "Look, buddy, we don't know anything about these things. If we push too hard, we're liable to be carried off in pieces. What say we stroke it most of the way and come up to the homestretch even? Then, as we hit the straight, we can go to the whips and go for the win."

Parnelli replied, "Fine, that sounds good to me."

So they played it cool most of the way around. As they entered the last turn, Parnelli turned to Foyt so they could take off together. But at that moment, Foyt was giving his horse a whack with his whip. Foyt's horse bolted ahead. Angrily, Jones began to drive his animal, but Foyt was too far ahead. Foyt won. Jones laughs about it now, but he has never really forgiven Foyt.

Foyt is the greatest athlete that this writer has ever seen. However, he has a lot of imperfections, too, being moody and temperamental. He has been fined and suspended for punching a promoter in a dispute over money, and another driver in a dispute over racing tactics. If he had not been who he was, he might have been barred from racing for such behavior. He has also been cruel to his crews. He has insulted his sponsors. He once drove a race on one company's tires while wearing another tire company's emblems. He has taken money from a sponsor to use a product and then returned the money because he thought he had a better chance to win with another sponsor's product.

Over the years he has mellowed somewhat, but he remains his own man, going his own way. Winning still matters more to him than anything else, perhaps more than it should. But if winning is not important in professional sports, what is? Why would men risk their lives in auto races? To lose like sportsmen?

Foyt may have scared men off the track, but he has never deliberately run another driver off to win a race. He may be surly and harsh with a writer or a fan before a race, but he will be pleasant and understanding the next day. He may be bitter after a loss, but he will be modest after a victory.

Balding now, marked like a battle-scarred tiger, but still full of energy and ready for fun, Foyt remains an awesome figure as he heads into the seventies. Not long ago, while sitting in the shade of some oil cans in a greasy pit area, he said, "I have a home and a family, but I also have a home in the cockpit of a racing car on a racing track and a family of friends who are drivers. They know what this thing is for me. If it doesn't leave me first, I'll leave it someday. But I'll miss it. There's nothing else in life quite like it, you know. It's a sonofagun, I wanna tell you."

To this author, Foyt is the greatest of the great ones in this special sport.

2

THE PIONEERS

Men have raced cars ever since the horseless carriage came into existence in Germany in 1885. Prior to that, men had experimented with steam-driven vehicles, but the development of the internal combustion engine produced the first automobiles as we know them today. However, it was a steam-powered car driven by the Marquis de Dion that won what was probably the first real automobile race, a seventy-eight-mile road contest from Paris to Rouen in France in June of 1894. The Marquis won the race at an average speed of 11.9 miles per hour.

The sport of auto racing accelerated with improvements in the engines and the appearance of cars designed and built by such inventive men as Charles and Frank Duryea, Ransom Olds, and Henry Ford in the late 1800s and early 1900s. The first real race in the United States was probably William Vanderbilt's 302-mile Vanderbilt Cup test through Long Island on October 8, 1904. It was won by Henry Heath in a French-built Panhard in six hours and forty-five minutes.

Today, few people realize how soon it was after the development of the first cars that men were driving their frail and clumsy vehicles at high speeds. The first listed mile record is 39.2 miles per hour, achieved by the nobleman Chasseloup-Laubat of France in 1898. In less than two years, just before the turn of the century, the record was advanced to 75 miles per hour. In 1904, Henry Ford drove his "Red Devil" over a frozen lake at more than 90 miles per hour. In 1906, Frank Marriot drove a Stanley Steamer at more than 125 miles per hour. In 1910, Barney Oldfield set the speed standard for the measured mile at 131 miles per hour. A year later Bob Burman raised it to 141 miles per hour. While these records were being set on straight runs, man's ability to negotiate oval tracks was improving, too.

Real road racing over open country roads dominated the early days of the sport and still lingers on in Europe today, but there was so much death and destruction that it was soon outlawed in the United States and gave way to enclosed oval tracks. The first American auto-racing tracks were short dirt "horse-racing" tracks. In 1903, Oldfield became the first man to break through the mile-a-minute barrier on a one-mile dirt track in a speed test in Indianapolis. In 1909, the two-and-one-half-mile Indianapolis Motor Speedway was opened as a dirt track. Oldfield set the first track record at 76 miles per hour. Bob Burman won the first feature race there at an average speed of 53.7 miles per hour over 250 miles. A driver and a mechanic were killed in that event before a crowd of sixty thousand persons. In only three days of racing, there was a total of five deaths. Because of this, the track was later paved with bricks.

In 1911, the first of the Memorial Day 500-mile classics was conducted. The speeds approached 90 miles per hour. Driving a Marmon Wasp at an average speed of 74.5 miles per hour, Ray Harroun won before a crowd of more than eighty thousand fans.

Beginning in 1910, when a wooden-board speedway was constructed in Playa Del Rey near Los Angeles, with lights for night racing, banked wooden saucers hosted most of the United States' greatest auto-racing events. All over the country, men competed for purses of over $25,000 before crowds of twenty thousand to one hundred thousand persons at speeds that soared to 130 miles per hour.

Impressed by the state of racing today, readers may be inclined to underestimate the past. As has been pointed out earlier, people seldom realize how fast men raced the early cars, how much money was at stake, and how large the crowds were that cheered the drivers on. It is possible that we will never again know a time when automobile racing attracts the public interest it did in the 1920s, long before the development of jet planes and rockets that could land men on the moon.

In a way, the early race drivers were greater than those who followed them because they were challenging a greater unknown. Americans were not driving 65 miles per hour on crowded highways then. Most persons had not even driven an automobile. The early race cars were frail and awkward creations. They had delicate power plants, erratic steering equipment, primitive braking systems, fragile wheels, and skimpy tires. They quickly went out of balance, caught fire, or exploded. They often broke up and careened wildly over splintering board tracks, rutty dirt tracks, and bumpy brick tracks.

Those who drove in the early days were usually punished severely. It took six hours to drive a 500-mile race, not three hours as is true today. And many of the major races ran 200, 300, 400, and 500 miles. The drivers had to wrestle their clumsy cars over bad ground while being pelted with rocks, thick splinters, and pieces of metal that fell off the cars. In those early cars men were as quickly injured or killed in crashes at 60 and 70 miles per hour as they are today at two and three times the speed. One driver, Louis Strang, was killed while driving at less than 10 miles per hour on a public road in Wisconsin. He had pulled over to permit a horse and buggy to gallop past, hit a soft spot on the shoulder, rolled over, and was pinned underneath his car and crushed.

At 60 and 70 miles per hour, those old cars could become airborne, roll over, and come apart in pieces. The drivers had little protective equipment (fireproof suits and crash helmets were unknown) and they didn't even wear leather or cloth aviator caps and glass goggles.

One cannot say that A. J. Foyt would not have been a successful racing driver had he been born fifty years earlier. He probably would have been because he is made of the stuff that produces great racing drivers. But one can say that today he is not challenged to the same extent as were the pioneers of the sport.

The names of these peerless veterans still sparkle with glamour. They include "Hurrying Harry" Harkness, who won the first United States driving championship in 1902, and Barney Oldfield, who won the second crown, and Harroun, who won that first Indianapolis 500, and "Wild Bob" Burman and "Terrible Teddy" Tetzlaff.

In 1902, Henry Ford built a racing car to challenge Alexander Winton, a Cleveland car maker who was recognized as the reigning racing champion of the day in his "Bullet" car. Ford selected a daring bicycle racer named Oldfield to drive for him, although Oldfield never had driven a car. Oldfield challenged Winton at Grosse Point, Michigan, in October, beat him, and became the new "champion." Oldfield, a former Toledo bellboy, was a colorful character. A cocky braggart who constantly chewed a cigar, sometimes while racing, he went on to set many speed records and win many races. He drove the famous "Green Dragon" car, and his name is synonymous with speed to this day. However, others soon came along who were superior to Oldfield.

In the early days many champion drivers, including Oldfield and Tommy Milton, drove for traveling racing troupes that crisscrossed the country staging daredevil carnivals of speed. Many of these races were rigged in favor of the star of the show. When the American Automobile Association began to supervise racing in this country between 1910 and 1920, participation in such activities was discouraged. However, Oldfield, who could always draw a well-paying crowd, hated supervision and often defied the authorities. He continued to barnstorm and sometimes received "lifetime" suspensions from sanctioned events.

Even in the early days of racing, the standard for regularly scheduled races on oval tracks in the United States was set by the Indianapolis Speedway, which had been built by a group of four men headed by a person named Carl Fisher. Before World War I, major events were conducted annually in Los Angeles and San Francisco, California; Chicago, Illinois; Minneapolis, Minnesota; Cincinnati, Ohio; Omaha, Nebraska; Long Island, New York; and other areas. Shortly after the war, yearly events commenced in Kansas City, Kansas; Charlotte, North Carolina; Altoona, Pennsylvania; Atlantic City, New Jersey; Laurel, Mississippi; Salem, Massachusetts; and many other cities. All were inspired by Indianapolis, but none has survived as successfully as Indy, which remains the classic contest of the racing world.

When Harroun won the first Indianapolis 500 he did so against many faster cars. Fortunately for Harroun, most of these were punished by the pace they sought to set and either were slowed down by long periods in the pits to replace tires and damaged parts or they broke down completely. Harroun, with relief help from Cyril Patschke in the middle stages, drove his black and yellow Marmon Wasp to triumph with a steady, smartly conceived tempo.

A former ribbon salesman from Ohio, Harroun had become the chief engineer of the mammoth Marmon operation and had great funds at his command. After winning the first prize of $14,000, he collapsed in a coughing fit in victory lane and retired on the spot.

Ralph Mulford drove a Lozier to second place in that first 500 and later went on to greater glory, though never a first place in the 500. David Bruce-Brown drove a Fiat to third place. Bruce-Brown was a wealthy New Yorker who had attended Yale. In 1908, while still an Ivy League collegian, he had set a speed record of 109 miles per hour at Daytona. A year after his third-place finish at Indianapolis he led the French Grand Prix for three-fourths of the distance before he ran out of gas. He raced in the second Indianapolis 500, but his car broke down early. Later that year, while practicing for the Milwaukee Grand Prix, he tried to pass Ted Tetzlaff and crashed to his death.

There were some who said that Tetzlaff had squeezed Bruce-Brown out of room. "Terrible Teddy" was a most controversial figure of the period, a tough, defiant character who broke commitments, did what he pleased, barnstormed to speed records and race victories, but actually won fewer races than his reputation would lead one to believe. He raced in four 500s and did not win any, though he was second in the 1912 race. He lived to retire and died of natural causes in 1929. Oldfield, who finished fifth in the only two 500s he drove, and who almost drowned when he crashed into an infield lake in Atlanta, also retired to die of natural causes in 1946.

Until the 1930s, most drivers raced with mechanics by their side to make minor repairs and keep them posted on the whereabouts of the other cars. However, Harroun was an innovator. He rigged up the first rearview mirror on his car and drove without an aide, launching the reputation of Indianapolis and other tracks as proving grounds for passenger car equipment, in that first 500.

Most of the winners of the early 500s had relief help, though. But Jules Goux, who won the third 500 in a Peugeot with the first four-wheel brakes, sent his crew to some visiting Frenchmen in the stands to secure some wine, and needed only the help of a half-dozen bottles of chilled champagne to prevail. In victory lane, he said, "Without the good wine, I would not have been able to win." Charles Merz finished in third place in somewhat lesser spirits because his mechanic had been hanging on the hood beating out a fire that had broken out in the engine.

The victory by Goux launched a cycle of 500s that were dominated by foreign drivers, including another Frenchman, Rene Thomas, who won in 1914, and Italian Dario Resta, who won in 1916. Goux and Resta drove Peugeots. Thomas drove a Delage. Other great cars of this period were the Marmon, Maxwell, Mercer, Mercedes, Montore, National, Frontenac, Lozier, Fiat, Stutz, and Duesenberg.

The names of the men who developed the cars, engines, and equipment of the early days still ring magically today—the Chevrolet and Duesenberg brothers, Henry Ford, Harry Miller, Leo Goosen, Harry Stutz, Harvey Firestone, Albert Champion, and Fred Offenhauser. But it is the nature of the sport that the drivers become the spotlighted heroes, not the men behind the scenes. Of course some drivers had better cars and help than others, giving them more opportunities to achieve fame. But historians can only record results.

Probably the first truly great American race driver was Ralph De

Palma, the only American to interrupt the early period of foreign frustration for our drivers at Indianapolis. He won the 500 in 1915. De Palma, like Mario Andretti today, was born in Italy, but was raised in the United States, became a citizen, and did almost all his driving in America. Thus, De Palma and Andretti can be considered American race drivers, though the point is open to debate. Certainly, De Palma was a great driver.

Born in Troia, Italy, in 1883, he and his family moved to New York when he was ten years old. He first became a great speedster with his legs as a track star, then a bicycling champion. He won the only motorcycle race he ever entered and then turned to cars. He enjoyed enormous success and became known as "the King of the Roaring Road." He preferred to call himself "the Hard Luck King," for he led almost every race he entered and lost many through one misfortune or another. However, with his sportsmanlike behavior, his extraordinarily good looks, and his large physique, he became a great public hero.

Aside from Indianapolis, De Palma won almost every major race available to drivers of his time. Perhaps his most dramatic victory was in the 1912 Vanderbilt Cup, in which he skillfully avoided overturning when one of his tires blew out in the homestretch and he crossed the finish line riding on the rim of one wheel. On another occasion he sneaked out of a hospital after a severe racing accident and drove in a race with a broken leg in a cast. He lost that one, though he led until his car failed him.

De Palma won the national driving title in 1912 and 1914. He also engaged in a bitter series of exhibition duels with Barney Oldfield, beating him more often than he lost and supplanting Oldfield in the affections of the fans. When De Palma's sponsors hired Oldfield as his co-driver just prior to the 1914 Vanderbilt Cup event, De Palma was so angry that he quit the team, bought back a famous old car that he had retired, his Mercedes "Grey Ghost," completely rebuilt it in three weeks, and whipped Oldfield in the race.

This was a stunning triumph of strategy. The two dueled fiercely most of the way. Near the finish, De Palma noted that Oldfield's tires were shredding. De Palma reasoned that Oldfield wanted to stop in the pits to replace his tires, but did not dare do so unless De Palma also had to make a pit stop. De Palma signaled wildly to his pit crew, then began to slow down and enter the pit area. Seeing this, Oldfield immediately pulled into the pits and stopped, too. But De Palma never stopped. He just pressed down on his accelerator and shot from the pit area. Angrily, Oldfield started up and took off in pursuit, but the finish was near and he lost by two hundred yards.

De Palma won twenty-six national championship races, more than any other driver could win until the 1960s, when new races were added to the list of possibilities. His record still endures as one of the three or four best totals of all time. He probably won a hundred races overall. In ten Indianapolis 500s, he led for a total of 613 laps, which remains the record to this day, more than 100 laps ahead of his nearest challenger. In the 1912 Indianapolis 500, he led for 196 of the 200 laps, a mark that has been exceeded only once. He was the first man to win the pole position twice as the fastest qualifier, and while he actually won the race only once, he nearly won several other times.

The first near-miss occurred in the 1912 race. With five laps left and leading by five laps, he broke a connecting rod, tearing a hole in his crankcase and causing an oil leak. With declining power, his Mercedes became slower and slower. Joe Dawson, driving a National, passed him twice. On the last turn of the last lap, less than a mile from the finish line, De Palma's car quit completely. De Palma got out sadly, shrugged, and with his mechanic began to push his car down the stretch. As they pushed, Dawson passed him three more times and finally took the checkered flag as the winner.

Dawson had led for only two laps, the fewest of any 500 winner in history. Although he won, the cheers of the crowd went to the gallant De Palma. More than a half century later, the picture of De Palma pushing his crippled car home lingers in the minds of men. As so often happens, he became a greater hero in defeat than he had been in victory, and he was more than repaid for his loss by the fame it brought him.

De Palma did win the 500 in 1915, though. Curiously, a connecting rod snapped and punctured the crankcase of his Mercedes near the finish again. But this time the car continued to run and he was able to hold onto first place until the finish.

In 1916, he did not even get a chance to run in the 500. He had held out for "appearance money," a guarantee of $5,000 just for racing, and wound up sending his entry form in after the deadline. The other drivers were asked if his entry should be accepted late, and De Palma's old rival, Oldfield, blackballed him.

In 1919, after a two-year interruption in racing because of the war, De Palma led the 500 at the halfway point, but was knocked out by wheel trouble. During this race a freak accident occurred. A wheel of Louis Chevrolet's Frontenac broke and a jagged end snapped a thin electric timing wire stretched across the start-finish line. One of the severed ends of the wire uncoiled and slashed the neck of a driver in another car, Elmer Shannon. An artery was opened and he almost bled to death before he could stop his car and be rushed to a hospital. After the accident, Shannon never raced in the 500 again. Howdy Wilcox won the race, his only victory in eleven tries. Wilcox was later killed in a race at Altoona in 1923.

In 1920, as De Palma circled the track with the field prior to the start of the 500, one of his tires was punctured by a sharp object on the track. He yelled "flat tire" to the official in the pace car, but the official happened to be the retired Oldfield, who shrugged and yelled back, "Tough luck," and did not delay the start to permit a repair as he might have done. De Palma changed his tire and got off a lap behind the field, but drove so furiously that he led within one hundred miles. With only thirty miles to go, he led by five miles, but then his engine caught fire. Twice, his nephew and riding mechanic, Peter De Paolo, crawled out on the hood and doused the blaze with a fire extinguisher while De Palma continued running. When the fire went out, however, the car ran dry. De Palma had used up too much fuel in his mad run. Again, circumstances had cheated him out of victory. De Palma also led the 1921 race by three laps at the halfway point before his car failed him.

De Paolo later drove the 500 seven times himself. In 1925, with relief help and the use of the first balloon tires, he became the first winner to average more than 100 miles per hour.

The frustration of losing the 500 is something many great American race drivers have in common. It is so hard to win, so much at the mercy of the fates. Among the glamorous names of racing history who drove in the 500 in the early days and failed were Oldfield, Tetzlaff, Burman, Earl Cooper, Harry Hartz, Eddie Hearne, John Aitken, Spencer Wishart, Eddie Rickenbacker, Ralph Mulford, and Arthur and Louis Chevrolet. Gaston Chevrolet won the 1920 race when De Palma fell out, but he was killed in a crash on the Beverly Hills boards later that very year. All things considered, De Palma was fortunate.

De Palma's sportsmanship is an aspect of his career that has become almost legendary. For example, a farm boy once suffered a broken arm while cranking the champion's car prior to the start of a country fair race. De Palma drove the boy to the hospital, returned just in time for the start of the race, won it, then left before receiving his prize to return to the boy's bedside. He arranged for all medical care and a private nurse before he left town.

On another occasion (during the 1912 Milwaukee Grand Prix), De Palma's Mercedes was passing Pasadena millionaire Caleb Bragg's huge Fiat when Bragg brushed De Palma out of control. De Palma's car catapulted over a barbed wire fence and he was hurled out and impaled on a cornstalk in an adjacent field. He was rushed to a hospital in critical condition. Approached by reporters as he was carried on a stretcher out of the ambulance, he murmured, "Tell the people Caleb Bragg wasn't to blame, boys. He gave me all the road."

After Oldfield retired, Burman took the ex-racer's old cars and set new records with them, renewing the old challenge to De Palma. The two men met in a famous match race on Sheepshead Bay's board track in October, 1915. They finished in a virtual dead heat. The officials debated, then declared De Palma the winner. But then De Palma did an amazing thing—he rushed up to the officials and announced that as they had crossed the finish line, the nose of Burman's car had been inches in front. The officials reversed their decision and gave first place to Burman.

The following year, while Burman was driving a Peugeot in the Corona Road Race, a tire blew out and his car went out of control, hitting a parked car and two power poles. He and his mechanic were thrown through the air to their deaths. Burman's wife rushed to his side and he actually died in her arms. Ironically, two years earlier Burman had told a reporter of a dream in which he died precisely that way and the reporter had printed the story.

De Palma continued to race and in 1921 he finished second to Jimmy Murphy, who became the only American to win a European Grand Prix event until forty years later. Ralph De Palma was still driving and winning races into his forties. He won the Canadian championship in 1929 at the age of forty-seven before finally quitting. He died in 1956, a legend in his own time.

Another two-time national champion of this period was Ralph Mulford, a gracious Georgian and a meticulous individual who often raced in the stiff high white collars favored by gentlemen of the period. Mulford, who was very religious, taught Sunday school and refused to race on the Sabbath, though most of the great races were run on Sunday. Nevertheless, he won enough races to win the United States title in 1911 and again in 1918. However, he raced in ten 500s without winning one. In the first race he managed to come in second, though. Strange as it may seem, he is most famous for having finished tenth in the second race.

In that 1912 event, in which De Palma broke down so near to victory, Mulford was the tenth and last car still running at the finish. He had completed only four hundred miles when he stopped at the finish line to ask if tenth-place money was his. Distressed because De Palma would get less for having done so much more, Speedway head Carl Fisher told Mulford he'd get the money only if he finished the full distance. His usual composure ruined, Mulford resumed running at a deliberately slow pace. He even stopped in his pits for some fried chicken. He finished after eight hours and fifty-three minutes with the great arena now nearly deserted and darkness closing in. He collected $1,200. De Palma collected only $380. After that, the rules were changed so that the race could be halted after the leaders finished, with the remaining places being awarded on the basis of laps completed. Mulford retired in the 1920s.

Following De Palma, the next great American race driver was Earl Cooper, who was born in Nebraska in 1886 and raised in California. A short, slender fellow, Cooper was working as a mechanic in a San Jose garage when he began his racing career. He borrowed a customer's car, beat his boss in a dealers' road race, and was fired. "From now on, I'll have to race for eatin' money," he told a friend. And he raced with enormous success, though he never attained the fame of his leading rivals.

In contrast to such cocky and outspoken daredevils of the period as Oldfield, Tetzlaff, and Burman, Cooper was shy and quiet. Unlike the others, he was not a reckless charger, but rather a cool tactician. He was able to figure out the maximum pace a car could endure on a given track in a given race and would try to hold that pace until his rivals failed in front of him. In seven tries he failed to win the 500, though he finished second in 1924, when he led by forty-four seconds after four hundred miles only to have a tire blow out.

Nevertheless, Cooper beat the best so consistently that he became the first three-time winner of the national championship, winning in 1913, 1915, and 1917. One of Cooper's most spectacular triumphs occurred in 1915 at the new "million dollar" Twin City Speedway near Minneapolis, where he beat Stutz teammate Gil Anderson literally by inches.

A super sportsman like De Palma, Cooper was once declared the winner of a race at Charlotte, but went to the officials and told them he had started behind Tommy Milton and had not passed him, so Milton must have won. The officials gave the nod to Milton. Another time, at

The incomparable A. J. Foyt.

(John W. Posey)

A. J. Foyt in action on dirt track at Sacramento Fairgrounds in 1964.

(Bob Tronolone)

Foyt comes out of a turn in the 1968 Rex Mays 300 at Riverside Raceway. *(Bob Tronolone)*

Ray Harroun drives his Marmon Wasp to victory in the first Indianapolis 500 in 1911.
(Indianapolis Speedway)

Foyt swings his Lotus-Ford into a turn during a 1965 Grand Prix race at Riverside Raceway in California.

Barney Oldfield and his mechanic pose at Ascot Park, Los Angeles, in 1916. Note the slogan on the side of the car.

Ralph De Palma in 1911.
(Indianapolis Speedway)

Eddie Rickenbacker at wheel of Maxwell he drove at Indy in 1915. *(Indianapolis Speedway)*

Ralph De Palma pushes his Mercedes down the homestretch at Indianapolis in 1912 after the car conked out with victory in reach. *(Indianapolis Speedway)*

Three-time U.S. champion Earl Cooper, who never won the 500, poses at the board track at Beverly Hills, California, in 1921.

(Ted Wilson collection)

Famous auto manufacturer Gaston Chevrolet poses on the old brick track at Indianapolis in 1919.

(Indianapolis Speedway)

The great Frank Lockhart in 1926.

(Ted Wilson collection)

Jimmy Murphy in 1922, the year he won at Indy. The year before he had won the French Grand Prix.

(Ted Wilson collection)

A rare photo shows the cars lining up for the start of the French Grand Prix at Le Mans in 1921. Winner Jimmy Murphy is in car 12.

(Ted Wilson collection)

Wilbur Shaw after a race at Ascot Park, Los Angeles, in 1934.

(Ted Wilson collection)

A classic photo of Wilbur Shaw's Duesenberg going over the wall at Indianapolis in 1931. Shaw came back to drive relief in a sister car a few laps later and scared the wits out of the other drivers, who thought they were seeing a ghost. *(Indianapolis Speedway)*

Tommy Milton at Culver City, California, in 1927. Milton and Jimmy Murphy were great rivals of the era. *(Ted Wilson collection)*

Lou Meyer, one of auto racing's immortals, at Culver City in 1927. *(Ted Wilson collection)*

Mauri Rose after qualifying at Indy in 1947. He went on to win his second of three victories in the 500 classic. *(Indianapolis Speedway)*

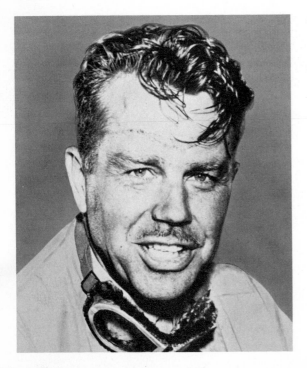

Ted Horn in 1947. *(Bob Shafer collection)*

This photo shows Rex Mays being thrown from his car in a fatal crash at Del Mar, California, in 1949.

(Phil Bath, Los Angeles Times—Bob Shafer collection)

Rex Mays was a great driver who never won the 500. Here he is at Indy in 1940.

(Indianapolis Speedway)

Junior Johnson straps on his helmet prior to the start of a NASCAR race. *(Ford)*

An aerial view of the old Daytona Beach course. *(Daytona International Speedway)*

The field streams into the start of the new two-and-one-half mile Daytona Speedway opened in 1959.

(Daytona International Speedway)

Lee Petty poses beside his Dodge toward the end of his career.

Curtis Turner, like Junior Johnson, began his career by outrunning Alcohol Tax Division agents while hauling illegal whiskey. *(Goodyear)*

Fireball Roberts in his Ford before the 1963 Daytona Speedway classic. He was killed the following year.

(Ford)

Fireball Roberts (22) slingshots past David Pearson in the NASCAR World 600 at Charlotte Motor Speedway in 1962.

(Bob Tronolone)

NASCAR great Richard Petty looks over his car before the 1969 Riverside 500. He won the race.
(Darryl Norenberg)

Tim Flock at Daytona Speedway.
(Daytona International Speedway)

Corona, Cooper was chasing Oldfield when Oldfield had to swerve and crash to avoid some spectators. Cooper promptly pulled over to see if he could help his rival. However, Barney not only wasn't hurt, but he couldn't understand such sympathy and angrily told Earl to get the hell back in the race. Cooper went on to win.

Cooper announced his retirement in 1918, telling reporters, "I'm saying good-bye to speed." Then he raced at Indianapolis in 1919. Then he retired again. He was attending a race at Fresno in 1921 when he was offered the car of a driver who had suffered a broken arm in practice. Despite more than two years' idleness, Cooper took the car and won the race, nosing out the great Jimmy Murphy. The now balding veteran was back in business, and, as it turned out, he was as good as ever.

Cooper might have become the only four-time national champion until A. J. Foyt came along if he had not lost to a dead man. In 1924 he fell only a few points short of the total reached by Jimmy Murphy, who had been killed in a race just before the end of the season.

Cooper did not retire permanently until he was forty, after he had placed third in the 1927 Italian Grand Prix at Monza. Even then he served the sport as an official for many years. He died in 1965, at nearly eighty years of age.

One of the most formidable racers of the period immediately preceding World War I was Eddie Rickenbacker. Eddie's parents were born in Switzerland, but he was born and raised in Columbus, Ohio. He eventually came to be known not only as "the Speedy Swiss" but also as "the Dutch Demon." He wore the first metal crash helmet ever worn at Indianapolis. He failed to win the 500 in three tries, nor did he win a national title, but he was verging on racing greatness when the war struck and he attained greatness in another way.

Utterly fearless, Rickenbacker crashed a steel cart into a gravel pit when he was eight, almost breaking himself into little pieces. He also made his own gravity-powered wooden racer using baby carriage wheels and he would send it hurtling down steep hills. Many years later he was influential in starting the soap box derby for boys. When his father died, Eddie quit school at the age of twelve to help support his family. His first job, in 1902, earned him five cents an hour. He worked in various factories and shops and even carved gravestones.

At fifteen, Eddie rode in one of the newfangled horseless carriages and was hooked. He got a job in a garage and studied mechanics by mail.

Later he found work with the Frayer-Miller Automobile Company and one of the owners, Lee Frayer, took him to the Vanderbilt Cup and Indianapolis 500 races. Rickenbacker drove relief for Frayer in the first 500. Later, he went to work for the Columbus Buggy Company, whose president was Clinton Firestone. Besides selling cars Rickenbacker also raced cars for the company.

Rickenbacker's first race actually took place in 1910 at Red Oak, Iowa. While he was negotiating a rutty curve a wheel collapsed and the car slid broadside through a fence, leaped a ditch, and rolled over, throwing him out. Later, he survived several such accidents.

In 1913, Rickenbacker drove a 300-mile race at Sioux City, Iowa, in which his car hit T. C. Cox's car and sent it crashing through a fence in an accident that claimed the lives of both Cox and his mechanic. Rickenbacker not only escaped, but won the race. On the advice of his mother, he had caught a bat, dissected it, and tied its heart to his middle finger for good luck. Later, the young daughter of a friend gave him a crucifix for good luck and he has carried it with him every day of his life since. And certainly he has had good luck.

Rickenbacker was just beginning a spectacular racing career when the United States was drawn into World War I. He sought to organize racing drivers into an aerial squadron and had already recruited De Palma, Cooper, Harroun, and others when service officials refused to cooperate. Actually, Rickenbacker could not fly. In fact, according to service regulations he was too old to be taught. However, he went overseas with General John "Black Jack" Pershing's group as a driver. He chauffeured air pioneer Billy Mitchell about and talked officials into permitting him to take flight training by telling them that he was twenty-five, not twenty-seven.

Despite an intense fear of height, airsickness, and a weak ear that ached horribly at high altitudes, Rickenbacker not only mastered flying, but took the light and fragile planes of the period and in seven months of 1918 fought 134 air battles over France. He shot down twenty-six German craft to gain the title of "American Ace of Aces" and countless decorations. Along the way, he had many close brushes with death.

After the war he did not return to race driving, but developed his own Rickenbacker car, which was sold successfully for a while before the venture failed. Then he bought the Indianapolis Speedway for $700,000 in 1927. He ran it until closing it down when the United States entered World War II in 1941. When the war ended in 1945, Rickenbacker sold the Speedway to Tony Hulman for the same price he had paid for it—$700,000

—refusing a greater sum from a construction outfit so it would not become a housing site. Under Hulman, the Speedway has prospered so much that there is no thought of using the property for anything but racing.

Although Rickenbacker was fifty when the Second World War began and could not take part in the fighting, he still managed to live dangerously. In 1941, he was a passenger on a plane that crashed into a hill near Atlanta, Georgia, and was badly injured. In 1942, he was a passenger on another plane that crashed into the Pacific Ocean near Samoa. He and others endured twenty-four days on a raft on the open seas without food or water other than what they could extract from the sea. They ate raw sea gulls and fish and drank rainwater. One passenger died, but Rickenbacker and the others were finally rescued.

It is no wonder Rickenbacker is considered indestructible. He has walked away from many other air crashes, just as he survived earlier crashes in racing cars. He has also survived business failures and is now the successful head of Eastern Airlines. And throughout his exciting life he has not always had the heart of a dead bat tied to his finger.

Another glamorous racing figure of the World War I era was Frank Lockhart. He was a tiny, handsome, clean-living hero of the Roaring Twenties who came to be called "the Boy Wonder." Lockhart was born and raised in Dayton, Ohio, near the farm of the father of the Wright brothers. When Frank's father died, his mother moved her family to California, where she earned money by taking in sewing.

As a boy, Frank built a soap box derby racer, and then a real racer made from an old Model T Ford donated by a friendly vegetable peddler. Frank and his brother dismantled the car where they found it and carried it, piece by piece, to their home many miles away. Frank's mother mortgaged the house to buy him racing tires and he began to race—and to win. Few people realized that he was actually afraid of racing. He used to go off into the shadows before the races to vomit secretly. But he raced daringly in spite of his fears.

In 1926, he went to see his first 500 at Indianapolis. He test-drove a car there and when the driver got sick he was offered the chance to drive it in the race. He did not know the car, but he knew how to race and he won the 500. Overnight, he became famous. In 1927, he returned to Indianapolis and led the 500 for three hundred miles until his car broke down. He had become the darling of the sporting world.

By then, Lockhart's ambition was to set the land speed record. Although semiliterate, he was a brilliant mechanic. Britain's Sir Malcolm Campbell had just set the record at 206 miles per hour. This was worth a fortune in advertising fees and Lockhart needed money. Even though his curly-haired good looks adorned the nation's sports pages, he was broke and had a new wife to support.

Lockhart secured financing for an attempt on the record, readied a car, and went to Daytona Beach early in 1928. On the day of his first try Lockhart's car skidded on wet sand and rolled into the ocean, where it sank. Lockhart was pulled out with cut tendons in his hand. He had his car pulled out of the water and took it back to Indianapolis for repairs. Then he returned to Daytona.

On April 25, he was ready to try again. His mother was sick at the time and she wired him for money. All his money had gone into his car, though. He wired back, "I have the world by the horns. You'll never have to push a needle again." He went out and was running 225 miles per hour when his car's right rear tire was cut by a shell, blew out, and sent the vehicle rolling crazily down the beach. Lockhart was thrown from the car and landed dead at his young bride's feet. He was only twenty-five years old.

Tragedy also ended the career of an even greater race driver of the period immediately following World War I. Jimmy Murphy raced only five years, yet in that short time the brave youngster became part of the most bitter rivalry in all racing history and set standards that would endure for all time.

Murphy's mother died when he was two. His father died in the San Francisco earthquake of 1906 and the orphan was raised by relatives in California. When Jimmy's uncle, a judge, bought him a motorcycle, the youngster became hooked on engines and speed. He quit school to work in a garage and began to hang around the racetracks of the Los Angeles area.

In 1916, Eddie O'Donnell, who with Tommy Milton, Eddie Rickenbacker, and Eddie Hearne made up the star-studded Duesenberg racing team, offered Murphy a chance to ride with him as his mechanic. Murphy jumped at the chance and for the next four years he rode with O'Donnell, Rickenbacker, and Milton. But he wanted to drive, too, and he grew frustrated over his place in the shadows of the famous drivers.

Milton was the most famous driver on the team and Murphy sought the seat alongside him as often as possible so he could tell him his desire to drive. Milton had learned his trade barnstorming with a racing circus. The now famous driver had once traveled three thousand miles and raced in five cities in eight days, for which he earned a mere $35. Milton knew what it was to be a young hopeful and he befriended Murphy. They were a most unlikely pair. Milton was a handsome, polished gentleman, modest and shy, almost introverted. Murphy was tiny, homely, and crude, but charming, cocky, and aggressive. Milton talked Fred Duesenberg into giving Murphy his first chance as a driver, but Murphy crashed two cars and was demoted to mechanic's status again.

In a race at Uniontown, New Jersey, while driving with another mechanic, Milton was far ahead of runner-up Gaston Chevrolet when Milton's car caught fire going down the main straightaway. He slammed on the brakes, which bent. The car swayed and rolled over and one of his legs was crushed. He was rushed to the hospital, where doctors wanted to amputate the leg, but Milton refused them permission, hoping for the best. Fortunately his leg did mend, though he spent more than two months in the hospital. This was in 1920.

While he was there, Murphy visited him and said he was so discouraged that he was going home. Milton told him he would speak to Duesenberg again and would threaten to quit the team if Murphy was not given another chance to drive. As a result, Murphy got his chance again and he made the most of it this time, beginning to win races. Meanwhile, Milton gave Murphy a chance to make extra money by working on a car he was readying for a speed run at Daytona.

Though he was still recuperating, Milton began to race again. To prepare everything for his attempt on the land speed record, he sent Murphy and Harry Hartz to Daytona with his car. There the car performed so perfectly that Murphy, encouraged by Duesenberg, could not resist the temptation to try for the title of world speed king himself. He took the car out and smashed Ralph De Palma's existing record of just under 150 miles per hour with a run in excess of 152 miles per hour.

When Milton saw the headlines, he was angered beyond reason. He had befriended Murphy and gotten him several good opportunities to drive. He had sunk every penny he had in the world into the speed project and was paying Murphy's salary. Yet Murphy had risked his car and taken the record Milton wanted so much. "I don't think the world ever has looked so black. I could have killed him," he said later. But when he rushed to Daytona, Murphy fled.

Milton then took the car and made a frenzied effort to surpass Murphy's mark, but at first he could not. The car was hampered by the salty damp air and sand it had absorbed. The press proclaimed that Murphy was Milton's superior, further infuriating Milton. He sealed his car in a tent, tore it apart, and rebuilt it. Finally, he resumed running. Although he had only one good eye, and it was irritated by a steel sliver that had been driven into it, he surpassed Murphy's mark with a run of 156 miles per hour. When the car caught fire he calmly drove it into the ocean to douse it.

In the following years, Milton would not speak to Murphy off the tracks and battled him fiercely on them. Both were highly gifted drivers, certainly two of the greatest American race drivers of all time. Milton won the national title in 1920 and 1921, the first man ever to win it two years in a row. Murphy won it in 1922 and 1924. He also won the French Grand Prix in 1921.

The two drivers seemed to take turns capturing the big races. Murphy won the pole position at Indianapolis in 1922. Milton won it in 1923. Murphy won it back in 1924. Milton won the 500 in 1921. Murphy won it in 1922. Milton won it back in 1923, with relief help from Howdy Wilcox in the middle stages, when his hands and feet blistered in the new white gloves and shoes he had donned for the classic. Milton is credited with being the first two-time winner of the event. But Murphy, who earned $125,000 a year at his peak and who had a fox-trot named after him, was the great public favorite.

In 1924, Murphy raced Milton and others on the dirt track in Syracuse, New York. He did not like dirt tracks and had not planned to race in that particular contest, but he was leading the race for the national driving title and felt he might need the points to assure himself the coveted crown. Murphy had one superstition in common with many drivers—he did not like to make travel arrangements until after each race. However, on that afternoon his sponsor had a commitment that forced him to leave early, so he pressed train tickets on the protesting Murphy, tucking them into his pocket. Murphy shrugged it off and drove in spite of his superstition. In the race, he crashed into a fence and a splinter of wood pierced his heart, killing him at the age of thirty.

Milton seemed personally shattered by Murphy's death. At first, he wept privately. Then he asked and received permission to accompany the body back to California, where he made the funeral arrangements and paid most of the expenses for the burial of his fallen rival. Perhaps he now regretted the grudge he had carried against Murphy all those years, no matter how justified. Tears streamed down his face as Murphy was lowered into the ground.

At the close of the season, Earl Cooper's point total was creeping close to Murphy's. But Cooper's bid for an unprecedented fourth national title fell just short and Murphy was awarded his second crown posthumously, matching Milton's mark.

At his peak, Milton was a daring and resourceful driver. In one of his victories at Indianapolis, he outsmarted another driver in classic style. Near the end of the race, Milton was weary and his car was losing speed. He knew that another driver, Roscoe Sarles, had a stronger and faster car. But he also knew that Sarles, who had demolished two cars on the Speedway walls in the previous 500, was unsure of himself. As Sarles closed in, Milton deliberately slowed down slightly. As Sarles drew even, Milton turned to him, smiled, patted the tail of his car, and accelerated away. Discouraged, Sarles did not again challenge. Later, he admitted he had decided to settle for second place because Milton seemed so fresh and confident and his car seemed to have so much power left. Such clever driving was characteristic of Milton in his prime. But after Murphy's death, Milton became another person altogether.

He continued to drive for a few years, but his enthusiasm was gone and he was not as successful as he had been. Milton loved race driving and it hurt him to retire, but once he stopped winning there seemed no point in taking the risks anymore. Although he had turned down an opportunity to buy the Speedway, he did return to it to serve as chief steward for a while. He was typical of drivers who are hooked on the narcotic of racing and cannot shake it, no matter how many painful experiences they have endured. In later years he once said, "The hardest job I've ever had is being a retired race driver. I want to drive every race I see. And I see every race I can. I can't stay away from the tracks even though it's torture to be there." He died in 1962.

His retirement and Murphy's death in the 1920s marked the end of a golden age in racing—approximately a quarter century of pioneering in which the first great American race drivers were developed.

3

CHAMPIONS OF THE
CHAMPIONSHIP TRAIL

In the early days, when tracks were constructed from wooden boards, there were a number of unusual problems associated with the sport. The board tracks used to break up and carpenters would have to hammer them back together between races. Sometimes cars and drivers would even drop through broken boards. The great Wilbur Shaw once recalled a race in which youngsters sneaked from the stands, went under the track, and poked their heads up through holes in the boards. The drivers would be roaring along and suddenly they would see heads without bodies seemingly sitting on the track and they would swerve in horror and some crashed.

By the late 1920s and early 1930s American race drivers were competing mainly on dirt ovals, and the board tracks fell apart, rotted away, or burned down. There were some paved tracks, such as Indianapolis, which was lined with bricks, and these were rough. But most of the tracks were dirt, and these were even rougher. Just as road racing has been symbolic of European auto racing, dirt racing has been symbolic of American auto racing. For years, American race drivers learned to drive on dirt tracks. It is a special form of racing, bumpy and dirty. The cars slide sideways through turns so they will be pointed straight when they reach the straightaways, throwing up rooster tails of dirt and pebbles that shower the spectators in the lower seats. It was a cruel kindergarten for the American race drivers who developed mainly in the 1930s and 1940s.

In this second great era of American racing, the so-called "championship trail" took shape. Other forms of racing became popular, too—for example, driving the bulkier sprint cars and smaller midget cars on half-mile and quarter-mile tracks and racing at the famed Ascot Speedway in Los Angeles, which served as the incubator for many great drivers. But it was racing along the championship trail in Indianapolis-style cars on dirt or paved tracks of a mile or more that crowned the true national driving champions each season and drew men to their racing destinies. These races took place at Indianapolis; Springfield, Illinois; Langhorne, Pennsylvania; Milwaukee, Wisconsin; and a dozen other places sanctioned for title events by the American Automobile Association. The championship trail has also been called a "heartbreak highway," for many men have left their high hopes along this rutty road. Some have left their lives.

The typical racing cycle seems to follow a pattern. Usually two great drivers come to the forefront at the same time to dominate the sport. Following the Oldfield-Burman, De Palma-Cooper, and Murphy-Milton dueling periods, Wilbur Shaw and Louis Meyer emerged in the spotlight as the most spectacular racing figures of the late 1920s and early 1930s. Both reached Indianapolis in 1927. Ironically, Meyer got his first chance as a relief driver for Shaw in Wilbur's first 500. Even more ironically, Meyer won the next year, the first 500 he started himself, in a car originally assigned to Shaw and sold to Meyer's sponsor only a few days before the race. From then on, the two were strong rivals.

Meyer actually emerged as a star first, winning the 500 in 1928, 1933, and 1936, and the national championship in 1928, 1929, and 1933. Shaw won the 500 in 1937, 1939, and 1940, and the national title in 1937 and 1939. In a dozen 500s, Meyer finished first three times, second once, and fourth once. In thirteen 500s, Shaw finished first three times, second three times, and fourth twice. His Speedway record is probably the greatest of all. In one six-year stretch, he got his three firsts, two seconds, and a seventh.

Shaw and Meyer rank near the top on the all-time list of United States drivers. In 500 competitions the two men drove more than five thousand miles each. Shaw led the classic for a total of 508 laps, second only to De Palma's record of 613. Meyer led for 332 laps, sixth in the all-time rankings. Neither ever held the speed records at Indy, however.

Both men won many other races, but they were conservative drivers who, after they had attained fame, stuck mainly to the major events. Consequently, they are most closely associated with the Indianapolis classic, which has dominated American racing.

Shaw was born in 1902 in Shelbyville, Indiana. His father was a happy-go-lucky wanderer who deserted his family when Wilbur was still very young, and the boy was raised by his mother. Indiana is racing country and Shaw soon succumbed to the fever. While in his teens he took a job as a mechanic and built his first race car out of junk parts on the second floor of a warehouse. Once he had built it, though, he had to figure out how to get it outside. He knocked out a window, built a ramp, and lowered the car to the street, almost wrecking it. He took this "junker" to Indianapolis in 1921 and was chased from the Speedway. Then he took it to Lafayette, Indiana, and on the first lap of his first race he flipped the car and it was demolished.

However, Shaw continued to hound the racetracks of the area, pleading with drivers, owners, and mechanics for a chance to drive. The older drivers used to get their kicks by letting him hang onto the tails of their cars while they practiced, driving wildly in an effort to throw him off.

Finally, he began to get rides. His first Indianapolis ride was in the same car that had carried Jimmy Murphy to his death at Syracuse in 1924. "I felt I had been sucked into a hundred-mile-an-hour tornado. I was never so scared in my life," he later admitted. Nevertheless, with relief help from young Meyer in the middle stages of the race, he finished fourth.

In 1931, Shaw and Jimmy Gleason drove identical Duesenberg cars, numbered 32 and 33, in the 500. On the backstretch of the sixtieth lap, Shaw passed Shorty Cantlon, Red Shafer, and Fred Winnai and had drawn abreast of Ralph Hepburn when he drove too deeply into a turn. He skidded over the wall and out of sight, sailed twenty-five or thirty feet through the air, tore down some telephone wires, and landed right side up with what Shaw remembers as a terrible sound of rending metal. But he and his mechanic were not seriously injured. Shaw suffered only a cut leg. Meanwhile, he had sucked Winnai's car over the wall, too, but he also survived the crash.

Shaw returned to the pits in bandages and immediately Gleason's sister car was called in. Gleason jumped out and Shaw jumped in. Back in the race, he soon passed Cantlon and Shafer on the backstretch, drew up to Hepburn again, and passed him successfully this time. As he passed the other drivers, he noticed that each of them backed off sharply, but he did not know why. Later, they explained that they had just seen him go over the wall, possibly to his death, so they were startled to see what seemed like his ghost passing them a few laps later in the same place and in what they assumed was the same car. Meanwhile, Shaw went too deep into the turn again, skidded, but managed to straighten out this time only inches shy of the wall. He turned to his new riding mechanic, who was pale with horror, and said, "If you'd seen what I did on that turn a little while ago, you'd really be shaken." Shaw had no chance to win in relief, though he finished sixth.

It seemed that nothing was going right for Shaw at this time. When he didn't crash at Indy, his car often broke down. In 1932, he led the 500 until his engine went sour with only fifty laps to go. He finished second with a sick engine in 1933. He finished second again in 1935, when rain curtailed his late move for the lead. He led by eighty-one seconds in 1936 when his hood tore loose, putting him out of contention. One year he was ineligible on suspension for having driven on "outlaw" tracks. Then his young wife died in premature childbirth.

These were hard times for Shaw, but he kept driving. Speed was his life. He raced motorboats and airplanes as well as cars, and even jumped from planes in parachutes. In 1934, he and Harry Hartz set a stock car record by driving 2,026 miles at an average speed of 84 miles per hour in a twenty-four-hour endurance run over the Utah salt flats.

Meanwhile, Meyer had come into his own. He had taken Shaw's car and had won in his first 500 start in 1928. He finished second in 1929 and fourth in 1930. In the 1930 race, Billy Arnold became the first to win at an average speed of more than 100 miles per hour without relief help. The next year Arnold led again until, less than a hundred miles from home, an axle broke on his car, sending a wheel soaring over a wall and into the yard of an adjacent house, where it struck and killed an eleven-year-old boy who was playing there. Arnold crashed over the wall and suffered a fractured pelvis. The next year, he crashed over the same wall and suffered a broken shoulder. After that, he retired. Meyer skidded and crashed that year, too, but was unhurt.

The 1933 race turned out to be the most tragic 500 ever. In a qualifying run, one car cleared a wall and the driver and mechanic were both killed. During the race, another car cleared a wall, again killing both driver and mechanic. Then another car crashed, killing the driver and seriously injuring the mechanic. However, Meyer had a good car under him and won the race easily.

In 1934 and 1935, Meyer's cars ran poorly. But whenever he had a good car, he was a careful, calculating competitor who got the most out of his machine, waiting for the "hot dogs" to burn themselves out. When Shaw's hood tore loose in 1936, Meyer surged past to become the first three-time winner of this most difficult of races. Lou Meyer had peaked, attaining a height few drivers reach in their lifetimes.

Now it was Shaw's turn. His luck turned at last. He had run four minutes faster than Meyer on the track in 1936, but had spent seventeen minutes longer in the pits. Afterward he said that the failure to install three cents' worth of fresh rivets in the hood of his car had cost him a fortune. The next year, he completely rebuilt his old car and set a qualifying record of 122 miles per hour, though "Wild Bill" Cummings immediately surpassed it. Later, a car went out of control into the pits, missing Shaw by inches and killing two men in its path. Years after the accident Shaw said that he could close his eyes and see every detail of it. But he was a racing driver and he went on competing, in spite of such experiences. That year, he provided racing fans with one of the most exciting races and dramatic finishes in Speedway history.

Shaw was more of a charger than Meyer, but just as smart. He was leading Ralph Hepburn by almost two minutes with only twenty laps left in the classic when his oil pressure fell and he realized that he was running out of oil. His only hope was to slow down. Quickly, he calculated in his mind how much he could afford to give away to Hepburn each lap and still preserve his lead. He then slowed down by precisely that much and Hepburn crept closer and closer. Shaw was not caught by Hepburn until the last turn of the last lap, with the crowd standing and screaming. Shaw was still running, though, and at that moment he pressed on the accelerator and suddenly pulled away from the startled Hepburn, beating him under the checkered flag by 2.16 seconds, the closest finish in Speedway history.

For the 1938 Indy, Shaw ordered an Italian Maserati, but when it arrived, its engine was too small to be competitive and he had to return to his old car. It was a tired machine by now, though, and he was outrun by Floyd Roberts to the wire. In the next 500, one year from his happy victory celebration, Roberts was cut off by another car, crashed, and was killed. For that race, Shaw had obtained a new and more powerful Maserati. He drove it carefully for a while, but then turned it loose with 175 miles to go and more than a minute to make up on his old rival, Meyer. He caught Meyer with 40 miles left, and the two dueled dramatically most of the rest of the way as the fans urged their favorites on. Three laps from the finish, Meyer tried to pass Shaw in a turn and spun out to a stop along the wall. Meyer never drove another race.

Shaw's Maserati was the first foreign-made car to win the American classic in twenty years. He returned with the same car in 1940 in an attempt to become not only the first driver to win the 500 in consecutive years but also to become the second three-time winner. He succeeded. He passed the lead car, driven by Rex Mays, on the thirty-fourth lap and by the seventy-fourth lap he had a lap or more on everyone except Mays. Then Shaw's engine died on a pit stop and by the time he got back in the race he was in third place. But just past the halfway point he regained the lead, pulled far ahead, and won.

When Shaw's cars were right, he was almost unbeatable. In 1941, he came very close to becoming the only four-time winner in Indy history. One wheel on his car had been found to be defective and it was marked with chalk so it would not be used. On the morning of the race, a fire raged through "gasoline alley." A fireman's hose washed the markings off the defective wheel. In the race it was used.

Shaw dueled Mays and Mauri Rose for half the race, pulled away, and was two minutes ahead of the field with 125 miles to go in quest of his third straight victory when the spokes of the wheel tore loose and caused him to slide out, spin, and whack the wall twice with tremendous force. Luckily, although the fuel tanks burst, there was no fire. However, Shaw was paralyzed from the waist down from a blow he had received on the spine. It was weeks before he began to recover. Shaw never raced again.

When the United States entered World War II the Speedway was closed to racing for four years. This and the retirements of Meyer and Shaw ended more than a decade of dueling by two of the greatest American race drivers who ever lived. However, neither could tear himself away from racing.

For Shaw, the Indianapolis 500 was "not only Memorial Day, but my birthday, Christmas, and all good days rolled into one." Following the war, he was approached by Eddie Rickenbacker and asked to buy the Speedway to save it for racing. In turn, Shaw prevailed on Terre Haute businessman Tony Hulman to purchase the track. Shaw himself served as president of the Speedway, running the annual race until he was killed in a plane crash in 1954.

Although retired, Meyer continued in the sport in another way. The greatest engine ever raced at Indianapolis was the Miller, developed by Harry Miller, Fred Offenhauser, and Leo Goosen. The rights to its design were purchased by Offenhauser and the engine was renamed the Offenhauser. Then it was purchased by Meyer and Dale Drake and renamed the Meyer-Drake Offie. This high-powered, specially designed racing engine was constantly improved over the years and was the dominant power plant on the championship trail until Ford came along with its automotive millions to challenge it for supremacy in the 1960s. Even Ford could not discourage the Offie, however, and it remains a key source of competitive strength to the greatest drivers to this day.

Before Meyer and Shaw retired, several other great race drivers arrived on the scene. Among these was one cut in their mold, Mauri Rose. Like Meyer and Shaw, once he attained gold and glory at Indianapolis he swiftly ceased most of his other racing activities to concentrate on the major events. Like Meyer and Shaw, he was a specialist—a conservative and shrewd driver.

Not all of the United States' greatest racing drivers have been daredevils. They have been brave, of course, but only a few could survive for long with wild ways. The best have usually driven with their minds as well as their courage. There are chargers and there are waiters. Most of the greatest winners have been waiters. They have charged when necessary, but have been protective of their equipment and patient with their strategy.

Rose, born in Columbus, Ohio, was a small man who had a moustache, smoked a pipe off the track, and while driving wore a strange visorless helmet like a derby without a brim. He began to race as a wild man, heavy-footed and reckless. He crashed frequently and was lucky to survive. He took many years getting to the top and when he did, it was only after having taken stock of his situation and adopted a more cautious and thoughtful approach to racing. Few men can change their ways, but Rose was a bright man who could. He was always watching, absorbing all that went on at a track, learning, improving.

There is an interesting story about Rose that may shed light on another famous driver of a later era. Years after he retired to become an engineering specialist with various automotive and racing firms, Rose sought out J. C. Agajanian, the sponsor of a wild and reckless young man who was having trouble adapting to the special demands of the Indianapolis track. He told Agajanian, "I've been watching your boy and I think for his first year he's fantastic, and I'd like to talk to him because I think I can help him. I'm not doing anything around here and I don't mean anything to anybody anymore, but I know this racetrack and I know this race and I think I can take some of what I've learned out of my head and put it back in his head." Agajanian accepted and put his driver, Parnelli Jones, into Rose's hands. Rose tutored Jones intensively, and Jones eventually went on to greatness.

Rose is the only driver ever to compete in fifteen consecutive 500s. Only two other drivers, Cliff Bergere and Chet Miller, drove in more 500s. Both drove in sixteen, though not consecutively. Rose drove a total of 6,050 miles in the 500. Only Cliff Bergere, who drove 6,142 miles, has bettered this mark. Although Rose never held the speed record and is not among the all-time leaders in number of laps led, he is one of only four men to take the checkered flag three times at the Speedway.

Rose entered his first 500 competition in a curious way. In 1933, the great Howdy Wilcox, already qualified for the race, was refused permission to run because in his prerace physical examination doctors had discovered he had diabetes. Speedway president Rickenbacker ruled that the car could start with another driver if it was moved to the rear of the field. It was a large field, the last year the number of starters exceeded thirty-three. Rookie Rose was installed in Wilcox's seat. Right up to race time, the other drivers threatened revolt if the popular Wilcox was not permitted to compete, but Rickenbacker stood firm and the rebellion ended at the last minute. Rose started in the forty-second and last position and, through hard driving, moved up to fourth place. He had just passed the 125-mile point when his engine came apart under the torture to which he had subjected it.

The following year, Rose lost the 500 to "Wild Bill" Cummings by only twenty-seven seconds. Disappointed by coming so close, he may have pushed too hard for some years after that because he broke down repeatedly —usually soon after the race began. After eight years of competing at Indianapolis, he had only a fourth and a third place to go with his early second.

In 1941, Rose's ninth year at Indianapolis, his car broke down early in the race again and it seemed he was finished for another year. However, he was asked to take over Floyd Davis's car, which was in fourteenth place, two minutes behind the leader, and going nowhere with 180 miles left in the race. Rose took the car and did one of the greatest driving jobs in the history of the classic. He moved up steadily as others broke down in front of him, including Shaw, whose wheel collapsed, tossing him out of the lead and the race. Rose passed the great Ted Horn and Rex Mays, took the lead, and sped home the winner by more than a lap. He is credited here with half a victory, but some consider this the first of three 500 triumphs for Mauri.

Now that he was finally established as one of the great drivers, Rose had to wait out the four-year interruption of the war. When it ended he returned confidently to driving and was able to obtain the finest cars. In 1946, he was competitive at Indy until his steering failed. His car spun out and crashed, throwing him out unhurt. The following year, he and teammate Bill Holland, in sister Blue Crown cars sponsored by former driver Lou Moore, contested one of the most controversial 500s of all time.

Holland, who was a thirty-nine-year-old rookie, led by two miles at the four-hundred-mile mark when Rose began his move. Actually, Holland thought he led by more. As Rose closed in, sponsor Moore became concerned that his two lead cars would begin to duel, perhaps precipitating disaster. In long races, drivers rely on the scoreboard and signals chalked on blackboards held aloft by their crews to determine their position, the distance remaining to run, and the amount by which they lead or trail. Holland had not learned to use the scoreboard yet, and he relaxed contentedly as Moore's crew flashed him signs indicating he could take it easy and that everything was okay with his lead. When Rose caught and passed him, Holland waved him on, thinking he was still a lap ahead. He was not, however. He was never told that he actually trailed Rose and when he saw his teammate take the checkered flag and coast into victory lane ahead of him, he was furious.

Moore admitted later he simply did not want to risk both his cars in a late duel for the lead and would not have given signals to spur on either unless a third and rival car had entered the picture. Holland never forgave Moore and he felt unhappy toward Rose, though he continued to drive Moore's cars as Rose's teammate because he felt they were the best at that time. But, hard as he tried, Holland still fell almost two minutes short of Rose again the following year as the Blue Crown team enjoyed its second straight one-two finish.

In 1949 Holland and Rose were again running one-two when Rose's car broke down with twenty miles to go. Holland finally went on to win over Johnny Parsons by three minutes. Parsons, Holland, and Rose finished in that order the next year as rain curtailed the chances of the Blue Crown pair's overhauling the leader at the 345-mile mark. With this race the domination of Indy by the duo ended.

After having finished first once and second three times in four years at Indy, the fiery and moody Holland drove only one other time in the 500, finishing fifteenth. He barnstormed beyond the jurisdiction of the AAA, which governed United States championship racing at the time, turned to the outlaw tracks, and concluded his career in obscurity.

After his "third" triumph, Rose drove in the 500 three more years. One year he was third. In his last year, 1951, a wheel broke on his car and he overturned. He was not seriously hurt, but he retired on the spot.

Rose had enjoyed considerable success, especially in the 500. In contrast, Holland had come extremely close but fell frustratingly short. Great drivers have always had great frustrations at Indianapolis. Before Lou

Meyer and Wilbur Shaw retired, another pair of drivers arrived on the scene to dominate American racing even more than Meyer and Shaw, except that they were never able to win the 500.

The Speedway career of Rex Mays began in 1934 and that of Ted Horn one year later. Mays drove the classic a dozen times. He never held the speed record there, but he won the pole position four times, the only driver ever to do so. He led the race nine times. He usually led early and broke down early. He finished twenty-third, twenty-eighth, thirtieth, thirty-third and last. He finished second twice in a row. But he never won.

Horn had a better record. He drove the classic ten times and, while he won the pole only once and led only three times, after his rookie year he never finished less than fourth. Over nine straight years, he finished fourth four times, third four times, and second once. But he, too, never won. In those nine years, he completed a total of 1,799 laps, missing only one lap when he was waved in at the finish because rain was falling.

Horn was less of a charger than Mays. In some ways, he never came as close to winning the 500 as Mays did. Perhaps if just two or three more cars had broken down in front of him, he would have come closer to winning. In any event, although greatness eluded Mays and Horn at Indianapolis, they found it elsewhere as they traveled the country, driving every kind of race they could find. Their spectacular duels dominated the era and they captured the imagination of the sporting public as few drivers ever have.

Horn was born in Cincinnati in 1910 of wealthy German parents as Elyard Theodore Von Horn. He was raised in Pittsburgh and later in northern California. Taught in private schools, he grew up to be a charming, handsome, blue-eyed blond, articulate, immaculate, and talented. From an early age he admired race drivers and turned to the tracks as soon as he was old enough. Like so many others who went on to greatness, Horn crashed in his first race and in many races thereafter. He was injured in a crash at Langhorne when a piece of railing went through his shoulder and broke his collarbone. He was injured at Nashville and was in critical condition for months.

For years, Horn had trouble getting good cars and he survived only because he was a mechanical genius who worked wonders with the cars he did have. For the first ten years, he seldom won and was always broke and in debt. Still he persisted. "I have to race. I'm too lazy to work for a living," he'd say, smiling wistfully.

Meanwhile, Rex Mays came flashing out of southern California into national prominence. Just as handsome as Horn, more hungry at first and more daring, Mays became a matinee idol much sooner. The clean-cut Mays was pleasant and personable. If he met a person once, he remembered his name six months later and would reach out to shake his hand. He always had time for fans and friends. But if he said ten words in a day, it was a big day for him. Mays was shy and modest and really did not give much of himself away to anyone. He always said, "I just want to be one of the bunch." After races, he'd go home to his wife and children in Burbank, California, and live quietly. He was a sincere, impressive person and much admired within the racing fraternity. For example, the tough veteran, J. C. Agajanian, says, "The only real hero I ever had in sports was Rex Mays."

Mays won at Milwaukee, Langhorne—everywhere except Indianapolis. And he was certainly the fastest driver at the Speedway in those years when the speeds were soaring up to and past 130 miles per hour. He won the national driving championship in 1940 and 1941. Had there been no war, Mays might have won at Indianapolis and probably would have compiled a record few drivers could have equaled.

Immediately after the war, Ted Horn came into his own and began to surpass Mays, winning the national driving titles in 1946, 1947, and 1948 to become the only driver to win three straight crowns. Like Mays, Horn won everywhere but at Indianapolis. In contrast to Mays, though, he was a conservative driver. Earlier in his career, he had shown a certain lack of discipline, but, like Mauri Rose, he had altered his ways to become a superb tactician. Before each event, he would walk carefully around the track, studying every foot of the course, and during the race he would baby his car. He was also unusually superstitious and hated having women and children around the pits. Among other things, he disliked the color green and refused to shave or allow his picture to be taken before a race. And afterward he would insist on shaving before posing. Often Horn refused to start in races and dropped out of others even when his car was running well, simply because he had a bad feeling about the race. "Horn's hunches" became famous and often frustrated his crews. But whenever Horn decided to drive in a race, he had a good chance of winning it.

Horn seemed to fear racing, but he loved it, too, and wouldn't give in to his fear. In 1948, he won twenty-five of the thirty-three races he entered. In October of that year, he had his wife and children with him at Du Quoin, Illinois, for a race because she was pregnant and he was worried about her. She had run out of clean clothes to wear when she asked his permission to wear a green dress to the race. He said he supposed it would be okay. At the track, he asked permission for her to park their car and sit with the children near the pits so he could be near her, and the officials said they supposed it would be okay. Distracted, he did not tend to his car as he usually did and did not replace some old wheel spindles as he had planned to do.

While the cars circled the track, getting into position before the race began, a serious threat of rain hovered overhead. Somehow, the cars got mixed up in a ragged pattern, went around three times, and were still trying to unscramble themselves when the starter decided not to hold them back any longer and sent them on their way in a disorderly tangle. They had not gone very far when Horn's car went crashing into a fence, throwing him out onto the ground. He had no marks on him, but he was dead. A wheel spindle had broken.

Horn had already accumulated sufficient points to be awarded his third national title posthumously later that season, as had been done after the death of Jimmy Murphy less than a quarter century earlier. Four months after Ted Horn's death, his third daughter was born.

Rex Mays refused to continue the race that killed his old rival. He would not talk to anyone and went away by himself. As usual, he kept his deepest feelings, possibly his secret fears, to himself. When he returned, he seemed to have been altered by the experience. He was a person who always smiled. Except when he was in action, it is hard to find a photo of him in which he was not smiling. But after Horn's death he was subdued, almost spiritless, and his expression became grim. He did resume racing, but with none of his former fervor.

In June of 1948, Mays, still shaken by Horn's fatal crash, was driving in a race at Milwaukee when Duke Dinsmore's car hit a wall and flipped. The driver was thrown out of the car onto the center of the track. Mays promptly crashed his own racer into the wall to avoid hitting Dinsmore, jumped out, and daringly ran onto the track to Dinsmore's side, standing there protectively and waving off the cars that sped onto the scene. He survived his daring deed, neither he nor Dinsmore was run over, and Dinsmore later returned to racing.

In November of 1949, little more than a year after Horn's tragic accident, Rex Mays drove in a rare auto race on the dirt horse-racing track at Del Mar, California. His front wheels seemed to hit a rut, his car took off, and he was dumped out before it crashed. Mays never wore a seat belt because he always said it was safer to be thrown clear. Now he was thrown into the path of oncoming cars and one or two hit him. Later, doctors determined he had been killed not in the crack-up but by being run over. He was thirty-six at his death.

With these two deaths, the second great era in American race driving came to an end. It was now four years after the war and new race drivers were about to take over the racing scene. The shape of American auto racing was changing. Great drivers would continue to ride on the championship trail through Indianapolis, but others would begin to drive the big stock cars to glory in the Deep South. Americans would drive sports cars and Grand Prix cars in the Far West and in Europe. Still others would begin to hurtle curious cars called dragsters through races that ran a mere quarter mile and lasted six or seven seconds, not three, six, or even twenty-four hours.

4

DAREDEVILS OF
THE DEEP SOUTH

Legend has it that southern stock car racing began when rebel bootleggers could find nothing better to do on Sunday afternoons with the souped-up jalopies in which they ran whiskey all week. There is probably more fact than fancy to this. Bootleg whiskey long has been big business in the Deep South and many of the first auto-racing heroes from that part of the country admit to having run booze in their early days.

Curtis Turner is one example. "Pops," as he is called, was born in 1924 near Floyd, Virginia, where he got the reputation of being the best of "the good ol' boys" at hauling hooch. He drove a souped-up 1940 Ford coupe with big springs in the back and knew the back roads like he knew the back of his hand. On pitch-black nights, running faster than 100 miles per hour, he could easily lose the state troopers. After all, he had been at it since he was ten years old.

"Some ol' state trooper ran me thirty-nine times, but he never come close," Pops recalled once. "I used to talk with that ol' trooper and he'd say, 'I'm gonna catch you if it's the last thing I do, Curtis.' Later, that ol' boy committed suicide, and some people say it was because he could never catch me. I don't know about that, but thirty-nine times sure's a lot."

Not that Turner never was caught.

He used to take sugar from the Little Creek Naval Station in Norfolk, Virginia, drive back into the hills, and trade it for "white lightning," which he'd sell to the sailors. Authorities found out about it and set a trap for him. They let him load up at the base with five hundred pounds of sugar and tried to arrest him on the way out of the gate. But he crashed the barricade and took off with bullets flying around him. The police set out in pursuit and Turner flew through the Norfolk suburbs, across the county line, and lost them in the foothills of the mountains.

By then every law officer in the area had been alerted to look for him. Turner had shaken the first group, but then had to shake a second, with more fireworks. He ran out of gas and hid in the hills. He siphoned fuel from a parked school bus and took off again. But when he got home, the cops were waiting for him and grabbed him. He was fined $1,000 and given a suspended two-year jail sentence.

Turner had heard that some of the "good ol' boys" were racing their booze-runners Sunday afternoons in a cornfield near Mount Airy, North Carolina. So he went to see what was happening, and from that point on he was committed to racing. He was in his late twenties.

Another famous driver, Junior Johnson, began his career in a similar fashion. He was the champion hootch-hauler of Wilkes County, North Carolina. He had a specialty: when the Alcohol Tax Division agents were closing in and ran him into a blockade, he'd hold the accelerator to the floorboard, spin the wheel, skid into a screaming about-face with the insides of the car threatening to burst through the metal, and head right back where he had come from.

"Ah'd say nearly everybody in a fifty-mile radius of here was in the whiskey business at one time or another," Junior once commented. "When we grew up here, everybody seemed to be more or less messin' with whiskey, and myself and my two brothers did quite a bit of transportin'. It was a business, like any other business, far as we was concerned. During the depression here, people either had to do that or starve to death. It wasn't no gangster type of business or nothin'. Gettin' caught and pullin' time, that was just part of it. Me and my brothers, when we went out on the road at night, it was just like a milk run, far as we was concerned."

Junior remembers his father as a hard worker. "There ain't no harder work in the world than making whiskey," he says. Starting about midnight, the "milk deliveries" began. A man who could complete his route was worth his weight in corn. Junior had a hot car. "They wasn't no way you could make it sound like an ordinary car," he admits. So he sacrificed secrecy for speed and roared through the nights, waking up sleeping citizens in backcountry cabins. Finally, in 1955, agents spotted his still and arrested him. Johnson served ten months at the federal reformatory in Chillicothe, Ohio. He'd already started racing, and when he got out he went back to it. Johnson was in his mid-twenties.

Curtis Turner and Junior Johnson are living legends. They are big men, with hands like hams and bellies that hang over their belt buckles. They are big in the South, where they are authentic American folk heroes.

Babe Ruth and Bill Russell are nobodies compared to what Pops and Junior are in that part of the country. Both began their careers before the big tracks and the big money, but they were big stars before some of today's hot kids could balance a bicycle. They burned up the old dirt tracks, where the good ol' boys bashed one another's cars just for fun; and the farmers in overalls, sitting in the stands swigging soda pop and beer, hooted for the sheer hell of it. When the new breed came along to run the smooth high-banks for fortunes, Turner and Johnson were still around able to run with the best of them.

Stock car racing began to boom around the country in the late 1930s and early 1940s. But at first it was considered far less respectable than Indianapolis or Grand Prix racing. It was thought of as a brawling side-light for tough guys who raced their family cars without rules. World War II interrupted its growth. After the war, Bill France, a former driver, mechanic, racing car owner, and promoter, revived racing on the Daytona Beach course, where many of the early speed runs had been conducted. France masterminded the formation of the National Association for Stock Car Auto Racing in 1948, governed the growth of NASCAR, and continues to serve as its president.

The success of the sport mushroomed from the creation of Darlington Raceway in the heart of cotton and tobacco land in South Carolina in 1950. This is a one-and-three-eighths-mile paved track, narrow and tough, and hosted the first 500-mile stock car race. Then, in 1959, France built Daytona Speedway, a massive two-and-a-half-mile track modeled after Indianapolis, but with much higher banks, especially on the turns. As a result it is not necessary to slow down much in the corners and the track is far faster than Indy. The next year, Atlanta Raceway and Charlotte Speedway, one-and-a-half-mile high-banked paved tracks, came into existence. In 1965, a fifth major southern track opened, the North Carolina Motor Speedway, a one-mile paved oval in the sand hills near Rockingham. And in the last year of the 1960s the construction of a sixth superspeedway was completed, a two-and-a-half-mile track at Talladega, Alabama.

Each of these tracks hosts two top races a year at 400 to 600 miles. They are the most important tracks in the Grand National circuit, which is the heart of southern auto racing. However, the Grand National tour also takes in a few courses in other parts of the country, including Riverside Raceway in California and Watkins Glen in New York. There, road races are staged each year on courses of longer than two miles around. The Grand National tour includes forty-five to fifty races, big and small. Most of them take place on paved ovals of a mile or less, some as short as a fifth of a mile around, and in the South a few races take place on dirt tracks.

NASCAR sponsors other forms of stock car racing, too, but its Grand National circuit is by far the biggest and best stock car circuit in the world, and the racing drivers who have been developed on this tour rank with the best in the world. Some have performed better on dirt tracks than on paved tracks, and others have been better on short tracks than long. Some drivers who rarely won in the larger, prestige races have won often enough on the shorter tracks to take NASCAR Grand National championships. They could do this because, even though there are more points awarded in the longer races, there are many more of the shorter races.

Short-track racing is a special form of racing, primitive and punishing, and NASCAR's first champions took this route to the top. Their like will not be seen again, for, with the coming of more superspeedways, the short tracks are bound to be reduced in status to a lesser circuit. As always, when the old gives way to the new, there must be regret for the shape of things as they once were.

The Daytona Beach sand classic was first held in 1949. Red Byron won it and went on to win the first NASCAR Grand National driving championship that year. Bill Rexford won the second Grand National crown in 1950. Then Herb Thomas won in 1951 and again in 1953, and Tim Flock in 1952 and 1955. Thomas won a total of forty-nine Grand National races, Flock forty. In 1955, Flock won eighteen, setting a single-season record that endured for a dozen years until Richard Petty eclipsed it.

Flock was typical of the early NASCAR champions, most of whom had grown up in hard times. He was born on a farm. He says, "My father died when I was a child, leaving nine little Flocks and Big Mama. She worked in a mill for nine dollars a week and nine little Flocks almost went to an orphanage."

The elder Flock had been a tightrope walker at one time, and his children must have inherited his daredevil ways. Four of the Flocks became auto race drivers—Fonty, Bob, Tim, and sister Ethel, who was named after the high-test fuel. Another sister, Reo, made thirty-nine parachute jumps. A brother, Carl, raced boats.

Tim began to race cars in 1950. He won the Daytona Beach sand classic in 1954, but was disqualified because of an illegal part in his car. He was infuriated by the ruling and decided to quit racing. He went home to Atlanta and opened a service station. In 1955, he heard that Carl Kiekhaefer, who operated a powerful racing team, was looking for another driver. Tim applied for the spot, got it, and went on to his greatest successes. "The competition was brutal in those days, though that was before the superspeedways began to dominate things," he pointed out.

"I had the best equipment. I know for a fact that Kiekhaefer spent $278,000 to finance his operation in 1955. I don't know why. He just enjoyed racing and he was in it to give him something to do. He gave all his drivers what they won. The purses were a lot smaller. The biggest purse I ever won was $6,800 one time in Detroit. In my big year, 1955, I won $55,000, which probably is equivalent to $200,000 today."

If not for an unusual difficulty that year, Flock probably should have won one more race than he did. "I had a monkey that rode with me," Tim recalls. "His name was Jocko Flocko. I had a seat for Jocko and a seat belt. During a race at Raleigh [North Carolina] he got loose from the seat belt, became frightened, and got on my shoulder and around my neck. I had to stop and put him out. I finished second. My record would have been nineteen wins that year if it hadn't been for Jocko," Tim says with a laugh.

Despite such monkey business, Kiekhaefer ran a taut team. "I can recall when he'd rent an entire motel for his drivers and their wives before a race," Flock says. "He'd put the drivers at one end and the wives at the other. He'd take a room in the middle and if the drivers and their wives got together, he'd know it. The more races I won, the tougher he was on me."

Tim was driven so hard that he developed an ulcer and his weight slipped 20 pounds below his usual 160. "I remember winning a race on Saturday night in Syracuse, New York," Tim recalls. "There was a race in Bay Meadows, California, the next afternoon. Kiekhaefer chartered a plane for me. Fonty [Tim's brother] was already there and had qualified my car." Tim won in Syracuse, but lost in Bay Meadows.

"Early in 1956, I was exhausted and ill," recalls Flock. "I just walked into Kiekhaefer's hotel one day in Charlotte and told him I was through and walked out." He raced only occasionally after that before retiring.

During Flock's time at the top, Lee Petty came along to surpass him. A lean, hard man, Petty recalls how his career began: "We had a garage. We built a lot of hot rods and specialized in tune-ups. I used to bang up cars on the back roads, but I'd never driven in a race. They had a race at Greensboro, North Carolina, one day. I'd had it in my mind that I'd try a race one of those days, and that day I said I thought I'd give her a go. My brother said, 'You wanna' try?' and I said 'Why not?' So I did. I was thirty-three years old."

Even in racing, life sometimes begins at thirty-three.

Lee flipped in his first NASCAR start in 1947. In 1949 he drove in the first Daytona Beach race and crashed. But he was a patient and determined man who did not get discouraged easily. He was an extremely smart driver, and soon he was winning races and placing consistently high in the annual driver standings. In fact, for twelve straight years he never finished lower than fourth. He was first three times, second twice, third four times, and fourth three times.

Lee won the Daytona Beach event in 1954, a wild race in which the lead changed hands thirty-five times with the cars broad-sliding through the sands at a brutal clip. That year, at the age of forty, he won his first driving title. In 1958 he won his second and he repeated his feat in 1959 with his third. Only one other has won as many, though six drivers, including Lee's son, Richard, have won two. Lee won fifty-four Grand National races before he retired—the record until Richard surpassed it.

In 1959, Lee won the first 500-mile race on the brand-new superspeedway at Daytona. Seven men swapped the lead back and forth thirty-four times. Two men, Lee Petty and Johnny Beauchamp, traded first place back and forth eleven times during the last 125 miles. The cars crossed the finish line side by side. There was no camera at the finish line then and it was three weeks before officials, after studying photos taken from various angles, decided Lee Petty's car had crossed the line a few inches in front of Beauchamp's.

Petty was a rugged driver. At Charlotte that year, his last championship year, Junior Johnson was taking up a lot of the track, preventing Petty from passing him. So Petty started to bang the fender of Johnson's car. This sort of thing is impossible in Indianapolis championship cars because the exposed wheels would cause the cars to hurtle out of control. But it is possible to do it within reason in big stock cars with fenders and bumpers. Unfortunately, Petty's bumper bent Johnson's fender in, cut a tire, and blew it, causing Johnson to spin out into a guardrail. Johnson returned to the pits, changed tires, got back on the track, and ran Petty into the infield. The drivers scrambled out of their cars and came together. Johnson had grabbed a pop bottle and was wielding it. Luckily, before either could be seriously injured, the Charlotte chief of police broke up the fight, arresting Junior for assault with a dangerous weapon.

In 1961, John Beauchamp spun Lee through a fence. Lee's left knee-cap was torn off, some ribs were broken, and it was six months before he got out of the hospital. His knee never was fully flexible again, and Lee, who was in his early fifties, retired, leaving the driving to his son, Richard, who already was on his way.

A driver whose career was similar to Lee Petty's was Buck Baker. He came to the forefront of NASCAR racing during the heyday of Lee, Tim Flock, and Herb Thomas. Baker drove for more than twenty years. He drove in the first Grand National race, a dirt track event held at Charlotte, North Carolina, in 1949. He did not retire until the late 1960s, when he was a grandfather and one of his toughest rivals was his son, Buddy.

A former Greyhound bus driver, Elzie Wylie "Buck" Baker stands in the top ten of NASCAR's all-time rankings with forty-six Grand National victories to his credit. But his long and spectacular career includes many victories on other circuits besides the Grand National. He won the Southern 500 at Darlington in 1953, 1960, and 1964. His last victory is made more remarkable by the fact that he was forty-five years old at the time. The only other driver to win this classic three times is Herb Thomas. Baker won the Grand National driving title in 1956 and 1957 and he was second in 1955 and 1958.

Baker, who had had some hair-raising experiences flying his own plane, never seemed nervous on a racetrack during his career. "I never saw nothing out there to scare me much," he once said. Although he was a superstitious driver who felt that green cars and the number 13 were unlucky in racing, he once drove a green number 13 car for Smokey Yunick, an outstanding mechanic, because it was a good car and he didn't want to pass it up.

Baker was lucky to have good cars in the beginning of his career, as a driver for the Kiekhaefer team. But he was a maverick, and when the big, rich teams sponsored by automotive concerns came into being and began to dominate NASCAR Grand National racing, they were reluctant to hire the old man. Since he was reluctant to beg a spot, he went his own way as an independent for a while. When he no longer was competitive, he quit.

Near the end, he said, "The fastest car doesn't always win the long races, but I sure hate to spot my competition ten miles an hour. And you can't buy groceries with points won at the small tracks."

Since then, his son has helped keep him in groceries. In his prime, Buck Baker stood five-feet-eleven and weighed 175 pounds. His son, Buddy, stands six-five and weighs 235 pounds, which makes him one of the biggest stock car drivers. And he's one of the better ones, too. In 1967 he won the National 500, and in 1968 he was victorious in the World 600, the longest of the stock car races.

After Thomas, Flock, Petty, and Baker had won the last of their driving titles, Rex White won the 1960 crown. White won a total of twenty-six Grand National races, including the Dixie 400 at Atlanta in 1962 near the end of his career, and he was one of the better competitors of his day. The next great NASCAR drivers were Joe Weatherly, who won driving honors in 1962 and 1963, and Glenn "Fireball" Roberts, who never won the top prize. Both were killed in 1964.

Weatherly, a short, husky, homely fellow who always wore brightly colored sport shirts and saddle shoes when he drove, was an immensely popular competitor who came to be called "the Clown Prince of Racing." He was also affectionately known as "Little Joe." He was a fun-loving character who adored the spotlight. Weatherly began racing motorcycles in the late 1940s and became a national cycle champion. Later, he switched to cars and drove all kinds on many different types of tracks, but he disliked the Indianapolis cars, which he called "big cucumbers."

Reminiscing, Weatherly once explained, "I got started on my motorcycle with the wilder type of boys. We'd go cross-country. I'd take the bike out on Friday afternoon and bring it back with the handlebars broken, the frame bent, a wheel twisted, or an engine blown on Monday morning. I'd also have a few things broken on me. See this scar running from my left eye to my chin? It came on a street, not a track. I stopped driving on the streets after I got three speeding tickets in one month and my license suspended for a year. I began to fly a plane so I could get to the races and save my speeding for the tracks, where it's safer."

In a race at Savannah, he somersaulted his car six times, soared over a twenty-foot fence, and walked away from the wreckage in a drainage ditch. "All I got out of it was two bloodshot eyes," he laughed. He drove all night—685 miles—and the next night was driving in a race at Moyock, North Carolina. "If you want to cash in, you got to be there when the man puts his hands out with the money," he explained.

Weatherly came up the hard way. He performed very well on the short tracks and later he proved himself on the superspeedways when he won the Rebel 300 at Darlington in 1960 and 1963 and the National 400 at Charlotte in 1961. The latter race was perhaps the highlight of Weatherly's career. He led almost all the way, then fought off Richard Petty through twenty of the most furious laps NASCAR racing has produced. He never let Petty past and won.

Actually, he won only twenty-four Grand National races in his career, but he placed high consistently in many other races. In 1961, Weatherly finished the season in fourth place and reached the top ten in points for the first time. He was thirty-nine years old. In 1962 and 1963 he finished first. In 1963 he won only three races, but on twenty occasions was one of the top five cars to take the checkered flag and wound up with the title.

In January of 1964, the two-time defending NASCAR champion entered the Riverside 500 in California. During the week preceding the race, he sat trackside and said, "Nothing comes easy to anyone in racing and certainly nothing ever came easy to me, but it's a great sport and now that I'm on top all the struggles seem worthwhile."

Weatherly was asked if he felt fear. "Yes," he grinned, "but ah don't let it get the upper hand of me. They build these cars pretty good and the people who run the sport do everything they can to keep it safe. Shucks, you wouldn't want it too safe. What would be the fun of it then?"

A short time later he was interviewed by Chris Economaki, the editor of the *National Speed Sports News* and a broadcaster, who noted that Weatherly was one of the few drivers who did not wear a shoulder harness, though he did wear a seat belt. Weatherly said he got fidgety in the seat of a race car and moved around so much that he felt extra harness would hamper him. He also said, "The harness might snap your neck in a quick stop."

Midway in the Riverside 500, the throttle of Weatherly's Ford jammed as he traveled through a turn at 100 miles per hour, and he slammed into the retaining wall in front of the bleachers with such force that grandstand patrons were showered with glass from the windshield of his car. He was wrenched forward and killed by head injuries. He was forty-one years old in his final race, which his wife witnessed. They had no children. Later, a stock car museum that Joe had promoted at Darlington was opened and named, in his honor, the Joe Weatherly Museum.

Another great driver, Fireball Roberts, was as introverted as Joe Weatherly was extroverted. Born in Florida in 1929, he picked up his nickname as a semipro fast ball pitcher, but it seemed appropriate later in his racing career and gave him considerable color. Roberts was a powerful, six-foot, two-hundred-pound man who dressed simply and wore his hair in a crew cut. He drove like a demon, pushing his cars to their limits and often beyond. He also drove colorfully. However, out of a car, he was moody, often rude, and very much of a loner. Roberts was a sharp business-man who made racing a good business. He gave short answers to reporters, dodged publicity, and often avoided fans. As this became obvious he was sometimes booed by crowds, but he shrugged it off. "They pay for the right," he said. In spite of this, many fans cheered him because he was such a dynamic driver. During his career he became a very controversial character, constantly bathed in a spotlight he hated.

Roberts studied automotive engineering for a while at the University of Florida, but dropped out after two years. He preferred racing cars to building them and began racing in 1947. He was in on NASCAR's birth the following year and came into prominence in the Southern 500 at Dar-lington in 1950, when he started in the sixty-third position and finished second. At one time or another he held the speed record at almost every track in the South. For three years in a row, he was the fastest qualifier in the Daytona 500, and won the same honor five times at Darlington's Southern 500.

Throughout his career, Roberts led Grand National races for a total of 1,644 miles, nearly twice as many as any other driver up to the time of his death. He often broke down while leading a race, but he did win a total of thirty-two, including eight superspeedway races, more than any previous driver. His record shows the following impressive victories: the Southern 500 at Darlington in 1958 and 1963; the Rebel 300 in 1957 and 1959 at Darlington; the Dixie 300 at Atlanta in 1960; the Daytona 500 in 1962; the Firecracker 250 at Daytona in 1959 and 1962; and the Day-tona Firecracker 400 in 1963. He won on every superspeedway in exist-ence then except the one in Charlotte, North Carolina.

Some of the greatest NASCAR drivers have never won the driving championship because they concentrated on the superspeedways and did not work the small tracks as relentlessly as others did. This was true of Fireball Roberts. He tried sports car racing at Sebring, in the twelve-hour endurance contest, and at Le Mans, finishing sixth in the twenty-four-hour grind in 1962. But he often passed up the smaller Grand National races. So he seldom finished in the top ten in points. However, the superspeedway races are faster, richer, and more dangerous than the short-track races, and only drivers who have performed well in the big ones can be considered among the great American race drivers. Roberts certainly qualified in this respect. He was the first southern stock car driver truly famous beyond the South.

The Fireball, who chain-smoked and had developed an ulcer, hid his worries from the world. He once said, "When everything is working perfectly, I'm no more afraid than I am driving the family car on a highway. When something goes wrong, it scares the hell out of me," he said with a smile. "And something's always going wrong. But that's what makes it fun."

But as time went on, he spoke less and less of it being "fun." Near the end, Roberts, who always seemed nerveless in race cars, admitted, "I get scared in racing. I'm scared most at the beginning and at the end of races. I'm always scared, but what I dread above all else is fire."

In May of 1964 Roberts was driving at Charlotte, which he called his "jinx" track because he had held the pole position five times and had finished second twice, but had never won. His car tangled with those of Ned Jarrett and Junior Johnson and crashed in flames. Ned Jarrett's car caught fire, too, but he leaped out to help pull Fireball from the inferno and beat the flames off his "fireproof" suit.

Roberts was rushed to a hospital with severe burns over more than half of his body. He fought valiantly for forty days. He seemed on his way to recovering when he developed severe infections and then contracted pneumonia after a skin graft operation. He died at thirty-five.

Roberts had divorced his wife and left only a young daughter behind. He had once remarked, "No one knows me very well." This was because he didn't let many know him very well. But some drivers knew and understood him. He was comfortable only among other drivers and many attended his funeral near his home in Daytona Beach, Florida. Fred Lorenzen, who had been injured in a Daytona race the day before, left a hospital bed to attend the funeral. Driver Ned Jarrett said, "Fireball was the most respected driver there ever was or maybe ever will be. He was the ideal. A lot of drivers copied him, but few had his ability. He had as much to do with making stock car racing the major sport it is today as anyone else in the world."

Meanwhile, Junior Johnson and Curtis Turner raced on. Like Roberts, neither ever came close to the driving title, but when the money was on the line they were there. Both drove so hard that their cars often broke down while they were leading. Even so, Johnson won fifty races, a mark topped by only three others, and Turner won seventeen, despite missing four years while on suspension.

Johnson's impressive string of victories includes the following: the the second Daytona 500 in 1963; the Dixie 400 at Atlanta in 1963; the

National 400 at Charlotte in 1962 and 1963; and the Rebel 300 at Darlington in 1965. He led the World 600 in 1963 until he ran out of gas with five miles left. He thought he had won the Southern 500 at Darlington in 1962 until officials announced eight hours later that there had been a scoring error and someone else had won.

Turner, who often ran on outlaw tracks, won more than 350 races in his career, but only a few big ones in Grand National competition. He won the Southern 500 in 1956 and the Rebel 300 in 1958, both at Darlington. Accidents didn't seem to slow him down. He broke his back at Charlotte once, and as soon as he got out of the hospital he resumed driving. At one track, he crashed through a fence and immediately crashed through again from the other side to get back in the race.

Johnson and Turner came along too early to win a share of the big money. For example, in a dozen years in the big time, Turner earned less than $100,000. However, both of these enterprising former bootleg runners managed to become rich along the way—Johnson as a chicken farmer near Ronda, North Carolina, and Turner as a lumberman near Roanoke, Virginia. Turner actually made and blew several fortunes. He invested $1 million in planning the Charlotte Speedway and went deeply into debt trying to build it. When he tried to obtain a loan from the teamsters' union, they agreed on condition that he organize a drivers' union. This he tried to do, for which he received an indefinite suspension from NASCAR boss Bill France.

For four years, Turner rebuilt his fortune and ran a few outlaw races. Then France unexpectedly reinstated him in 1965. No one thought that Turner, who was forty-one years old, could possibly come back, or would even attempt to do so, but he did. In the 1965 inaugural race at the new superspeedway at Rockingham, North Carolina, Turner, taped up from cracked ribs suffered in an earlier race, battled young Cale Yarborough for 500 miles and came out on top. Two years later, he became the first driver to crack the 180-mile-per-hour barrier at Daytona as he paced all qualifiers to win the pole in the hottest race on the tour. In the race itself, however, he broke down.

Now that he was back in racing, he was as tough as ever. At Winston-Salem, Bobby Allison found his path around Turner blocked a few times and began to bump the veteran in an effort to nudge him out of the way. Angrily, Turner pulled off the track onto the infield and waited for Allison to come around. When he did, Turner accelerated and rammed him. A riot almost developed among the fifteen thousand fans, and both drivers had to be ejected from the race before peace could be restored.

Yet there is a story told that shows another side of Pops Turner. Once he and some friends left a party to attend an unimportant minor-league dirt track race in Richmond, Virginia. There are not many Negroes in racing, especially in southern racing, but Turner noticed a black team struggling with the worst-looking race car he'd ever seen. "I believe some boys need some help," Turner said. He jumped the fence and went into the pits. He didn't tell them who he was, but he began to work on their car. He got the engine running well, and when the race was called, he jumped in the car and won it. He was handed the winner's check, turned it over to the team, and disappeared into the night. The next week, when another driver asked if he could drive their car, the black owners were firm. "No, sir," one said, "this car is reserved for the big man in the white shirt and fancy cuff links."

Junior Johnson and Pops Turner always drove hard and partied hard. For some years, Pops teamed with "Little Joe" Weatherly, swinging through the circuit, racing hard, ramming each other for fun, taking their winnings, and having a ball. Before one race, Joe filled the water cooler in Pops's pit with mint juleps. Pops had pulled into the pits for fuel and was about to sip what he thought was water when Joe pulled alongside and yelled, "Hey, Pops, gimme a swig of that stuff."

Pops and Little Joe had a place near Daytona where they used to throw parties during the annual Speed Weeks there. They'd hire bartenders after hours, but Little Joe liked to serve drinks by squirting them from a fire extinguisher into a flower vase. "That way you don't have to pit so often," he explained. They'd blow $5,000 a week on parties, but felt money was only for spending anyway. "I've made a few fortunes, but it never lasted long. I like to live high," Pops says.

Once, Pops and Little Joe took out rented cars and drove down a highway banging into one another broadside. Eventually they limped back to their motel in their crippled cars and Joe drove his right into the swimming pool. Pops fished him out and put him to bed, and the next morning they were back racing again. When Weatherly was killed, something seemed to go out of Turner. He retreated a little farther behind his big stetson and dark glasses.

He and Junior Johnson were the last of the real good ol' boys. Junior retired in the late 1960s. He was in his middle thirties and he said, "Ah've always been a charger and ah don't want to race any other way, but they're going too fast for me now and ah jus' don' feel ah can go as hard as ah could a year ago or the year before that."

Fireball Roberts and Little Joe Weatherly had died. But Pops Turner couldn't bring himself to quit. He was lucky to survive a horrible accident at Atlanta in which he flipped ten times. This frightened his sponsors out of giving him good cars, but as the 1960s ran out the brawling bachelor was still chasing the checkered flag, still throwing wild parties at his plush home in Charlotte. "If I was to die tomorrow, I'd have been the happiest son of a bitch who ever lived," he says.

Turner is a throwback to the caveman days of stock car racing, just twenty or so years ago, and the end of this era, the first great era of auto racing southern style, awaits only the end of his driving career.

5

RICHARD THE LIONHEARTED

The big racetracks with the big cars and the huge crowds are a long way from where Richard Petty lives in Level Cross, North Carolina, which is near Randleman, which is so small its telephone switchboard is in High Point, which is not the largest place in the state, either. A visitor would take the main highway, cut off onto a small road, turn off a smaller road, off that, and when he got to a general store and gas station with a Coca-Cola sign out front, he'd find still another road, a dusty, bumpy little cow path, and take that to the Petty spread, which is three houses, a big garage, shade trees, green grass, and brown dirt.

Lee Petty and his wife live in one house, and their sons Richard and Maurice and their wives and families live in the other houses. The three men and a half-dozen employees work on stock racing cars in the garage most of every week. Almost every week they tow one of the cars away in a truck, perhaps to the nearby airport, and then to a track where Richard will race. It is very countrified, peaceful and quiet, except when they fire up one of those racing engines, *varoom, varoom, varoom.* The Pettys work and play here, and then Richard really goes to work on racetracks to make some more money to play with.

Richard Lee Petty, who dislikes being called Dick, is a tall, husky fellow, six-feet-two and 195 pounds. He is very handsome, with a lot of curly brown hair, and has a relaxed, friendly manner. He smiles a lot and speaks with a soft but not overpowering southern accent. He is the greatest stock car driver who ever lived, but even so, there is very little pretension about him. Some even think he is greater than A. J. Foyt or Mario Andretti or Dan Gurney. He might be, except that Richard Petty has never driven anything but stock cars, mostly in the Deep South. So he just hasn't demonstrated the versatility necessary to be granted the highest laurels. Like Foyt, Petty is a family man, but he is a far less wild man, on and off the track, and he tolerates defeat somewhat more graciously.

"I don't know anything about greatness," he has said with a smile. "That's for others to decide. My daddy was a race driver, so I became a race driver. If he'd been a grocer, I might have been a grocer. If he'd been a baseball player, I'd probably of wanted to be a baseball player. But he was a race driver, so here I am. I grew up around cars. I been working on 'em since I was twelve years old and driving 'em since I was twenty-one and it's all I know really. I jus' go out and do the best I can and often as not it's been good enough. Oh, I have pride in my record, but I really just consider myself a workin' stiff.

"Maybe there's glamour in racing, but I don't see much of it. All I see is the inside of an engine and the inside of a car, all hot and banging, and other cars and a narrow stretch of road, and some pit signs and some flags. I hear the cheers when I win, but I'm usually too tired to think much about it by then. The money's good, of course. We can have anything we want. The fact is, we don't want much. We're just country folk, really. And I regret that racing keeps me away from my family, from my wife and three kids, half the time. So I have them travel with me whenever possible. It's a hard life, but there's harder lives."

Richard was born in North Carolina in 1937, around the time his father began to race. In high school he was an all-star football lineman and a good all-around athlete. After graduation he attended business college. He met his wife, Lynda, a cheerleader, in high school, and married her soon afterward. They now have a son and two daughters. He helped work on his dad's cars for a few years and then one night, when there were two races available and Lee could run only one, of course, Richard told his father that he'd like to try the other one. Lee looked at him and thought a moment and then said, "Well, we have a few old cars laying around, so we'll fix one up and let you give her a try." So they did that. Richard recalls, "So I went to one and he went to the other. He didn't even see me run my first race. Anyway, I didn't win. I didn't win much for a while."

As Richard Petty can attest, it is not easy to break into the big time. Drivers take what cars they can get and try to make enough of an impression to be offered a ride with one of the big teams, which have the only cars good enough to win consistently. Richard was fortunate in that he had an entrée into racing. Some drivers have slept in their cars and gotten by on beans and ham sandwiches to save money for entry fees on the way up.

Many of them have never gotten anywhere and have quit and gone home in disappointment. But Richard had good support. "The first couple of years I must have torn up about twenty or thirty thousand dollars of dad's racing equipment and I didn't bring home any money," he says. "But he just let me find my way. If it'd been anybody else, I guess I'd've been shot out of the saddle and never made it, but dad carried me."

Father and son raced against each other for four years, and Lee never gave Richard a break on the track. Once, at Atlanta, Richard took the checkered flag just ahead of his dad and coasted right into the pits. Lee kept charging around for another lap, then went up to the officials and demanded a recount, claiming the checkered flag had come out one lap too early and the race hadn't been completed until he just finished it. They checked and, sure enough, Lee was right. So they took the trophy away from Richard and gave it to Lee and declared him the winner. Questioned about his act, Lee snorted, "I don't reckon I regret it. When he wins, he can have it, but he ain't gonna have it give to him."

Richard smiles and says, "Dad taught me you have to earn everything you get. They were hard lessons, but I don't regret them."

In 1960, Richard won his first Grand National race and began to do well. "That was my third year on tour and I earned about $35,000, which came close to getting dad even on me, and I've done all right ever since," Richard recalls. Lee, who didn't even start driving until he was thirty-three, was in his late forties and had won forty-nine Grand National races, which was the record then, plus three driving titles, which is still the record. Then he was severely injured in a crack-up and had to retire in 1961. "I may have been old as most athletes go, but a lot of race drivers have had their best years in their late thirties and done well into their forties," Lee says. "Experience is more important than muscle in this business, but when I had to quit, it was up to Richard, who was still just a kid, really."

Richard has recalled, "I knew I had to make the living for the family then and it gave me a lot of desire."

In 1960 and 1961 Richard placed second and eighth respectively in driving standings. He placed second again in 1962 and 1963. The latter year he won fourteen races, by far the most he had won in any single season of his first nine years on tour. Although his victories did not occur in super-speedway races, he was driving forty or fifty races a year and placing consistently high in the small events on the short tracks. In this way he piled up points and made a fair amount of money—up to around $50,000 a year. Finally, in 1964, he broke through at the start of the season by dominating the last 350 miles of the Daytona 500 and winning easily at a new record speed of more than 154 miles per hour. This was his first superspeedway triumph, exactly ten years after his dad had won the first Daytona 500. Richard had triumphed at the age of twenty-six, whereas Lee had been thirty-nine. Winning eight other races and placing among the top five finishers in thirty-seven out of sixty-one races, Richard won his first driving title and made almost $100,000 that year.

However, he was driving Plymouths for the Chrysler Corporation at the time, and when NASCAR outlawed the big engine Chrysler was using, the company withdrew from racing. Out of loyalty, Richard withdrew, too, and stayed out through most of 1965. "I'm wastin' time," he said sadly, and went drag racing, drawing big crowds and making good money. However, at a small drag strip in Dallas, Georgia, in April of 1965, a wheel of his car broke off and went into the crowd and the car swerved into a ditch, up an embankment, over a fence, and right into a knot of spectators, smashing into a small boy. As Richard sat dazed on the ground outside his smashed car, someone said, "You just killed a boy. How do you feel about that?"

Petty replied, "Just go see how that boy is."

The boy was dead, though, and others were hurt.

Late in the season, Chrysler and Richard returned to racing. "It's my work," Richard explained. "It's a hard sort of business. It's hard when you lose friends. Sometimes you can profit by mistakes. I know when Jimmy Pardue got killed, he busted through a guardrail at Charlotte. They rebuilt the guardrail stronger. Next race, I hit it in exactly the same spot, but it held me. Myself, I've been lucky. I've had accidents, but I've never been upside down and I've never been hurt bad. I've never felt scared of racing. If I ever did, I'd quit. The only thing I regret in racing is killing that little boy. It wasn't exactly my fault. It was one of those things that can happen in racing. And it was on a circuit that isn't as safe as ours. But I sure regret it."

Back in racing at the tail end of the 1965 season, Richard won a few races, and then came back into his own in 1966. At the beginning of the year, at Daytona, he set a new record by qualifying at more than 175 miles per hour. During the race he overcame early problems and the time spent during seven pit stops to change eight tires and charged from far back to win a rain-shortened Daytona "495" at an average speed of more than 160 miles per hour. Richard Petty became the first man ever to win that classic twice. Later in the year, he won the Dixie 400 at Atlanta and the Rebel 400 at Darlington, as well as lesser races.

In 1967 Petty was simply incredible, surpassing several NASCAR standards. At one point, he set a tremendous record by winning ten straight races. He wound up winning twenty-seven in all, breaking Tim Flock's one-season mark of eighteen, and along the way he eclipsed his dad's career mark of fifty-four. He won the Rebel 400 and Southern 500 at Darlington and the Carolina 500 at Rockingham, plus a bundle of 100- and 200-mile races on the small tracks. He placed in the top five in thirty-eight of forty-eight races, won his second driving title, and set another record by earning more than $130,000 in purses.

Richard returned in 1968 to win sixteen more races, including the American 500 at Rockingham, and won nearly $90,000 to become the first NASCAR pilot to pass the half-million-dollar mark in earnings. In January, 1969, he won the Riverside 500 road race and kept right on winning. At one point he won two races within eighteen hours in Tennessee—the Smoky Mountain 200 at Maryville on a Saturday night and the Nashville 400 on a Sunday afternoon—each by a car's length. The next victory, a 250-lapper on the quarter-mile asphalt oval at Bowman-Gray Stadium in Winston-Salem, North Carolina, gave him one hundred Grand National triumphs in his career, far more than anyone else had ever won. He wound up the year with ten victories and $109,000 in earnings.

Richard Petty was just thirty-two years old and had been driving for only ten years, yet he had won at more than twenty different tracks, including every superspeedway except Charlotte. Few other drivers have ever won more races on superspeedways. On top of that, Petty was certainly the best NASCAR driver on the short tracks.

"I got all the money I'll ever need, I guess, but I'm too young for a rocking chair, and I still got a lot of go in me," he said.

In 1970, the engine in Richard's car went sour after only eighteen miles of the Daytona 500, but Richard then joined Lee and Maurice in the pits to help mastermind new star Pete Hamilton to a stunning upset triumph in a Petty team car. In the Rebel 400 at Darlington, Richard's car got out of shape, hit an inside wall, flipped several times, and came to rest upside down with Petty lying half out of it and unconscious. He was carried away on a stretcher, but, incredibly, suffered only a severe shoulder injury and was back racing a month later, and back in the winner's circle, after a 400 at Riverside, six weeks later.

"It shook me up, but it didn't shake me out of wanting to go on racing," Richard drawled.

Most of his career, Richard drove a bright blue Plymouth, a new one almost every year, and he became known as "Little Boy Blue." He was loyal to Chrysler even when Ford produced faster cars, but in 1969 he finally switched to Ford. In 1970, he switched back to Plymouth. Some say he could win in a Volkswagen.

Richard Petty is a smooth driver and makes few mistakes. Some call him a rattlesnake because he seems to coil, waiting to strike. He has a "feel" for racing. One admirer has commented, "Ever see a good bartender pour whiskey without using a shot glass? He doesn't have to look and he can pour a hundred and you ain't never gonna git a drop more than what's coming to ya. He has the feel. Richard, he has the feel, too."

Richard says, "If a boy told me he wanted to be a race driver, I'd say forget it. It's tough to break in and it's dangerous while you're learning and it takes a long time before you know if you're any good or not. In the end, I think, you've either got it or you don't. You can't train for it, and all the practice in the world won't help if you don't have it. It's not only raw ability, but sort of instinct for knowing when to pass and when to not pass and when to charge and when to lay back and just how much your car can take that day in that race on that track. You have to push everything as far as it'll go and if you push any further, forget it. And if you don't know when is too far, nothing good's gonna happen to you.

"I know cars better than most drivers because I work on my own cars more than most, and that helps because I can sort things out quicker than most others. I've had real good equipment, which really helps, of course. One thing's for sure, no driver ever got to the finish line first without a good car under him. You can't beat anyone walkin'. And there's nothin' more discouragin' than to run your butt off in a long race and get to near the end first and have the car give out on you. That happens lots, even with good cars. I led the Volunteer 500 at Bristol, Tennessee, for 450 of the first 496 laps, then had my engine blow on me 4 laps from the finish, and I coasted 3 laps still ahead before it stopped. But I won a few like that, too. It's the sort of sport you got to determine your way to the top sometimes."

Right after winning one race in horrible, humid heat at Nashville, he collapsed and had to be revived with oxygen. The promoter of the race had a couple of cute girls circling the track atop a car and asked Richard if he wanted to ride with them and he said, "No, thanks, I just want to lie on the ground so they won't have far to go to dig me under." Another time, after winning an equally hot race, he sneaked away from the victory ceremonies and lay down in a truck with a wet rag over his face. Someone came over and asked him why he hadn't kissed the beauty queen. And Richard said, "If I couldn't do it right, I figured I just wouldn't do it."

It is a hard sport, with some races lasting four or five hours, and Richard is as hard as he has to be, just as his dad was. Once, after a tough race, he and Ned Jarrett had a fist fight. Another time, when a race was called off, angry spectators closed in on the drivers and track officials and some drunks began to swing tire irons. Richard waded into the drunks and wiped them out. An official said, "He's as good a fighter with his bare fists as I ever saw."

Lee and Richard Petty head up the most remarkable family in auto-racing history, superior to those of Buck and Buddy Baker, or Indianapolis 500 winner Jim Rathmann and his brother Dick. Only Bobby and Al Unser, 1968 and 1970 Indy champions, along with their father, uncles, brothers, and cousins, who have dominated the Pikes Peak Hill Climb, currently have a chance to surpass them. Al seems assured greatness.

Richard's mother says she wasn't upset when her husband turned race driver at the age of thirty-three. "I told him, if that's what he wanted to do, to go ahead and do it. But I'll admit I thought he was just skylarkin', and I had no idea it would come to all of this," she once said laughingly while standing outside her house and looking sort of helplessly at the garage and cars. "When Lee had his accident in '61, I wasn't surprised. I always knew it could happen. That was a hard time, but it could've been worse. And when Richard was starting and Lee was so hard on him and people demanded so much of him, I was upset, but I guess it was all for the best."

She sat down and sighed. "I'm afraid for them, certainly. It's hard on any woman in any racing family. There's nothing we can do except wait and hope for the best. But it's no good trying to make a man not do what he wants to do. And my men are good at this business and have worked hard at it and don't take any unnecessary chances. And it's a good life. People have the wrong impression of it. Maybe it started out wild with a bunch of bootleggers and all, but it's a real clean sport now. There's a lot of manliness to it, and my family has been something special in it and have been able to stay real close because of it. I feel real proud."

Richard's wife has said, "His job is racing and my job is to raise his family right and be a good wife to him. I want Richard to go to each race knowing his family is well cared for. We go to as many races as we can because we want to be together as much as we can. And I really get a kick out of the races, just like any fan. Maybe I get more excited because of Richard, but in the longer races I sometimes get sort of bored and restless just like anyone else. But it's sure not a boring business, even if it is a sort of restless one. It's a dangerous business, of course. And I worry about him. More than I'll ever let on. But I know he's good and can take care of himself. And I appreciate the good living he makes for us."

Lee Petty, lean, hard, closemouthed, cigar chewing, said, "All you can do is the best you can. I'm right proud of Richard, of course. If I could've won more races, I'd of won 'em, and maybe Richard would've never caught me. But I won every one I could and Richard has come on and won more, so more power to him. O' course, I got a late start," he added, allowing himself a rare chuckle. "I'll admit I get more nervous in Richard's pits than I ever did drivin' myself. When you're drivin', you feel in control of the situation. Now all I can do is see that things is prepared as proper as I can and then watch and encourage and throw out a little advice maybe he'll take and maybe he won't, and some of the time he'll be right anyway."

Richard stood in the cool of a shade tree, breathed in the fresh air, looked at the open country around him, and said, "We could move to the big city, but we like it here. We can all be together here. I don't think nothing of jumping in a car and driving eight or nine hundred miles for a race. Maybe we seem sort of stuck out here in the country, but you don't like to get above your raisins, you know. We do quiet things. Racing's excitement enough for us. The house is all paid for. The kids is all paid for. I'm still young and I've been having myself a high old time."

He was wearing a sport shirt, Levi's, and high boots. On Peachtree Street in Atlanta, wearing a suit and tie, he'd knock the ladies dead, but he'd rather not. He walked behind the garage where, in a weedy hollow, lay a large pile of twisted and broken cars and metal debris that would gladden the heart of a junk dealer. "Anytime I get to feelin' too cocky, I can always come back here and look at this and sober up," he said. How many of the wrecks had he put there? "About half," he grinned. "I done my share of winnin', but I done my share of this kind of losin', too," he said. "It's a good sport, though. Used to be rough, but it's cleaned up a lot. The fans are clean and real sportin'. The drivers are clean and real businesslike. We're all a better class of people now."

"Ain't no way they could be worse," joked Lee, who was standing nearby.

Richard squinted into the sun. "We run this thing like a business. We run every race we can. Some good drivers pick their spots, saving up for the big ones. That's one way. Our way is to run 'em all. You keep sharper that way. And make more money. Lots of people figure the reason I've won so many races is because I've run so many, which is true to a point, but I've also won a better percentage of my races than anyone else, too. Winning's our business. Greatness, I don't know nothing about that.

"I've thought of going to Indianapolis, though not for a long time. Not to prove greatness, but to win a one-hundred-and-fifty or two-hundred-thousand-dollar first prize. But they wouldn't just hand it to me, you know. And I don't know if I'd like those little 'June bugs' down so low to the pavement and out in the open with open wheels all around me. I kind of like being enclosed in a lot of metal. Anyway, I'd have to take too much time away from our circuit. I don't know that racing. I know this one, so it's best I stick to it."

It was time for him to get back to work. "We work eight or nine hours a day, five or six days a week, just like anyone else. I look after the chassis of the cars and drive 'em. My brother, Maurice, looks out for the engines. Mom watches over the books, and pop watches over all of us," he said with a smile. "If I could make more money running a supermarket, I'd run a supermarket. My best thing is driving cars. I make my living at it. It's a business, like any other business."

6

THE BRAVE BUSINESSMEN

There's no denying that stock car racing is a brutal business. Stock cars are big machines weighing around thirty-five hundred pounds each, and as many as fifty of them may be crammed into a single track on the NASCAR Grand National circuit. Because of the high banks on some of these tracks, they are the fastest tracks in auto racing. In the last year of the 1960s, drivers were negotiating the 2.5-mile Daytona Speedway and the 2.6-mile Alabama Speedway at around 200 miles per hour. Veteran driver Cale Yarborough says, "When I started in racing about a dozen years ago, I never thought I'd be driving anywhere near that fast. They keep improving cars and tracks, but I don't know if they can keep improving men. I don't know how much faster a man can go and still control a car. Sometimes it seems we're hurtling out of control. The G forces really press on you. You grip the steering wheel so hard, your arms and shoulders wear out. And it scares you."

Adding to the problems has been the technique of "drafting" developed by Junior Johnson and now popular throughout the circuit and virtually unique to stock car racing. Booming along, the big cars create a vacuum behind them. By moving in close behind another, a trailing car is sucked along and uses less fuel. It also pushes along the car in front, and both are given extra momentum. It is extremely dangerous to run with a car's nose pressed to the tail of a preceding one at, say, 225 miles per hour down a straightaway, but confident NASCAR stars do it. And as the trailing car swings out to pass the lead car, the trailer carries the suction with him, which can "slingshot" him past the leader. Thus, it is considered more advantageous to be a close second than to be leading on the last lap of a big race. And NASCAR Grand National superspeedway classics are the most closely competitive of any races and are often settled on the last lap as a drafting car "slingshots" around the pacemaker.

Most of the new tracks are well planned. A few of the older tracks are extraordinarily difficult. Richard Petty says, "Daytona has been the easiest because it was the biggest and widest and smoothest. The competition is very intense and very fast, but not especially dangerous. If the drivers are about equal, all you can do is let it all out as far as it'll go and you either have the best car or you don't. Darlington is something else. Every turn is different, so every turn is difficult. And there are places you just don't dare to try a pass. And places you don't dare make a mistake.

"But no superspeedway is as tough as some of the small tracks. When you run a half-mile track one hundred or two hundred or even four hundred laps, you sprint and struggle every inch of the way. I think Freddie Lorenzen was the toughest driver I ever faced on a superspeedway. And Ned Jarrett or David Pearson on a short track. These are, or were, specialists. Good businessmen out for a buck, you know."

The money is there, all right. Auto racing has been drawing approximately forty million paid spectators each season in the United States, second in sporting attendance in this country only to horse racing, which has gambling as its main lure.

NASCAR is the busiest auto-racing operation, sponsoring more than 1,000 events each year, which pay out around $4 million in purses and draw some twelve million spectators. USAC operates a select circuit of just about 125 events each year, which pay out around $2.5 million and draw around three million fans.

USAC's championship trail remains the major league of American racing, with twenty-five or so events each year. Aside from the Indianapolis 500, these events distribute around $1 million in purses, with the winner of each race receiving an average of around $5,000 to $10,000 per victory. There is only one Indianapolis 500, which draws around 300,000 fans, pays out around $1 million, and rewards its winner with more than $250,000. The superspeedway in Ontario, California, may prove to be a comparable draw and produce a similar jackpot.

By contrast, the Daytona 500 draws more than 90,000 fans, pays out around $250,000, and rewards its winner with about $50,000. However, there are more big races on the Grand National tour, which has around fifty races in all and pays off about $1.25 million. More drivers have been earning approximately $100,000 a year in NASCAR than in USAC racing.

On both circuits, fat contract guarantees, extra sponsorship money, and lush endorsement money are available to the top drivers, swelling the individual incomes of some to around $250,000 a year. In no other sport is big business so vitally interested.

Even with the entry of Ford into USAC racing and the heavy investments by Firestone, Goodyear, and other product manufacturers in the championship trail, the big automotive companies are more deeply concerned with NASCAR racing than with any other circuit. The main reason is that NASCAR Grand National drivers use cars that look like the cars the average person drives on the public highways. The winning car in a Grand National superspeedway race on Sunday tends to be a hot item in dealers' showrooms the following week, especially in the South. In the early years, drivers piloting Oldsmobiles, Chryslers, and Hudsons won most of the titles. In recent years, drivers have raced Chevrolets, Pontiacs, Plymouths, Dodges, Fords, and Mercuries to take the crowns. Over the years, Fords have won far more races than any other cars.

However, the men running the racing teams for the automotive companies remain southern stock car veterans, owners, and mechanics. Some of them are former drivers, such as John Holman, Ralph Moody, Ray Fox, Bud Moore, Ray Nichels, Smokey Yunick, Cotton Owens, Banjo Matthews, Lee Petty, and Glen and Leonard Wood, who run the fastest pit crew in captivity. And the drivers who man or have manned the cars for these brilliant men remain the spotlighted stars: Richard Petty, Ned Jarrett, David Pearson, Bobby Isaac, Bobby and Donnie Allison, James Hylton, Fred Lorenzen, Cale Yarborough, and Lee Roy Yarbrough. Some of them are reminiscent of the daredevils of the Deep South's past, but all of them are good businessmen.

Isaac, for example, never has won a superspeedway race, but he came close to beating Pearson for the 1968 NASCAR driving title, and he won the most races in the 1969 season. "I never played a game of anything in high school. I always wanted to race," the veteran North Carolinian explains. "I was racing on the side while I was working in the cotton fields for forty dollars a week. Some day we'll have only superspeedways on the Grand National circuit. Right now, I drive forty or fifty races a year, some of them worth only one thousand dollars, but it all adds up so long as I win my share, which I do. It's a job and I make a good living at it."

"I consider auto racing a business," Ned Jarrett said a few years ago as he sat in the infield at the Atlanta Speedway with the big cars booming all around him. "I like to conduct myself in a businesslike manner. It is good business for me to enter as many races as I can. The more races I enter, the more money I can win and the more points I can earn toward the championship. I have a good organization behind me that enables me to run all kinds of races on all kinds of tracks with good equipment that gives me a chance of winning. I enjoy racing and, except for the sacrifices I must pay in my family life, a long schedule is no hardship on me. I believe ambition is half the battle. I firmly believe that if a person knows what he wants to do, he can do it if he is willing to apply himself and make sacrifices and maintain his determination. I have been successful, and with success comes confidence. I am a very confident person."

The South does not seem to change as quickly as other sections of the country, and this is not necessarily bad. The flavor of southern auto racing is reminiscent of what it was twenty years ago. A person can still hear the Sunday revivalists preaching on the car radio as he drives to the track past signs addressed to coon hunters. Confederate flags still fly at the tracks, and "red-necks" still give out with rebel yells. But the cars in the traffic jams are big and shiny, and the women with the bare-chested, beer-drinking, soda-pop-guzzling guys in the stands are fancily turned out in the latest-style flared pants, short shorts, and miniskirts. Although a Pops Turner may still be stomping around, there are fewer new drivers cut in his image than there are in the image of Ned Jarrett.

During his racing days, Ned Jarrett presented such a squeaky-clean appearance that he made people tingle all over. He is tall, dark, and handsome, and he smiles a lot. He is proud, but modest, intelligent, and soft-spoken. He used to play ball with his sons. He opens car doors for his wife. He is so polite that he used to return sportswriters' phone calls. He still does, even in retirement. In his racing days, he made Frank Merriwell look like a bum. Those people who think race drivers are hard and mean, a little crazy, and that southern stock car drivers are fat and full of booze and profanity should meet Ned Jarrett. Five minutes with him and he'd have them convinced that race drivers, northern, southern, or Martian, are in a class with scientists, brain surgeons, and spacemen. They did not call him "Gentleman Ned" for nothing.

Ned Jarrett is a country gentleman. He stands six-feet-one, weighs 185 pounds, and dresses conservatively. He is married to a bright, attractive blonde named Martha, who used to be president of the organization of race drivers' wives, an auxiliary that raises funds for the families of needy racing people. They have two sons and a daughter. They live in a three-bedroom home on treelined Brook Drive in Camden, South Carolina. On Sundays, they attend St. Timothy Lutheran Church. During his racing career, townspeople who didn't know him well could easily have mistaken him for a rising young banker or an insurance executive. He was neither. He was a race driver. Jarrett was born in 1932 on a farm near Newton, North Carolina. One of four children, he was the only member of his family to catch racing fever. "As far back as I can remember, I loved to drive—a team of horses, a wagon, a tractor, anything," he recalls. "I can remember clearly dad letting me drive the family car to church when I was only nine years old. I played basketball and baseball, but my heart was always in auto racing. You have to remember that stock car racing was the only big-league professional sport in the South until the 1960s. Oh, college football always has been big, and a lot of southern boys have always gone into baseball. But to me, as to a lot of boys who got taken to dirt track races or big track races around their hometowns, race drivers were absolute gods. The big baseball and basketball and football stars never were as big in the South as Fireball Roberts and Junior Johnson, and even today a Richard Petty or a Lee Roy Yarbrough is about as big a hero as they come in our part of the world. Nowhere in the country are the auto racing stars revered as in the South."

At seventeen, Ned quit high school to join his father and brother in a lumber business they had started. Secretly, however, Ned had his heart set on getting into racing somehow. His brother-in-law and another fellow owned a sportsman racer. These are cars that have smaller engines and may be smaller and older than the ones that compete on the Grand National circuit. The partner ran short in a poker game one night and offered to sell his interest in the car for $400. Ned, who had some money saved up, did not have to be asked twice. He was nineteen when he drove the car, a re-built 1939 Ford, in his first race in 1952 and finished tenth. However, his father did not approve of this dangerous business and talked him out of it. Ned was not old enough to argue. However, he did convince his father to let him continue to work on the car so long as he did not drive it. Ned played it straight for a while, hiring a driver. One night, though, the driver was sick, and Ned subbed for him and finished second. From then on, he resumed driving.

Jarrett braved the big time in 1953, entering a car in the Southern 500 at Darlington. However, the car broke down after eight laps and Ned placed last. Discouraged, he stuck to the smaller sportsman car circuit for six years, and won the driving title in that division in the last two years. His renewed confidence finally built up to the point of overconfidence and one Friday night in 1959 he wrote a check for $2,000 to buy a car that had been raced by Junior Johnson. He planned to reinvade the Grand National circuit. Unfortunately, he had only $900 in the bank. However, he could enter two weekend races worth a total of $1,000. He won both, borrowed $100, and got to the bank in time to cover the check. The car was his and he was on his way.

In 1960, Jarrett borrowed some money to finance a full Grand National tour and went on the road, a poor boy trying to make good. His car broke down many times, but he rapidly became a smart driver who could nurse it to its limits, and he managed some high finishes. In fact, he was running second in the World 600 at Charlotte until he blew a tire and hit a wall eight laps from the finish. He won $20,000 that year. But it had cost him $22,000 to operate. Still, he had made a good impression and began to get better sponsors after that.

In 1961, he won only one race all season, a 100-mile dirt track event at Birmingham, Alabama. However, week after week he nursed his car to high finishes. It happened to be a year in which the top drivers were dividing the victories fairly evenly. At season's end, only his second in the big time, Jarrett had the most points and so was the new driving champion. This was a great surprise to everyone and it was considered a fluke. However, Jarrett began to win a lot of races after that, and he began to place consistently high in the driver standings.

In 1964, Ned Jarrett won fifteen races, the second-best single-season total in history. He also won his first superspeedway triumph, the Dixie 400 at Atlanta. And in 1965, he came back to win thirteen more races, including the Southern 500 at Darlington, and his second driving title. By the time he retired after the 1966 season, Jarrett had won fifty Grand National races, which was the third highest number up to that time.

During his career Jarrett won only two superspeedway classics. In the Dixie 400, he started seventeenth. When Fred Lorenzen was sidelined early, he took his crew and equipment to Jarrett's pits in order to help out. Ned fought a tortuous battle through the field to take the lead just past the halfway point, then had to hold off Richard Petty in the late stages. The lead changed hands thirty-five times in all. When Petty's tires failed him, Jarrett went on to win—on Lorenzen's tires. In contrast to this hard-fought battle, Ned won the Southern 500 by fourteen laps. And he was close to winning others. He led the Daytona 500 with three laps to go in 1963, but ran out of fuel and finished third. In 1965, he missed placing among the top five finishers in only one of eight superspeedway classics. That year, he was out of the top five in only twelve of fifty-four races, big and small.

The fact is, Jarrett was a short-track specialist, close to the best NASCAR ever has had. While he was never a rough driver, he scored best on the rough tracks. He was a smart, conservative driver and wasn't the pushy sort who would jump out in front early and make others chase him. He was fraternal and would run with the pack, taking the lead in a modest way only if it was made available to him. When the rough tracks tore up others' cars, Ned would still have his car running smoothly.

He was not only very good at his profession, but very proud of it, too. He enrolled himself, his wife, and even his pit crew in one of Dale Carnegie's "How to Win Friends and Influence People" courses, concentrating on the lessons in "How to Stop Worrying and Start Living" and public speaking. He'd often travel up to ninety thousand miles a year, spending much of his time making speeches on racing and traffic safety at schools and at dinners. He may have been the best ambassador of goodwill NASCAR has ever had. He won the organization's Heroism Award for stopping to help pull Fireball Roberts out of his fatal and flaming crash in 1964.

"It's a good sport and a clean sport," Jarrett has said. "Most of the fellows in it are very sporting. It's a dangerous way to make a living, but it's not as dangerous as sensational stories would have you believe, and ours is the safest circuit of all. I'm proud of my association with this profession." Jarrett was thirty-four when he retired, a fine career behind him.

Another driver, cut from somewhat similar cloth, is David Pearson, the NASCAR champion in 1966, 1968, and 1969. Pearson was born and reared in a small mill town, Whitney, South Carolina, near Spartanburg. As a boy, he built powerful hands and arms and shoulders hefting heavy spools of cotton. He quit school at sixteen to get married and become a race driver. He still lives in Whitney with his wife and three sons.

David Pearson is a quiet, gentlemanly, clean-cut fellow and his handsome face shows traces of his Cherokee Indian ancestry. He is not the public spokesman for the sport Jarrett was only because he does not have Ned's polish. "I jus' don't have the education to speak at banquets and such, and it depresses me, 'cause I love racing," he comments. He is bothered by his lack of schooling and is almost painfully shy and withdrawn except with racing people.

"From the time I was a little shaver, racing was all I ever wanted," Pearson recalls. "Me and my buddies used to sneak over the old board fences at the Spartanburg Fairgrounds and watch the stock cars flying on that dirt track, and I always knew that was for me." He used to sweep out his older brother's body repair shop just so he could be near the bent-up racers that were brought in. He used to race anyone who'd challenge him or take up a challenge, even if his prospective bride was in the car. Helen Pearson says, "David sure got in a lot of races on the streets and never lost a one that I can recall. It always scared me to death and I'd yell for David to stop and let me out. He'd laugh at that. We got married in 1952 when we were teen-agers. David would still take up a challenge up on the flat-lands above town."

Four months after their first child was born, Pearson bought an old racing car for $40 and told his wife that he was going racing. Helen offered to go to work to support him if he'd forget it, but he wouldn't. He fixed up the car, entered it in a race, finished second, and won $13. "I was scared," his wife recalls, "but then I saw how thrilled he was when we were driving home and I realized how slow he was driving. I realized he'd finally found a place to satisfy his lust for speed, so I was relieved."

David's mother offered him $30 if he'd sell the car. He took her money, sold the car for $70, and with his profits bought another racer. For several years, he worked all week and raced on weekends, mostly on outlaw tracks. "I didn't know anything about weights in a car or anything else when I started," Pearson recalls. "Some of my buddies were helping me and they knew about what I knew. We thought we had to lean to the left like all good race cars, so we all jumped up and down on the left running board of my old jalopy and actually knocked it over to one side. That's how I went about setting up a car."

The first time he drove a Grand National race, the World 600 at Charlotte, the generator fell off, and David and his "crew" put it back on with a wire coat hanger and finished the race.

"I ate a lot of dirt on the way up," Pearson recalls. "On the way up you eat dirt and push old worn-out cars on dimly lit tracks and hope you get a break before you get killed. The old tracks tear up the cars and it keeps you working just to keep going. If you're a winner, it's even tougher. You're like the gunman in a western movie. You have the reputa-tion and everyone is after you to see if you're really good. Some of the small tracks even put a bounty on your head—a bonus to the driver who knocks off the top man."

After joining NASCAR's sportsman car circuit and winning thirty of forty-two races and the South Carolina state championship, David moved onto the Grand National trail. He drove twenty-two races without a victory in 1960, but showed enough promise to be offered a place on a factory team in 1961. He startled the stock car racing world in his sophomore season by winning three superspeedway classics—the World 600 at Charlotte, the Dixie 400 at Atlanta, and the Firecracker 250 at Daytona.

His wife remembers that first big score at Charlotte quite vividly. "I watched the race from the infield," she recalls, "and I wasn't scared until a driver had a real bad crack-up. Later he lost his leg. I shuddered at David having to continue the race after such a horrible accident, but he was leading and he did go on to win. Everyone came running up to me and started yelling about how much David had won. I couldn't even see them because tears were rolling down my face. An official came to take me to the winner's circle. When I got there, David was kissing some gal movie star. I remember a reporter asking me if I was crying because he was up there with a beauty queen. I was so happy I couldn't answer him. David and I had both dreamed that he might someday be in the spotlight. I wanted him to enjoy it. Later, though, I told him not to overdo it."

She laughs wistfully. "That first race, David earned twenty-eight thousand dollars and a new convertible. His cut was twelve thousand, including the car, the first new one we'd ever earned. When he told me he wanted to put the money into a house I was thrilled. We decided our home would be in the same mill village surroundings that we both knew and loved. I was really proud of David when he told me he didn't care for a big house with a lot of fancy trimming. Maybe he knew it wouldn't always be as easy as it was that year, but he's never changed, no matter how much money he's made. None of it came easy."

Pearson earned almost $50,000 that year and was nicknamed "Little David" because he'd knocked off the goliaths. "I don't know how I did it," he says. "I wasn't that good. Only I didn't know it. I'm a charger. I had a good car. I charged with it. It held up. I won. I soon found out I had a lot to learn, however."

During the next six years, he did not win a single superspeedway race. In fact, in 1962 and 1963, he did not win a race of any sort. In 1964, he won eight. But in 1965, he won only two. He was getting better, however, and coming close in the races he lost. And in 1966, he won fifteen races, his first driving title, and almost $60,000. In 1967, Pearson fell out with Cotton Owens, for whom he had been driving Chrysler cars, and sat out much of the season until he settled on a Ford team spot. And in 1968, he came back strong to win sixteen races. He finished among the first five in thirty-six of forty-eight events, won his second driving crown, and earned $118,842, the third highest total in racing history.

Along the way, Pearson ended his long drought on the superspeed-ways in striking fashion by capturing the Rebel 400 at Darlington to become the second driver in history to win classics at all four of the South's original big tracks. He was so relieved and happy over his record that he wept in his pits. Then in 1969 he won the Yankee 600 in Michigan and the Carolina 500 at Rockingham to become the first man to conquer the first six ovals on the circuit. With these and nine other triumphs, he won his third driving title and $183,700. Early in 1970, he won the Rebel 400 at Darlington.

Still, Pearson's reputation is that he is a short-track specialist, the best NASCAR has ever produced on dirt tracks and on road courses. A big man, he is extremely tough and, though he pushes hard, he is an unusually smooth stylist. His cars seem to glide through courses. It is not always smooth sailing, however. To win a 250-lap race on Richmond's half-mile track he had to struggle through five pit stops to change sixteen tires. He won a 300-lap race on the one-third-of-a-mile oval in Asheville, North Carolina, by steering with his left hand and turning the ignition on and off with his right hand to accelerate and decelerate after his engine jammed in a wide-open position. In 1969 he also won a 500-lap race on the one-mile track in Bristol, Tennessee, despite a week-long siege of flu and 102-degree fever on race day.

But in spite of his impressive victories, Pearson has never become a superstar, perhaps because he shuns the limelight. He regrets his lack of education and feels embarrassed by his rough edges. He avoids small talk with fans, interviews with reporters, and public appearances. Yet he is one of those race drivers who are happy only around racing tracks and in the company of members of the racing fraternity, and with these people he does relax and his fun-loving nature comes out. For example, he will "borrow" the camera of a track photographer, shoot pictures of every pretty girl he can find, slip the camera back in place, then amuse himself by imagining the poor fellow's reaction when he develops his film.

A publicist named Jim Hunter was once chauffeuring Pearson on a highway when a policeman pulled them over. As the officer stuck his head in the car window, David said very seriously, "I sure am glad you stopped him, officer. I've been trying to get him to slow down since we got on the road. He's been driving so fast I've been scared out of my wits." Hunter got a whopping ticket.

Pearson especially used to enjoy himself with Cotton Owens, his long-time boss. A writer would corner the pair in a garage and Owens would say, "I picked this here boy up out of the gutter. He was a has-been at twenty-five. If it hadn't of been for me and the good equipment I give him, he'd be racing go-karts back east somewhere. Everything he has, he owes to me. If it wasn't for old Cotton, Little David would be no one."

Hearing this, David would make a face and answer, "Why, this here old boy had a little two-car garage and was living with his family in a shack when I came along. If it hadn't been for my fine driving, he'd be pumping gas out in the sticks somewhere and trying to tell the one or two people that would pass each day what kind of a fine driver he once was, which he really wasn't. Now that he's got me driving for him, he's got a big engineering company and a fine home. He should pray for me every night."

It seemed sad to many when they separated, but Pearson had been losing the big races and he and Owens were beginning to blame each other and they finally split up after a series of arguments. Now that he is with Dick Hutcherson, Pearson has been capturing the classics. "That still don't mean Owens was wrong," Pearson says. "It's a funny game."

He adds, "Stock car racing is two ends of the world. You win and you're at the very top. You're surrounded by fans. You're a great driver and a great guy. You blow an engine, blow a tire, strip a gear, hit a wall, or do one of the thousands of freakish things that can keep you from victory lane and you're a nobody. You take your busted racer to the garage area and sit in solitude to dream about the next week, the next race, the next bit of glory. You earn every nickel you make and deserve every ounce of credit you get. Nothing comes easy.

"It's like a giant carnival, on the move from town to town. Every track is different and you have to set up to meet a new challenge every week. There are nights of sleeping in the truck or working until daylight in the garage just to pick up a fifteen-dollar tow fee to get you to the next race. It takes most of what you win, even when you win consistently, to keep on the road from race to race, and to keep your car in condition to run again and again. There's a lot of work and heartache from the bottom to the top. One race you're a hero and another you're a bum."

By the end of the 1969 season, Pearson ranked among the all-time winners in Grand National racing with fifty-seven victories, three driving titles, and $569,777 in earnings.

In any discussion of the great moneymen in NASCAR racing, Freddie Lorenzen must be given credit as the first to enter the big time. In contrast to Pearson, Lorenzen was a long-track specialist who asserted his greatness on the superspeedways, where gold hides in every corner. If a race was less than 200 miles long, he didn't bother with it. He entered only fifteen to thirty events a year.

Fred Lorenzen was that rarity in southern stock car racing—a northerner. He was born December 30, 1934, in Elmhurst, Illinois, and later settled in Chicago. His father was an electrical engineer. Fred played basketball and football in high school, but he liked cars, and went to auto races whenever he could and listened to radio broadcasts of the southern stock car classics. "I heard all about Fireball Roberts, Joe Weatherly, and Curtis Turner, and they were big heroes to me," he explained once.

"When I was still pretty young I got my hands on a midget car and I used to wheel it around the neighborhood pretty fast until the cops took it away from me. When I was sixteen, I started carpentering with my brother-in-law and joined the union. A friend sold me a race car cheap, a jalopy, and I took it racing and rolled it over, but I was on my way."

Lorenzen raced hot rods at Soldier Field in 1955 and the next year he won a couple of track titles around Chicago. Then he ran in NASCAR minor-league events in the East and Midwest in 1957. He switched to USAC and won the 1958 and 1959 stock car crowns. But this was before USAC beefed up its stock car circuit, and Fred was dissatisfied with the returns. "The best year I had, I won fourteen thousand dollars, a trophy, and a gold watch," he said with a grin. So he switched back to NASCAR and headed south to hunt his fortune on foreign ground.

Lorenzen took his savings, bought his own car, prepared and drove it himself. Fortune eluded him, though, and he failed to win a race in 1960. He had won $8,000 and spent much more than that. He recalled, "I slept in the backseat of the car and ate peanut butter sandwiches half the time. It was no good. I sold my car and trailer for $7,500 and quit racing. I owed $10,000. I paid off $4,500 of it and went home. I needed a used car to get around in. I bought one for $2,500. By then, I had $145 in my pocket and $5,500 in debts. I was some big shot."

Then Ralph Moody called him up and asked if he'd like to drive a new Ford for the powerful Holman and Moody team. Lorenzen was surprised. He couldn't imagine what he'd done to impress anyone. But he knew it would be a long time before he squared his debts by hammering nails, so he grabbed the chance and returned south. Given good equipment, he quickly began to move up in the standings. In 1961, he won only three races, but one was the Rebel 300 at Darlington. His purses were worth $30,000 and after taking his 40 percent, he paid off his debts and opened a bank account.

In 1962, he won only two races, but one was the lucrative Atlanta 500, and his earnings passed $40,000. In 1963, he struck gold. He won six races, including the Atlanta 500 and Charlotte's World 600. His earnings of $113,750 set a NASCAR record. From then on, Lorenzen was the man to beat in superspeedway events. He won the Atlanta 500, the National 500 at Charlotte, and the Rebel 400 at Darlington in 1964, the Daytona 500 and World 600 and National 500 at Charlotte in 1965, and the American 500 at Rockingham in 1966.

Once he was at the top, Lorenzen looked as if he belonged there. He was a rich and handsome bachelor, husky and tanned, with a loose mop of brownish blond hair. Away from the track, he knew how to smile. He had a nice apartment in Chicago, stayed in plush motels on the road in the South, wore good clothes, ate well, and was popular with good-looking ladies. He liked to have fun and could afford it. For a while he piloted his own plane, but sold it because he found it an impractical expense. Basically, he was conservative in his outlook on life.

"I've been broke and I didn't like it," he smiled. "I invest my money so I'll never be flat again. I haven't spent a dime of the money I've earned racing. I live on other money, from endorsements and such things. I don't live big. I bum a couple of cigarettes a day. I drink a lot of beer, but no hard liquor. I share my flat with a friend. I date, but I don't get hung up. I don't want to get married while I'm driving. I'd like to be financially set when I quit. I love driving, but it's a business with me."

Lorenzen's best friend in racing was the great USAC champion, A. J. Foyt. Like A. J., Freddie was tough and smart, moody and a bad loser. He was very serious about racing and tended to be tense and irritable while preparing for a race, and hard on those around him when things were going wrong. He'd go into a race cocked and ready to fire, and would shoot the works to win. Lorenzen was a perfectionist. By concentrating on the big tracks, he learned them well and he always had his car primed. He was not a charger, but would lay back for the right moment to move. He was the ultimate master at drafting, and the only lap he really cared about was the last one.

In the 500-lap, 250-mile Volunteer 500 at Bristol, Tennessee, in 1964, he trailed Richard Petty by three laps with four laps to go when

Petty's engine blew. Richard coasted for three laps, but came to a stop on the last lap and Lorenzen came on to win. He led only the last lap, but it was enough. In the 1962 Atlanta 500, he took the lead just before the race had to be halted at 328 miles because of rain and was declared the winner. In the 1965 Daytona 500, he took the lead in time to win the jackpot when rain washed out the classic at 332 miles. By then, he was popularly known as "Lucky Lorenzen."

However, he was more than lucky. He was shrewd and as tough as he had to be. In the Old Dominion 500 at Martinsville, Virginia, he drove without any brakes and won the race. In the National 400 at Charlotte in 1965, he saw that he either had to run with Foyt or Foyt would run away from him, so he dueled A. J. for a hundred miles, bumper to bumper, swapping the lead back and forth, until he helped Foyt up to the wall near the finish. A. J. crashed and his pal Freddie won. In that shortened 1965 Daytona 500, Lorenzen and Marvin Panch crunched sides near the finish, but, whereas Panch had to drop out, Lorenzen limped into the pits, had the torn sheet metal pulled off one side of his car, and raced back out to maintain his lead.

They also called him "Fearless Freddie." In 1961, he blew a tire at Atlanta and landed on a fence. The same year, after taking the checkered flag at Darlington, he flipped upside down. In 1964, at Daytona, he came upon a wreck, slid into the infield grass, and was rammed by another car. He was hospitalized with two cracked bones in his back and severed tendons in a wrist that required surgery. Two days later, he ducked out of the hospital to serve as a pallbearer at Fireball Roberts's funeral. Soon Freddie was driving again, and in his first race, a 500-lapper in brutal heat, he won with his back strapped in a brace.

If Lorenzen had the lead in a race, he wouldn't move over for anyone. At Atlanta once he blocked off Junior Johnson and Junior was furious. He drawled, "All ah know is that what Lorenzen pulled here, he pulled a couple times down at the beach [Daytona]. He sort of swerves and fishtails raht in front of me, tryin' to keep me from goin' round him. If he hain't agonna get outta mah way, ah'll jus' bore straight through him. If he ever does it again, ah'll knock hell out of him."

Freddie just laughed and kept on driving his way, and no one ever did knock hell out of him. "The thing is," he explained, "if you're in front, you want to stay there, and if you're behind, you want to get in front. So you do what you have to do as best you can, and sometimes accidents happen. But you don't go out of your way to look for them. You try to avoid them. This is a tough business, of course, but it is a business, and you can't win any races in the hospital."

There is that word again—business.

Lorenzen's practical attitude toward the sport is demonstrated by the following story. Once at Darlington, he was well ahead of the other drivers, and still running hard. He wore out a tire late in the race and almost lost because he had to make an extra pit stop. At the next race, he found a big, bold sign on his dashboard that read, "Think! W.H.M.!" He asked sponsor Ralph Moody what it meant. Moody said it meant "Think! What the hell's the matter with you?" Lorenzen laughed and saw to it that the sign was in all his cars from then on. He even had a hole sawed in the floorboard of each of his cars so he could keep his eyes on his right front tire, the one that takes the most pounding in stock car racing. He left little to chance.

Relaxing in a motel in Atlanta one evening, he explained his racing strategy. "At Indianapolis, they prepare a month for the 500. That's the way to go. Big preparation for a big race. I'd like to win Indy. It's my kind of money. But that's a different kind of racing. A different kind of car. I'm used to fenders on my wheels and a roof over my head. I'm used to high banks. I can't take the time to learn it. So I'll let it go. The glory doesn't mean garbage to me. I'm only interested in money and I'm best prepared to win in NASCAR.

"Most of the guys drive fifty or sixty races a year. They run big risks for little cash. The driving title is worth a few bucks in appearance money, but not enough to make it worthwhile. More glory, but you can't spend glory at the market. By running only the big ones, we have a couple of weeks to prepare and plan and practice for something worthwhile. I'm fresh and my crew is fresh and my car is fresh.

"The car is the most important thing. That makes your owners important and your mechanics important. I don't just mean guys who know their business, but guys who take extra pride in excelling. I got the best behind me. Some guys say this is why I win. Sure, I can run an engine until it blows and they'll pull another one off a truck for me. The independent can't do this. I know that. I went that way, myself. But in the end, you all wind up on the track with the same stuff and you win or lose on the track.

"To succeed, you've got to have ability and you've got to push yourself. A lot of guys have my ability, but not many have my desire. You got to have ambition and determination to get ahead and be willing to make any sacrifices it takes and that's true in any sport or any business. Then you need experience. There is no substitute for experience. You have to know how to plan a race depending on what you've got going for you and you have to know how to adjust your plan as a race develops. You just don't pick that up by jumping in a race car."

Lorenzen continued, "Finally, you have to have guts. This is a tough racket and we lay our lives on the line to make good in it." He paused and rubbed his hand over his eyes and was quiet a moment before resuming. "You crash and you get scared. Your friends get hurt or killed and you get depressed. Hell, there are guys gone I miss so bad it hurts inside. But you got to have the sort of hardness to live with that and go on or you can't be a good race driver. In racing, you don't look backwards. You look to the next lap and stand on it."

In 1966, Lorenzen entered only sixteen races, but won eight of them, including the American 500 in North Carolina. He earned $72,385 that year.

Red Sullivan, a longtime friend of Lorenzen's and his chief mechanic, said, "Fred's always been a hard man with mechanics. He double-checks everything. He's very businesslike. He's always been a jitterbug. He's high-strung and he vibrates. He has this severe drive to win and he really gets turned on. Lately, however, he seems to have mellowed. He's a little more patient with everyone. When things go wrong, he says, 'That's the way it goes,' and shrugs it off." When Sullivan's comments were passed on to Lorenzen, Fred smiled and said, sort of wistfully, "Maybe it's time to quit."

In 1967 he failed to win any big races and felt that he had lost his edge. It was indeed time to quit.

Throughout his career, Fred Lorenzen had won only twenty-six Grand National races, but eleven of them had occurred on superspeedways, which constitutes a NASCAR record. He had won more than $400,000 before retiring at the age of thirty-two.

Suddenly, in 1970, he returned to big-time racing. He may have lost money in the stock market slump, but denied money was his motivation. "I just plain missed racing," he said. "It's hard on me, but I missed it."

The most recent big moneymen, besides Pearson and Petty, are Cale Yarborough and Lee Roy Yarbrough (who are not related). Like Lorenzen, both concentrate on the big races. During the last couple of years of the 1960s, what one didn't win the other usually did, and the loser would usually take second place. In the most bitter duel for domination of stock car racing the sport has ever seen, they have set records for speed and money throughout the South. Neither man is afraid to take a fling at Indy, either. Both have raced there, and while neither has gotten very far, it is not a bad bet that one eventually will, showing a versatility that thus far has eluded the greatest of the southern stockers.

Cale, the one with the extra *o*, certainly isn't afraid of anything. Born William Caleb Yarborough in March of 1939 on a five-hundred-acre tobacco farm in Timmonsville, South Carolina, he grew up cropping tobacco and cutting timber. He would ride bulls in the barnyard and pull their tails to make them buck. He used to swim in a nearby river and dive in headfirst from an eighty-foot-high cypress tree. The water was only five feet deep. He and his pals used to catch snakes bare-handed. Poisonous ones counted double. He claims he once wrestled an alligator.

Later on, a skydiving friend asked Cale if he'd ever tried the sport. Cale said he hadn't. That day he made his first jump. He's made twenty since. Once he tried to land in a bay and wound up on a roof in a shopping center. He had always wanted to own a plane, so he and a friend bought one. They climbed in and Cale started it up and took off. After they'd been flying awhile, enjoying themselves, Cale suggested that the friend might want to take a turn and land it. The pal admitted he couldn't fly. Then Cale admitted he didn't know how, either. So Cale landed it. Rough, but safe. Later, he learned to fly and now pilots his plane all over the United States.

In high school, Cale was an all-state fullback and had college offers, but he didn't like school so he skipped them. He did play semipro football for a while. He became an amateur boxer for a while and won most of his fights by knockouts. However, ever since his dad had taken him to see the Southern 500 at Darlington when he was ten, all Cale really wanted to be was a racing driver. "I used to dream a lot," he once said. "I would sit on a tractor plowing cotton and dream fantastic, impossible things—like my name in headlines for winning races, and piloting my own plane to races— and I'd plow right into the next field."

Cale began racing in the local soap box derby. Then he got a motorcycle, learned to do tricks on it, and toured some carnivals. Before he left high school, he had gotten himself a jalopy that he would drive to school, work on during lunchtime, then race nights and weekends on bush-league tracks. At seventeen, four years before he was eligible, he lied about his age and began running NASCAR minor-league events. He even drove in the 1957 Southern 500. An official who knew he was underage twice yanked him out of the car. Twice Cale got back in. Finally the official chased him clear out of the arena. Officially, Cale placed fifty-seventh.

For six years, Yarborough raced on the small backwoods tracks, working on the side. After he went broke running a turkey farm, he decided to make racing his full-time career. He was married by then. He went straight to Ford racing director Jacque Passino and asked for factory support. Passino was impressed by the stocky youngster's brashness and said, "I'll help you, but the first time you mess up, you're history."

In Yarborough's second race for Ford, Ned Jarrett blew an engine in his path and Cale slid out of control and flipped three times. When he called Passino and told him what had happened, Passino said calmly, "No problem. We'll give you another car." So Cale drove this one until the Rebel 300 in 1964, when he was sidelined with a burnt piston. He told Passino that it had been all right the week before. Passino asked him if he had checked it before the race. Cale admitted he hadn't. "You just messed up," Passino said.

Cale went back to the bush tracks, and then quit in disgust. He was working and playing semipro football when Passino called to offer him a second chance—as a handyman with the Holman and Moody team. Cale took the offer. In 1965, he got another chance as a driver and finished second in three superspeedway classics. He also crashed at Darlington, right over the fence, but he survived. The next year, Ford sat out part of the season, then returned to racing and reassigned Yarborough to the Wood brothers team. The combination clicked.

Yarborough won only one race in his first nine seasons in Grand National competition. He won only two in his tenth season, 1967, but one was the Atlanta 500 and the other was Daytona's Firecracker 400. He beat Dick Hutcherson by one car length in the latter event.

In 1968, he won six races, including the Atlanta 500 and the Firecracker 400 again, plus the Daytona 500 and Darlington's Southern 500. He had qualified for the big one, Daytona, at a record of nearly 190 miles per hour. With three laps to go in the race Cale passed Lee Roy Yarbrough and beat him home by three seconds. He won with an average speed of more than 140 miles per hour, despite eleven slowdown periods because of accidents and ten pit stops to replace burned-out tires. Cale also beat Lee Roy in the Atlanta race by nineteen seconds, and Lee Roy claimed that Cale had made an illegal pass under the caution flag. Lee Roy protested angrily, but to no avail. Cale won Daytona's Firecracker classic at an average speed of 167 miles per hour, making it the fastest race ever. Lee Roy was·no closer than the pits, where his car sat disabled.

In 1969, Cale won the Atlanta 500 for the third straight year and the Motor State 500 at the new track in Michigan. He won at Atlanta by three seconds over David Pearson. He won the Michigan race when he and Lee Roy collided on the last lap. Lee Roy was passing him on the outside when the sides of the two cars mashed together. Lee Roy went sailing up into the wall and Cale kept sailing on to the finish.

However, 1969 was Lee Roy's year. No one ever has dominated superspeedways the way Lee Roy did in 1969. Nor has anyone ever made the money Lee Roy did in 1969. Still, Cale didn't do so badly. He had started out poorly, for in his first seven seasons of Grand National racing he had never earned more than $10,000 a year. In three of those seasons, he actually earned $200 or less. But during his eighth season, he earned more than $25,000 and was on his way. He made $20,000 his ninth season, $50,000 his tenth season, a record $136,000 his eleventh season, and more than $100,000 again his twelfth season, 1969.

In December of 1969, in the inaugural Texas 500 at Texas International Speedway, Cale's car blew a tire and crashed into a concrete wall at 185 miles per hour. Cale suffered a smashed shoulder blade, breaking and splintering other bones in three places. One doctor observed that he had never before seen such an injury in a person who survived. At first, it was felt Cale would be sidelined six months to a full year. By February of 1970, he was back in action in the Daytona 500. In March he was second in the Atlanta 500 and in May second in Charlotte's World 600. In June, he won the Motor State 400 in Michigan. "I was worried, but I've always felt you can accomplish what you believe you can, and I believe in myself," he said.

At the age of thirty, Cale was living the good life. No driver on the circuit was more popular. Just five-feet-seven and weighing 215 pounds, with thinning blond-brown hair and pale skin that was always sunburned, the extroverted veteran had more businesses going for him than most businessmen. He had a southern-style mansion in Timmonsville, where he could live the life of a country squire among four dogs, including two Saint Bernards, a pony, a 140-pound bear cub given to him by Junior Johnson, a daughter given to him by his wife, and a startlingly beautiful wife given him by fate. She was a former cheerleader who used to cheer Cale when he was running for touchdowns.

Now, Cale was running for cash and enjoying it even more. "Ah'll tell you," the fearless one commented, "ah'm a businessman and ah race for money and ah don't mind that glory one bit. But ah think if ah were a millionaire, and we raced in private, ah'd still be racing. It does something to me inside."

It was doing a lot for Lee Roy Yarbrough, too, the one without the extra *o*. Like Cale, he took a number of years to get going, but once he got going he began to pick off all the plums. Also like Cale, he chooses his spots in selected starts each season.

Lee Roy Yarbrough was born in September, 1938, in Florida. A poor boy, he quit school in the tenth grade to go racing. At fourteen, he built a hot jalopy, lied about his age to get a driver's license, and began to run bush-league tracks. Like his dad, he drove a truck. On the side, he worked as a mechanic, setting up race cars for better-known drivers. He won most of the races he entered on Jacksonville dirt tracks. One year promoters put a bounty on his head: "Beat Yarbrough and win a $500 bonus." Lee Roy won fifty-two races that year.

He turned to NASCAR and began to drive sportsman races in 1962. He won thirty-seven races that year, including a sportsman race that was run at Daytona as a prelude to the 500. Lee Roy was ready to move up to the big time, but it wasn't ready for him. A handsome, husky fellow, he came on strong as a cocky character. He was a loner who made few friends and he bragged to newsmen and ignored fans. Few people liked him and he couldn't get factory rides.

"In those early years on the Grand National circuit, I owned the car I was driving or had built it for somebody else, and blood, sweat, and tears were usually tied up in it," he explained. "I had to do all the work and I didn't have time to stop and talk to anyone. I didn't care for the social life and I still don't. I have to do a lot of talking around reporters that I don't really want to do. I know it makes me sound cocky, but I have to do the talking because I've never had anyone to do it for me. If I have confidence, my crew will have confidence. If I don't have confidence in my own ability, who will?"

In five years Lee Roy won only two races in the Grand National ranks and never earned more than $15,000 a season. He won only one race in 1966, but it was the National 500 at Charlotte. He won only one race in 1967 and only two in 1968. But one was the Dixie 500 at Atlanta. And he won a whopping $89,000 in prizes in 1968.

Still, he hadn't yet hit the top. Along the way, he frequently set speed records, but broke down in races. At Daytona in 1965, he set a world's record for a closed course with a run of 181.8 miles per hour in gusting twenty-mile-an-hour winds. When he did finish a race, he was usually nosed out at the end. In 1968, he lost to Cale in the Atlanta and Daytona 500s and the Daytona 400 by heartbreakingly narrow margins.

During this period of frustration, Lee Roy survived a dreadful crash in trials at Charlotte. "The fire extinguisher in my car exploded, the windows became fogged, and I couldn't see a thing," he explained. "I rolled down a window, hoping I could see something, but with my safety belt on I couldn't get my head out the window. I didn't have any idea where I was. I tried to steer to the outside wall and I hit it, but not hard. I kept hitting it and one of the last times the front end must have gotten under the railing and then everything took off." The engine, radiator, frame, and wheels came undone in parts and scattered savagely around the track. Yet Lee Roy was not injured. "I don't know how I did it, but here I am," he sighed afterward.

Yarbrough eventually joined a Ford team headed up by Junior Johnson. He and Junior parted, then came back together again. "We had to get it straight that setting records in qualifying and leading races most of the way didn't mean a thing unless we're in front at the finish," Yarbrough says. In 1969, with Herb Nab, onetime mechanic for Freddie Lorenzen, turning the wrenches, Lee Roy began to finish what he had started earlier and wound up with one of the most amazing seasons in NASCAR history.

It was a fierce Daytona 500 and eight drivers exchanged the lead seventeen times. Some drivers turned laps at close to 200 miles per hour. Fifty miles from the finish, Lee Roy lost the lead to Charlie Glotzbach, fishtailed along a wall, straightened out, and took out after Glotzbach again. He caught Glotzbach five miles from the finish, drafted him until the waning moments, then shot around him on the last lap and beat him to the checkered flag in much the same manner that Cale had beaten Lee Roy the year before. In the winner's circle, Lee Roy wept. "After last year, I just can't help it," he murmured. His hands were blistered and he was drenched with sweat. He was so exhausted that he needed oxygen before he could go on. His average speed, more than 157 miles per hour, was a new record for the Daytona 500.

Lee Roy seemed swept up by the momentum of that race. Four laps from the finish of the Rebel 400 at Darlington, he collided with Bobby Allison, but survived to win the race. Next he won the World 600 at Charlotte by two laps. But he lost the Motor State 500 in Michigan to Cale when he hit a wall while sweeping past his rival on the last lap. In the Firecracker 400 at Daytona, Lee Roy passed Buddy Baker with fifty miles to go and beat him by fifty feet, averaging more than 160 miles per hours in what had been a spectacular race.

Lee Roy was so sick from a virus before the Dixie 500 at Atlanta that he said publicly he doubted he could go the distance. Even so, he grabbed the lead at the midway point and went on to win by a half mile. He was still picking up momentum and, while testing tires in Talladega, he circled Alabama Speedway at more than 195 miles per hour for an unofficial record. Later, in the Southern 500 at Darlington, he hit an oil slick, slid into a wall, and mashed in the front end of his car. He returned to the pits, had the bent metal ripped off, and got back on the track. He had just darted around leader David Pearson when the race was halted at 316 miles because of rain and darkness and Lee Roy was declared the winner.

No driver had ever won so many superspeedway races in a single season, or so much money—a total of $188,605. Married to a pretty blonde, the father of a young son, suddenly wealthy after a life of struggle and disappointment, the sensitive hard-luck king of the high banks was suddenly the newest superstar in the sport that seemed to spawn stars more suddenly than any other.

It was 1969. Pops Turner hadn't quit yet. Richard Petty was still going strong. Guys like the Allisons were waiting their turn. Cale Yarborough was still booming along. And Lee Roy Yarbrough, who once said he remembered when he couldn't afford to buy a pair of shoes, could suddenly buy a whole shoe factory. "Ah guess it's a pretty good business after all," Lee Roy said, allowing himself a rare grin. "Goin' to work is fun now. All you got to do is go two hundred miles per hour and beat off a bunch of four-thousand-pound metal monsters for a few hours.

"I like everything about racing. I like the competition. I like the pay. I like the people in it. Dangerous? Certainly it is. But if driving a racing car worried me, I wouldn't drive one. Other people enjoy bridge or dancing. I enjoy racing at high speeds. I'm happy when I'm running 180. I'm relaxed. I get out and my uniform isn't damp. I don't sweat. It's my fun as well as my business."

7

THE GLAMOROUS SPORTSMEN

The most glamorous racing circuits of the world are the Grand Prix circuit for Formula One cars (similar to those that race on the United States championship trail) and the worldwide Sports Car circuit of endurance classics. The Formula One cars compete in Grand Prix races in England, France, Germany, Italy, Belgium, Monaco, South Africa, Netherlands, Mexico, Canada, and the United States (Watkins Glen in upstate New York) as well as other countries. The champion of the circuit is widely heralded as the "world champion" driver. Wider, heavier sports cars tour the world, too, contesting such lengthy classics as the 24 Hours of Le Mans in France, the 1,000 Kilometers of Nurburgring in Germany, the 24-Hour Daytona Continental, and the 12 Hours of Sebring, Florida. These races crown not so much a driving king as a manufacturers' champion; that is, the car, not the driver, receives the laurels.

While the dangerous open-road races have virtually disappeared from the world, closed-course road racing—on paved tracks or on closed public roads through city streets and picturesque countryside—makes up the Grand Prix and Sports Car circuits. Many people consider this the most challenging form of driving because, unlike the closed-oval courses featured in United States championship car and stock car racing, Grand Prix and Sports Car courses require drivers to shift up and down, and to negotiate a wide variety of fast and slow turns, right as well as left, over uneven ground. Since the invasion of Grand Prix cars and drivers into the Indianapolis 500, road-course races have been added to the United States championship circuit. Still, it was not until the 1960s that American drivers began to conquer this form of racing.

The prizes available in Grand Prix and Sports Car racing do not approach those of the USAC championship trail or the NASCAR Grand National tour, so there has been little incentive for American drivers to forsake their traditional form of racing for the European variety. However, contracts with automotive firms guarantee the greatest Grand Prix and Sports Car drivers earnings of from $50,000 to $150,000 a year. Consequently, a few American drivers have gone the European way in quest of fame and fortune. But between Jimmy Murphy's victory in France in 1921 and those of Phil Hill, Dan Gurney, and Richie Ginther in the 1960s, no American driver won a Grand Prix race. And only Hill, Gurney, Foyt, Carroll Shelby, and Masten Gregory were able to conquer the greatest sports car test, the 24 Hours of Le Mans, in the 1960s.

In the early years of Grand Prix racing, the outstanding drivers were Rudolf Caracciola, Tazio Nuvolari, Achille Varzi, and Louis Chiron. Caracciola was a German who dominated the loosely knit Grand Prix circuit of the 1920s and the 1930s as no other man did. Once, while he was practicing for the Grand Prix of Monaco at Monte Carlo in 1933, his Mercedes lost a front wheel, and he crashed into a wall and his right thigh was shattered. He spent seven months in a cast and limped back into action only in great pain. Then his wife was killed in an avalanche at a ski resort, further depressing this moody and luckless fellow. He came back in 1935 to win five Grand Prix races, four in record time. In the late 1940s, he tried Indianapolis, but crashed in practice when struck in the face by a bird and was in a coma for ten days. After retiring for a few years, he resumed racing in 1952, but crashed in Switzerland, smashing his left leg. He was in traction for eight months. He never raced again, and died in 1959 of a liver ailment at the age of fifty-eight.

Nuvolari was an Italian who overcame countless crashes in his thirty years of driving before he died of heart failure in 1953 at the age of sixty-one. He was a brilliant, almost demoniac driver who was nicknamed "the Devil's Son." He won a great many races in the 1920s and '30s, often with inferior equipment. He had never tried the 24 Hours of Le Mans when he entered in 1933. He was teamed with a driver named Raymond Sommer in an Alfa Romeo. They overtook the defending champion, Luigi Chinetti, on the last lap to win by nine seconds, the closest finish in the history of the classic to then. In his last years as a driver, Nuvolari suffered from tuberculosis and a stroke, and often had to be lifted into his car. But he continued driving until he won his last race, in Sicily, in 1950. He was taken home in an ambulance. After collapsing in his car before a race in England in 1951, he retired.

Recognition of "world champions" by virtue of success on the Grand Prix circuit was inaugurated in 1950. Since that time, Juan Fangio has been the outstanding competitor, winning twenty-three races and the title five times in the 1950s. Though he had won only thirteen races through 1969, Jack Brabham of Australia ranked second to Fangio in titles won with three—1959, 1960, and 1966. However, the closest challenger to Fangio as the supreme master of Grand Prix racing of modern times, if not of all time, came in the person of Scotsman Jim Clark. This driver set a new record by winning twenty-four Grand Prix races, two world titles, and the Indianapolis 500 as well.

Alberto Ascari of Italy won two Grand Prix crowns in the 1950s, while Graham Hill of England won two in the 1960s. Hill also won the Indianapolis classic. Jackie Stewart of Scotland, who came close to winning a 500, had become the new champion and the newly dominant driver in Grand Prix ranks by 1969. Stirling Moss of England, who never won the Grand Prix title because he preferred to represent his country as an independent and frequently had inferior equipment, nevertheless won many races and gained recognition as one of the immortals of modern racing before a crash caused him to retire in the early 1960s.

Ascari was the son of a racing driver. Like his father, he died at the age of thirty-six on the twenty-sixth day of the month. The grim Italian drove like a precise, efficient machine. He came to prominence after World War II in a Maserati, but won his world titles in Ferraris. He dominated Europe with a Ferrari and qualified for the Indianapolis 500 with one in 1952, but a wheel collapsed and he crashed. He survived many crashes in his career, including one through a stone barrier and into the harbor at Monte Carlo in 1955. However, the next week, while testing a car at Monza, Italy, he crashed fatally.

Fangio was an Argentine, son of an Italian immigrant, who went to work as a mechanic at eleven and began to drive in races, late, at twenty-five. His first great victory came in the Grand Premio International, a 5,932-mile open-road race in the Andes Mountains. He drove thirteen days for over nine hours a day to win recognition. In 1949, the year before the Grand Prix circuit began to crown driving champions officially, Fangio won six of ten Grand Prix races. When the driving title became an official competition, he won it five times. Stocky, bowlegged, balding, he was a master behind the wheel of a race car and outdrove almost all rivals, usually winning if his car did not break down. A loner and a hard man who drove himself hard, he retired home to Argentina at the age of forty-seven.

Clark, a small, solemn, withdrawn Scot, son of a wealthy farmer, was a brilliantly versatile racing artist who came to prominence with England's Colin Chapman in the light, fragile, but quick Lotus cars the brilliant Chapman created. They not only monopolized Grand Prix racing through the 1960s, but truly revolutionized the Indianapolis 500 with their performances there in the 1960s, capped by Clark's triumph in 1965. Clark was killed in a crash in Germany in 1968. As the great American drivers of the early part of the 1900s can be compared to Nuvolari and Caracciola for excellence, so must A. J. Foyt be compared to Fangio and Clark for excellence in modern times. It is the judgment here that Foyt, Clark, and Fangio should be ranked in that order in the all-time history of racing. But this is only one man's opinion.

The rise in popularity of European-styled sports cars in the United States and of sports car racing in the period immediately following World War II sparked the entrance of the first quality American drivers into European racing circles. But it was a number of years before one or two came along who could win consistently. Briggs Cunningham, designing, building, and driving his own cars, was the trailblazer, three times placing third at Le Mans. But he had limited success. In the 1960s, Lance Reventlow tried with his Scarabs, but didn't make it.

While most United States sports car racing has been concentrated in southern California, the area that has produced the most successful American Grand Prix and sports car drivers, the first two to achieve noteworthy success came out of the Southwest and Midwest.

Carroll Shelby and Masten Gregory raced against each other in the 1950s. Like many American sports car competitors, Gregory was the son of well-to-do parents. Born and reared in Kansas City, he quit high school to go racing, and when he came into a share of the family insurance fortune began to invest it in his own cars. In 1954 he competed in an Argentine endurance test, lost the race, but bought the Ferrari that won it and began to race it privately. He did well for a few seasons, and landed a Grand Prix ride in 1957. He seemed to be on his way to success, but then he began to crash repeatedly. He has seldom had good rides since.

Gregory did show promise in one Indianapolis race and shared two noteworthy triumphs, one in the Nurburgring 1,000-Kilometer Classic in Germany with Lucky Casner in 1961, and the other in the 24 Hours of

Le Mans in France with Jochen Rindt in 1965. In the latter race, he and his partner drove 2,906 miles at an average speed of 121 miles per hour. "The race was very hard and I didn't think we had it won until it was almost all over, but then, all races seem to be hard for me and I haven't won many," the exhausted and delighted Gregory said later. A tiny, bespectacled man who has never shed his Kansas twang, Gregory was married at seventeen and had four children, then divorced his wife and remarried. He finally settled down to live the good life in Paris, having gone through his $500,000 inheritance in style.

Shelby came from humble origins but has been far more successful, though not primarily as a driver. He was born in 1923 in little Leesburg, Texas, the son of a mail carrier who used a horse and buggy to deliver the mail. His father was fascinated by cars and Carroll learned to drive at fourteen. But he did not begin to race until he was twenty-nine, an unusually advanced age for that sort of thing. During World War II, he was a United States-based test pilot, instructor, and flight officer in the air force and once parachuted from a flaming plane. After the war, he married, ran a trucking business, then worked as a roughneck in the oil fields before giving in to a lifelong desire to try racing.

Shelby enjoyed considerable success in American sports car racing, winning the United States championship and setting a number of speed records at Bonneville, Utah. He raced sports cars and Grand Prix cars around the world for a time, won the Governor's Cup at Nassau in a Maserati in 1956, and achieved his greatest success by winning Le Mans with Roy Salvadori in an Aston Martin in 1959. Shelby became the second American to win this endurance classic since Jimmy Murphy in the 1920s. He and Salvadori covered 2,720 grueling miles at an average speed of 112.5 miles per hour to prevail over Phil Hill and Olivier Gendebien.

During his career, Shelby survived a number of crashes. At Riverside, California, on his first practice lap, he ploughed a brand-new $20,000 Maserati into a hill at 80 miles an hour, demolishing it and scarring his face with wounds that required seventy-two stitches to close. In the Mexican Road Race, he flipped his car four times and suffered numerous broken bones and a shattered elbow. He retired in 1960, suffering from a minor heard ailment. He ran a chicken farm for a while, but grew restless and returned to racing in the early 1960s—though not as a driver. "I liked the idea of building an American car that could be raced or used on the streets. And I wanted to see Carroll Shelby amount to something," he explains. He secured help from Ford and Goodyear, founded Shelby-American in the Los Angeles area in 1962, and made a fortune with an enormous and diversified operation.

Shelby developed the first truly successful American sports car, the Cobra, a long, low monster, no more comfortable than most sports cars, but stronger, surer, and swifter than most. He didn't care about creature comforts in his car. He wanted a performance car. "Whether you're building an outhouse or a car, you don't compromise," he said. While the ultimate victories escaped the Cobra, it scored important successes at Daytona, Sebring, Germany's Nurburgring, and Belgium's Spa. Later, he took over the Ford GT car and shaped it into a spectacular racing machine. He generaled an international army of mechanics, drivers, cars, and equipment that invaded Le Mans in 1965 and conquered it in 1966, 1967, 1968, and 1969, smashing the supremacy of Ferrari in worldwide sports car racing circles.

Shelby's Fords won the 24-Hour Daytona Continental in 1965 and 1966. They were also victorious in the 12 Hours of Sebring in 1966 with Texan Lloyd Ruby, a brilliant but luckless Indianapolis 500 pacemaker, and British-born Ken Miles as drivers. Fords won Sebring again in 1967 with Mario Andretti and Bruce McLaren as drivers.

Actually, Miles came very close to sweeping the three distance classics in 1966. In the 24 Hours of Le Mans, he and Denis Hulme were far ahead in one Ford when, under orders, Miles slowed down to permit another team Ford, driven by McLaren and Chris Amon, to catch up for a flashy side-by-side finish. After Miles had coasted his car across inches ahead of McLaren's car, he was walking with Hulme toward the awards stand when officials announced that, because the other car had started a few feet farther down the grid, it had covered more distance and so was the winner.

Miles was bitterly disappointed. This would have been the crowning triumph in an outstanding racing career that had begun on motorcycles in England eighteen years earlier. But he had been Shelby's chief test driver and lead team driver for many years, and there was not much he could say about the strategy publicly. He was a fine driver, who once said, "The only philosophy that pays off in racing is that you go fast enough to win and slow enough to finish." Two months after the Le Mans debacle, Miles, who had settled in Hollywood in 1952 and become an American citizen, was killed at the age of forty-seven in a test crash at Riverside, a course he had helped to lay out originally.

Restlessly, Shelby moved on to help Dan Gurney create his All-American Racers team and develop Eagle racing cars. These American cars won the Belgian Grand Prix (with Gurney behind the wheel) in 1967 and finished one-two at Indianapolis (with Bobby Unser and Gurney as drivers) in 1968.

Although Shelby has become an international racing tycoon, he still looks like a Texas cowpoke. He is a ruggedly handsome fellow with a mop of curly hair and a weather-beaten face and, with his drawling southwestern slang, he seems more at home in Levi's than in anything out of Madison Avenue. He may not have been one of the greatest American race drivers, but he has become one of the greatest men in American racing.

Another Texan, Jim Hall, achieved racing success in a similar style. During the 1960s Hall was Shelby's foremost rival. As heir to a Texas oil fortune, Hall grew up with a great deal of money and doesn't actually dislike money, but would rather earn his own. "Every time I read 'Jim Hall, Texas millionaire,' I get mad. I figure that belongs on the society page and I belong on the automotive page or someplace like that," Hall said once. He was in Las Vegas for a race at the Stardust Raceway. Tall and thin, six-feet-three and 160 pounds, with thick brownish blond hair and a ruggedly good-looking face, Hall sat on a pit wall staring at the wide, low-slung prehistoric insect of a car he had created, his latest Chaparral. Everyone else was looking at it, too.

Hall got up, pulled on his driving gear, squeezed his long frame into the cockpit of his low-slung car, and sped smoothly to qualify for the race. He is a talented, but conservative, driver who has probably never used all the ability at his control. After qualifying, he wheeled back into the pits, uncoiled, and resumed his perch on the wall as his crew turned back to the car. "I always wanted to be a top driver," he said. "I enjoy driving. Taking a tricky turn at top speed is an incomparable thrill. But now that we've gotten engaged in endurance races, I enjoy it less. I consider myself primarily an engineer now. I've worked very hard on developing a good sports car. Someday I might want to market it. I might be interested in designing and building Grand Prix or Indianapolis cars, if conditions were right, but the field I've chosen would seem to be sufficiently challenging to keep me busy."

Hall is a daring and imaginative innovator. He and his partner, Hap Sharp, a husky Oklahoman and an excellent driver, had ordered their first car from builders Tom Barnes and Dick Troutman of Culver City, California, and named it the Chaparral. Later, they developed a small but substantial organization, built a test track in Midland, Texas, and set about redesigning the car, then designing brand-new ones. Hall devised the first automatic transmission that would work in a racing car under racing stresses. And he devised the "wing," an adjustable airfoil supported by two vertical struts and attached to the rear portion of the car to hold it down, aid its traction, and assist in braking. In 1970, when everyone else had copied these wings, Hall took them off his new Chaparral and added a system of fans to the rear. He pioneered many racing car improvements that have been copied by others.

Hall was born in 1935 and reared in Albuquerque, New Mexico. As a boy, he loved cars. As a teen-ager, he got his hands on a Corvette and began to drive in road races—a rich boy playing race driver, everyone thought. Tragedy beset him just before he entered college. His father, mother, and sister were killed in an airplane crash. He and two brothers inherited the Condor Petroleum Company of Midland, Texas. To obtain a geology degree and fit himself to help run the family business, Jim enrolled at Cal Tech, one of the toughest schools in the country. He struggled with his grades, however, and midway through he switched to mechanical engineering, giving in to what interested him most. Almost immediately his grades soared.

After graduation, Hall spent some time in the oil business and even operated a sports car agency with Shelby in Dallas for a while. But he soon began to concentrate on racing. In 1963, he accepted an offer to drive a Lotus-BRM on the Grand Prix circuit and finished fourth in the German Grand Prix and sixth in the British. Then he decided that it would take him too long to learn the various Grand Prix courses and branched off in another direction. He ordered the first Chaparral for $14,500 and went off on the United States Sports Car circuit. Soon he was knee-deep in developing his own Chaparrals. Friendly but modest, he has a reluctance to discuss his cars going well beyond the bounds of modesty. "This is a very competitive business," he said in his southwestern drawl. "If I have something no one else has exactly the way I have it, I don't see any point in giving it away." He has been nicknamed "the Sphinx" by those to whom he would not talk.

Sitting atop the pit wall at the Stardust Raceway in the gathering twilight, Hall listened as the roaring engines stilled. A rival watched Hall's crew start to pack their gear and said, "With all his money, he could buy the skill and imagination that have enabled him to do what he does with racing machines." Clearly, Jim Hall was a rich boy who made good.

Later, Hall sat in his hotel and discussed his life. He had married young, too young. After three children, he had divorced and remarried. Now he and his wife, Sandy, worked together on his enterprises. They lived modestly in a three-bedroom apartment in Midland. To beat the hot Texas days, Jim got up before sunrise to begin working on his cars, but still wound up working ten to twelve hours a day. He piloted his own plane to races around the country. He explained, "You never stop learning. You have to keep improving your product. It's very difficult to stay ahead. You can't stop development for even a moment."

He leaned back and closed his eyes. "When I read or hear about my money, it irritates me," he said. "I'm darn glad dad was a success. His money has made things a whole lot easier for me. I hope I can do as much for my children. That's the American way of life. But money hasn't done all that much for me. Hard work and brainwork have done for me. Cars are not a hobby for me, they're a business. We're not sportsmen in this for kicks. I'm pleased I've done well, but I should have done better and hope to do so in the future."

He has been a good driver and a better engineer. He won the United States road-racing title one year, but was not in a class with, say, Mark Donohue, who was the reigning champion and a top Indianapolis prospect in 1969. Hall and Hap Sharp did drive one of the Chaparrals to victory in the 12 Hours of Sebring by twenty-one miles over the nearest car in 1965. That year, the Chaparrals won sixteen of twenty-one races entered, and six times Chaparrals finished first and second.

Hall's cars have won the *Los Angeles Times* Grand Prix at Riverside, California, the Laguna Seca Grand Prix at Monterey, California, a number of events on the fast-growing Canadian-American Series circuit, and many other major races. Although Chaparrals have failed to meet their biggest test, Le Mans, Phil Hill and Swede Jo Bonnier drove them to victory in the prestigious and grueling 1,000 Kilometers of Nurburgring, Germany, in 1966. It was the first triumph in the Grand Touring class scored by an American-built car.

Unlike Shelby, Hall has not produced public versions of his privately engineered cars and has not captured every race in sight, though he has sometimes come close. His has been a smaller operation. Moreover, Shelby is less secretive about his operation. He has operated with Ford. Hall has had help from General Motors and others, but he will not discuss the details of it with outsiders. In any event, Hall was doing well until a serious racing accident removed him from the scene for a while in the late 1960s.

Up to that time, Hall had had only one serious driving accident. He had spun out at 80 miles per hour at Mosport, Ontario, flipped over several times, and escaped with a broken arm. However, in 1966 he was not so lucky. In Las Vegas his Chaparral hit another car at 150 miles per hour, flipped, and landed on its tail, coming apart in pieces. Hall broke both his legs and suffered other severe injuries that hospitalized him for a long time and curtailed his racing activities for an even longer time, but he resumed racing in 1970.

To sum up, Jim Hall and Carroll Shelby have been great American racing men and good drivers on a fiercely competitive worldwide circuit, though perhaps not great drivers as Phil Hill and Dan Gurney have been.

8

ALL-AMERICAN BOYS

Phil Hill's mother was a deeply religious woman who wrote church hymns as well as popular songs. His father was a former newspaperman who had become sales manager for the Mack Truck Company. They met and married in Florida, where Phil was born in 1927. They moved to southern California and his father became the postmaster of Santa Monica. The family was fairly well-to-do, and Phil went to a private kindergarten. Phil's aunt also had money and lived in a plush old Spanish mansion in Santa Monica, and had a chauffeur-driven Packard in which she used to take Phil and his brother to school during depression days. While others played baseball, Phil learned to play music, but mostly he preferred to play with the family's fancy cars. At twelve, his aunt bought him a car he wanted, a shiny Model T, and Phil learned to drive it that day.

Today, Phil lives in his late aunt's old house. He is surrounded by classic antique cars that he keeps in prime condition, and by valuable old player pianos. One wall is full of spools of music for these pianos. He is a classical music buff. He says, "I like things that are beautiful and have permanence." He is a proud and friendly man, yet withdrawn and moody at the same time. He is also a brilliant man and speaks Spanish, French, Italian, German, and a couple of other languages. He would ask, "Does this make me a freak?" No, but he certainly does not fit the public's image of the race driver, even though he has been one of the greatest.

Phil Hill is the only American ever to win the "world driving championship" on the Grand Prix circuit. He also is the only American ever to win both the 24 Hours of Le Mans and the 12 Hours of Sebring three times, plus the 1,000 Kilometers of Nurburgring twice. He won the Grand Prix of Italy twice and the Grand Prix of Belgium once. He is beyond question the greatest sports car driver America has ever produced and is possibly the greatest Grand Prix driver. Dan Gurney, who may have been a more accomplished all-around driver, is the only one to dispute his Grand Prix ranking.

Hill says, "I was a fanatic about cars from the age of six. But I never really knew what I wanted to do with my life. I enjoyed watching races, but I never thought about becoming a racing driver. I just didn't move in those social circles."

Hill studied business administration at the University of Southern California, but was bored by it and quit. He rebelled against his family's social status. Perhaps for this reason, as much as any other, he began to race sports cars. "I was searching for public recognition," he admits.

But recognition didn't come immediately. Hill was tense and unsure of himself. He raced well in the Pan American Road Race in Mexico in 1952, but his stomach acted up and he had to go on a diet of baby food. His nerves were shot and, on doctor's orders, he retired from racing the next year. During this time, however, he realized how much satisfaction he got from racing.

Late in the year, Phil returned to racing. He was a natural driver and had a delicate touch with a racing car. He was young, brave, smart, and very determined. He also was very nervous. His friend Richie Ginther once said, "Phil always finds some little thing to worry about—like what he should say at the victory banquet if he wins."

Hill replies, "Of course I'm nervous. Who isn't before he has to perform? It's the same with a ballet dancer. Anybody. Before a race, we all lack confidence. I have no lack of confidence when I have the wheel in my hands."

He was a pure driver. Asked which were his greatest races, he often mentions some he did not win. "It is one thing to win with the best car," he says. "It is another thing to finish many positions higher than you should finish with a poor car. Outsiders often do not know when a driver has done his best work, but the driver knows." He wanted nothing to stand in his way. "Racing and marriage are incompatible, so I will not marry while I'm in racing." He stuck to his vow. Small and husky, yet extremely handsome and able to enjoy life, Hill put racing first.

Through most of the 1950s, he won major sports car classics in Sweden, Sicily, Venezuela, Argentina, Nassau, and throughout the United States and set speed records at Bonneville, Utah. He won the United States road-racing championship. In 1958, co-driving with Olivier Gendebien in a

Ferrari at Le Mans during a blinding rainstorm in the middle of the night, Hill won the race by stepping on the gas instead of the brakes. A French driver skidded to his death in that race, but Hill drove like a madman over the slick, tricky course and was so far ahead by the time the rain let up late the next morning that he and his partner could not be caught. They covered 2,547 miles during the twenty-four hours at an average speed of more than 106 miles per hour and won by 100 miles over their nearest competitor.

Of sixteen Grand Prix drivers on the circuit in 1958, seven were killed and two were severely injured. As a result, there was a shortage of drivers that year. In the past, Americans had never been eagerly welcomed onto the great European Grand Prix teams, especially the Ferrari team, the most prestigious of all. But because of the shortage of drivers, Hill was given a place on the Italian team. The Le Mans champion would have a chance to compete with Fangio and Moss and the other gloried names of world racing.

Hill's first chore was to drive relief for Luigi Musso in "The Race of Two Worlds" at Monza. He took over an underpowered car in eighth place and drove the 2.6-mile high-banked oval circuit madly to finish third, just behind Jim Rathmann and Jimmy Bryan. Hill's first Formula One race turned out to be Fangio's last, the French Grand Prix. Musso crashed and died of his injuries in this race. Mike Hawthorn won. After finishing fourth, Fangio retired. Hill finished seventh, but it was just a beginning for him. In Italy, Hill led early and finished third. In Morocco, on Ferrari orders, Hill stayed behind teammate Hawthorn to permit him to win valuable points toward the world title. Hill finished third and Hawthorn won the world title. Three months later, Hawthorn crashed in London and was killed.

In 1958, co-driving with Peter Collins, Hill also won the 12 Hours of Sebring in the rain. In 1959, he repeated his victory at Sebring with Olivier Gendebien, his Le Mans partner, as one of three co-pilots. Gurney was another. In 1959, he also won the Riverside Grand Prix, in California. At Le Mans that year he and Gendebien were far ahead midway in the race, but broke down. In Formula One racing in 1959, Hill was second in France and Italy and third in Germany. In France, a rock hit him in the face and bloodied his nose, but he pressed on in suffocating heat. He finished twenty-eight seconds behind Roy Brooks, the winner. In Italy, he had tire troubles, but was beaten only by the great Stirling Moss.

In 1960, at Monza, Italy, Hill broke through for the first Grand Prix victory by an American in almost forty years. For the race, a high-speed banked course had been incorporated into the regular road course. It was considered dangerous and many teams withdrew their top drivers. Hill's average of more than 132 miles per hour set a record as he dueled another American, Richie Ginther, for the victory.

That year Hill placed third in Monaco and fourth in Belgium, despite having to stop during the latter race to put out a fire in his engine before going on again. In Belgium, Moss crashed severely in practice and Chris Barstow and Alan Stacey also crashed and were killed. Jack Brabham won the driving crown again.

The next year, 1961, was Hill's greatest year. With Gendebien as co-pilot, he won Le Mans for the second time. Again it rained and cars crashed on the slick course. Hill and Gendebien dueled Ricardo and Pedro Rodriguez in another Ferrari most of the way. The bright red cars staged a vicious battle until early morning, when the Rodriguezes' car went sour. Hill drove across the finish line the victor after covering 2,781 miles at an average speed of almost 116 miles per hour. He won Sebring for the third time, again with Gendebien. Again he had to fight off the Rodriguez brothers and again their machine went sour.

All through the 1961 season, Hill dueled with his Ferrari teammate, Count Wolfgang von Trips of Germany. In Monaco, Hill was third behind Moss and Ginther. In Holland, he was second behind Trips. In Belgium, at Spa near Francorchamps, a winding, extremely fast course through the Ardennes Forest, Hill and Trips swapped the lead back and forth, although Hill was nearly blinded by a pebble that struck his eye late in the race. Hill finally prevailed for his second Grand Prix success. In France, Phil spun out and finished far behind the leaders. In England, he almost slid out and had to settle for second behind Trips. In Germany, the brilliant Moss won, with Trips second and Hill third. Going into the next-to-last race of the season, in Italy, Trips led Hill by six points in the race for the driving title.

Hill took off in the lead on the course full of curves and high banks. Trips got off to a late start. On the second lap, driving hard to catch up at 150 miles per hour, he brushed Jim Clark and both went out of control. Clark hit a dirt bank and stopped. Trips bounced off a guardrail, flipped onto a fence and into the crowd, and back onto the road. Trips and fifteen spectators were killed. Hill won the race and the world title. No American had ever won it before and none has won it since. But the new world champion had lost a friendly rival.

Hill served as a pallbearer at Trips's funeral. After that, the sensitive

American was asked if he would quit. Hill said he didn't know. Thoughtfully, he added, "Everybody dies. Isn't it a fine thing that von Trips died doing something he loved, without any suffering, without any warning. I think Trips would rather be dead than not race, don't you?" Finally, he said he would go on. "When I love motor racing less, my own life will become worth more to me, and I will be less willing to risk it."

However, the following year the introverted Californian did not enjoy the spotlight that focusd on him. "It hasn't changed me as a person, being world champion," he said, "but I'm not as hungry as I was, and more is expected of me." That year he was second in Monaco and third in Holland, England, and Belgium. He won Nurburgring for the second time and Le Mans for the third time, both again with Gendebien.

The "Ring" course is fifteen miles long, narrow and rolling, with 174 curves in every lap. The brutal race is staged yearly in the lovely countryside near Bonn. One year, Hill took author Robert Daley for a practice trip on the course. He pointed out where Peter Collins had been killed and noted that authorities had supposedly proved that his brakes failed. Hill said, "Collins knew his brakes were fading. He didn't slow down. He made a mistake, that's all. I'd rather believe he was killed through his own mistake than somebody else's."

At Le Mans that year the Rodriguez brothers led early, but broke down again and withdrew. At the halfway point, Hill broke the lap record with a 126.7-miles-per-hour run and his Ferrari began to pull away from the others. Then the clutch went bad and he and Gendebien nursed it through the last six hours. Only eighteen of fifty-five cars that started the race were able to finish, but Hill's and Gendebien's car finished five laps ahead of the others, having covered 2,766 miles at an average of 115 miles per hour. The former world champion had helped Enzo Ferrari, who ruled his team like a dictator, win six world manufacturing titles, but after an argument with the Italian, Hill left the team.

Suddenly, at thirty-five, Hill went into a decline. He drove a year for a new team with bad cars. Then he signed with the John Cooper team, which did not have competitive cars. He had survived a few bad crashes in his career, but usually had finished what he started. But now he had to press to make the most of little and he wrecked two cars, blew three engines, and did not finish above fourth in a Grand Prix race. He did not win a race for more than eighteen months. He argued with his sponsor and chief mechanic. Hill said, "The owners see us drivers as a bunch of funny little psychopaths who sooner or later get too chicken to stick their shoe in it.

They want to know when this happens so they can get someone else, so they pressure drivers in a hundred little ways." Cooper fired Hill, saying he had better do it before Hill killed himself.

Hill was still an outstanding driver, but his reputation had been tarnished. He could no longer get top factory rides, and he was too proud to beg. His pride was injured. When he went home, his friends were embarrassed for him and didn't seem to know what to say to him. He got rides from Carroll Shelby and Jim Hall and he did some outstanding driving, but he was usually beaten by superior cars. In 1964, with Pedro Rodriguez, whose brother had been killed in the Mexican Grand Prix, Phil won the 24 Hours of Daytona for the first time. With Jo Bonnier of Switzerland, he won the 1,000 Kilometers of Nurburgring for the second time in 1966. At the end of 1967, he drove a Chaparral to victory in Brands Hatch, England, clinching the manufacturer's title for Jim Hall. Then he retired, his unprecedented career safely at an end.

Nowadays Hill sometimes serves as a commentator for televised races. In 1969, he sat in his comfortable house in Santa Monica and said, "Unlike some, I never had that all-consuming desire to be the greatest, but I still enjoy being around motor racing. It was the best part of me for a long time. I thought about quitting for a long time. I wasn't like Richie Ginther, who didn't know he was quitting a minute before he quit and just suddenly quit. I had always said I'd quit when I got to be thirty-five, and there I was still driving at forty. I had driven for more than twenty years and I kept thinking it was not all that rewarding anymore and that it was time to retire. Finally, I retired."

In October of 1965, in the high altitude and thin air of Mexico City, Richie Ginther climbed into the cockpit of a white Honda racing car and prepared to attack the last Grand Prix race of the season. It was Honda's second season on the circuit, Ginther's sixth, and his first with the Japanese team, and neither had ever won a Grand Prix race. The sky was a dazzling blue, the air warm and so clear that a person could see the distant snow-covered mountains easily. While armed soldiers watched over the crowd of fifty thousand and mariachi music blared over the loudspeakers, Ginther waited warily.

At the start, his engine faltered for a split second as cars sped past him, then it grabbed hold, and he lurched forward and passed those that were there to be passed almost instantly. As he recalled later, "I put it down, man, and it was gone. I was all by myself by the first corner. At the end of the first lap, I looked back in the rearview mirror and I couldn't see anyone behind me. Lord, I thought, they must have all spun out."

No one had, though some were to do so later. Chasing Ginther's Honda, the Italian Lorenzo Bandini drove his Ferrari right off the course, while the cars of Jim Clark, Jack Brabham, Jackie Stewart, Bruce McLaren, Jochen Rindt, and others broke down. Near the end of the 208-mile grind, only Dan Gurney had a chance to catch his fellow American, but Ginther, negotiating the tricky terrain smoothly, drove an almost perfect race. Gurney closed to within two seconds, but Ginther drove well within his limits and burst across the finish line in front.

At the finish a band played a Mexican song about swallows that is played when matadors retire and great events, like the Olympics, come to an end. Ginther was mobbed and girls kissed him and flowers and laurel wreaths were thrust at him. The little fellow's boyish face was split into a wide grin and he could hardly believe his good fortune. He had waited a long time for this. Someone asked him if he wanted a cigarette and he said, "No, man, if I lit one of those my head would blow off." He was the fourth American ever to win a Grand Prix race.

Paul Richard Ginther was born in 1930 in Hollywood, California, and was reared in Santa Monica. He had a heart murmur as a boy, so did not compete in athletics. He was tiny anyway, growing up to be only five-feet-five and 135 pounds. In 1946 he met Phil Hill at a party and that meeting led him into auto racing. He lived near Phil and began to hang around with him, sometimes serving in his pit crews when not driving. Richie's father was an aircraft worker and, after graduation from high school, Richie followed in his footsteps for a while. Then he went to work for an auto agency and began to work on some cars the owner raced, and in 1951 began to drive for the agency.

Ginther spent two years in the early 1950s as a helicopter engineer, part of the time in Korea, then came back in 1953 to manage foreign-car shops and race. After helping Hill with one of his first Ferraris, he got a chance to drive, did well, and was sent to Italy as a test driver. In 1960, when Dan Gurney left Ferrari, Ginther joined Hill on the team. Halfway through his first race, the Targa Florio distance classic, he crashed into a tree. But at Le Mans he was second after eighteen hours, when his car broke down. In his first Grand Prix, at Monaco, he finished second.

Ginther won many races and came close many times in many big races, but seldom won a big one. In 1962, he switched to the British BRM team and drove for them for three years. In 1965, he switched to the Japanese Honda team, finally winning the big one in Mexico City and driving for them for two years. In 1967, he switched to Dan Gurney's new Eagle team.

Ginther was a brilliant engineer and a good driver, though he admitted, "I'm too conservative. I'm not a charger. I like to lay back and pace myself and pick off the front-runners as they falter. But, while you can gain a lot of places that way, you can't win many races. I've worked on these cars and engines more than most drivers and maybe I know too much about them. If I think I hear or feel something wrong, I'm very sensitive about it. I nurse a car to make sure it finishes. But, in my own defense, I've seldom had one of the better cars and I've lost some heartbreakers."

In the spring of 1967, Ginther sat in his little house on a peaceful treelined street in suburban Granada Hills, near Los Angeles. It was a quiet Sunday morning. Outside in the backyard, orange trees bore fruit amid grass that needed to be cut. Inside, the walls were covered with photographs and paintings of race car scenes. It was a nice house, but it seemed lonely. After eight years of marriage, Richie and his wife had been divorced. Racing and marriage: "It is very hard for a woman to be married when she is afraid a great deal and her husband is away a great deal," Richie said. "I have a four-year-old son. I get to see him a lot. But I miss him a lot, too."

He made some coffee and settled into a chair, sipping from his cup. He had on a brown sport shirt, blue Levi's, white tennis socks, and black moccasins. He is small, but lean and hard, and moves with grace and agility. Red-haired, crew-cut, freckled, and quick to grin, he has the sort of face one says will never look old. But his hair had turned ginger and was streaked with gray, and his face was weatherworn and heartache lined now. He is not a vain person and has never been interested in publicity. He is very intelligent and always thoughtful about his sport. He seemed a tiny tiger who had survived a long time in a jungle.

"I have a lot of spirit in me," he said. "I know it's a dangerous sport and I know I could get hurt driving, and I can accept these things, but I'm not going to put myself in a position where the odds are against me. I guess I want to finish more than I want to win."

He'd had a couple of serious accidents. At Monza, a tire tore up and jammed a wheel, and he went out of control and flipped over a guardrail. He suffered a fractured right collarbone and ribs and injuries to his arm and face. In England, a car he was driving went off the road into a ditch and flipped upside down, breaking some of his ribs. Another time in England, a car he was testing burst into flames. He managed to park it, but was hospitalized with severe burns for six weeks.

In May, 1967, a few weeks after the author spoke to him, the jockey-sized chauffeur was practicing at Indianapolis for his first try at the 500 when the engine of his Eagle came apart and hot oil splattered back around him. He parked the car and told the team leader, Dan Gurney, he'd had it. He decided to retire and did so immediately. His fine but frustrating career as a driver had ended, but he wanted to practice his profession in some capacity. "When you've been in this sport, you can't just turn around and walk away from it," he said. "Although it would be nice to go out and see what the rest of the world is like sometime."

Race drivers live in their own world and to outsiders some drivers seem more like princes than ordinary people. No one matches this description more than Daniel Saxon Gurney. Tall, lean, blond-haired, extraordinarily handsome and articulate, Gurney may be the most popular American race driver of all time, as well as being close to the best. A few years ago, "Gurney for President" buttons and decals were popping up all over. Of course, no one took them seriously, but the fact was that if the auto-racing fraternity were to nominate a man for president, Gurney would no doubt be that man.

Gurney became a great sports car driver in this country, and he went on to win Le Mans in 1967 with A. J. Foyt. He was the third American ever to win a Grand Prix race and, while he never won the "world" title as Hill did, he won four Grand Prix races, one more than Hill, which is the record for an American. He became the first man ever to win a 500-mile race four straight times. This was the Riverside 500 stock car classic, which he won five times in all. He also introduced American stock car racing to England.

Then he introduced English Grand Prix designer Colin Chapman to the Indianapolis 500, prompting many other foreigners to enter the American classic and helping greatly to revolutionize it. Gurney built his own American racing car, the Eagle, which won the 500 with another driver. He himself has not won this race, but he was second in 1968 and 1969 and third in 1970. He and his Eagles have won other races on the championship circuit. And he drove his Eagle to victory on the Grand Prix circuit, the first victory by an American driver in an American car on that international tour in more than forty years.

Gurney was born in April of 1931 in Port Jefferson, Long Island, and reared in Manhasset, Long Island. His father had studied voice in New York and Paris and was singing bass-baritone at the Metropolitan Opera when Dan was born. In 1948, when Dan was seventeen, the elder Gurney retired and moved his family to southern California, where he had planted an orange grove. His parents wanted Dan to study voice, but he drew away from his musical background early. He became interested in midget and stock car racing while still in Long Island, and later in hot rodding, drag racing, and sports car racing in southern California.

He eased through junior college without showing any great passion for his studies or a business career. He had to go into the army and wanted to become a jet pilot, but instead became a mechanic with an antiaircraft battery and served sixteen months in Korea. After his discharge, he found work in an aluminum factory, but he was anxious to get started in racing. He had raced with motorcycles and jalopies on the streets and backroads, had become known to the police, and wanted to go straight. "I can recall getting challenged over the phone late at night, getting out of bed, pulling a jacket over my pajamas, and going out to race some hot dog," he says with a grin now.

Gurney has always been interested in anything that moves fast on wheels. He has even raced "go-karts" on occasion, and in Nassau in 1959 he broke a toe while driving one of the little machines and was forced out of a big sports car race. He once drove a motorcycle to twenty-first place in a field of two hundred in a 165-mile cross-country California meet. In 1955 he scraped up enough money for his first sports car, a used Triumph, and raced for the first time at Torrey Pines in California. Later, he and a friend named Skip Hudson bought new Porsches and practiced them wildly. Gurney won some races, quit work, and sought sponsorship for a full-time racing career.

He test-drove for one sponsor and raced for another. He almost beat a star-studded international field at Riverside, California, but lost to Carroll Shelby in the stretch. Later he beat Shelby in Palm Springs, California. Then Phil Hill took Dan to Sebring and introduced him to a powerful sponsor who arranged a ride for him at Le Mans. Gurney didn't win, but he performed well enough to be invited to test-drive for Ferrari in 1959. He drove first for Ferrari's sports car team, then on the company's Formula One team. He went on to the British BRM team in 1960, the Porsche team in 1961 and 1962, and the Brabham team in 1963, 1964, and 1965. Finally he began to drive for his own All-American Racers' Eagle team.

Gurney won the French Grand Prix at Rouen in 1962 with a Porsche and again in 1964 with a Brabham car. He also won the Mexican Grand Prix in 1964 with a Brabham. But the Grand Prix triumph that gave him the most pleasure was in 1967 at Spa in Belgium, one of the fastest and most dangerous races on the tour. He won in his own Eagle. Foreign car domination of European racing has always challenged Americans like Briggs Cunningham, Hall, Shelby, and Gurney. When Gurney and Shelby planned their Eagle in 1964 and saw it come into being, Shelby stood over it and said, "There it is—the by-God American Eagle."

Gurney took his $50,000, twelve-hundred-pound, superbly engineered creation, with its little but potent British engine, and drove the swift, tortuous, nine-mile forest course. He survived a fouled-up fuel line and a balky gearbox—steering part of the way with one hand while holding the car in gear with the other—and set several lap records with speeds of more than 148 miles per hour. Near the finish he passed Jackie Stewart, who was driving a BRM, and pulled away to win by more than two miles at an average speed of more than 145 miles per hour. It was the fastest race in the history of the Grand Prix.

As a scratchy recording of "The Star-Spangled Banner" was played over the loudspeaker system, the delighted and grinning Gurney pulled blossoms from a bouquet of roses that had been handed him and gallantly tossed them toward pretty young ladies in the crowd, who swooned over the movie-star-handsome American. Only the week before, he had won the grueling 24 Hours of Le Mans with A. J. Foyt, and at that moment no one stood higher in auto racing.

In 1962, Gurney asked Colin Chapman, who had developed the Lotus, the lightest and nimblest Grand Prix car to that point, to visit Indianapolis to see the 500. When Chapman hesitated, Gurney offered to pay his expenses. The wealthy Chapman took him up on it. Why did Gurney do it? "I'm an American and this is the greatest American race, if not the greatest race of all, and I wanted to be a part of it and I wanted the great teams and drivers of European racing to be a part of it, too," Dan explained. Chapman was so impressed by the American classic that he repaid Gurney and set about building versions of his Lotus cars with new Ford engines for his lead driver and Gurney to drive in the 500.

In 1962 Gurney drove his first 500, and he broke down while driving a car designed by Mickey Thompson. In subsequent 500s he drove Chapman Lotus-Fords twice, finishing seventh once. But after a time he tired of being the second driver on a team and being given second-best treatment, so he decided to go his own way. Meanwhile, Jim Clark took second place at Indy in 1963 and 1966 and first in 1965; Graham Hill won in 1966; and other Grand Prix drivers such as Jackie Stewart, Denis Hulme, and Jochen Rindt and sports car drivers such as Jerry Grant, Ron Bucknum, Peter Revson, and Mark Donohue performed well and gave the 500 great flavor. At the same time, Ford engines became competitive with Offenhauser engines and the rear-engine lightweight replaced the front-engine heavyweight as the dominant car.

In 1968, Gurney quit the Grand Prix tour to concentrate on American racing. Goodyear and others had helped his All-American Racers, but it was an underfinanced operation struggling to compete with wealthy factory teams and could not afford to spread itself too thin. Gurney's Eagles have been driven to victory on the United States championship circuit by Roger McCluskey and Bobby Unser. Gurney himself has driven them to two victories in the Riverside 300, one in Indianapolis, one in Detroit, and one in Sears Point, California, all on paved road courses.

In 1968, Gurney's Eagles finished one-two in the 500 with Bobby Unser and Gurney driving, then took second in 1969 with Gurney behind the wheel again. But his great dream of winning the Indianapolis classic himself remained frustrated. Frustration was not new to him, though. In the 1962 Riverside 500 Gurney had been declared the winner and was then disqualified for having illegal equipment on his car. But after this unpleasant experience he went on to win this tough stock car test five times.

Major closed-oval course imphs are the only ones that have eluded Gurney in his varied career. I s been successful in different types of racing tests more often than Phi. ᴴil, though he has won fewer major sports car races than Hill. Among Americans, perhaps only Foyt has proved as versatile, though Foyt has never attempted a Grand Prix race. However, in his hard-charging career Foyt has won several times as many races as Gurney.

The fact is, Gurney has not won as many races as his reputation would lead one to expect. He himself admits this: "It's remarkable, really, the way writers and fans recognize me, but I wouldn't blame them if one of these days they woke up and said, 'All right, I love the guy, but when the hell is the SOB going to win something?' Oh, I've won plenty, but I should have won more. I've set speed records and led countless races in which my cars broke down. I'm considered the original hard-luck guy. But I'm not the only person in car racing this ever happened to. Many have been stricken with bad racing luck. It's part of this business. You have to be not only good but lucky to win."

Gurney had plenty of experience to back up his statement. For example, one year, on the Grand Prix circuit, he led in eight of ten events, but broke down in every one of them. Everything imaginable happened to his cars, right down to a newspaper being sucked into his car's front end in one event. One time he led the Grand Prix race in Belgium by forty seconds when his fuel line failed and his car stopped dead on the last lap. Another time, in Austria, he led by a full minute when his front suspension came apart. At Sebring in 1966, his car wouldn't start and sixty-two cars got off in front of him. On the first lap after he got started, he passed twenty-seven cars. Within seventy-six minutes, he had passed the other thirty-five. He was five miles ahead with five minutes left in the twelve-hour grind when his car went dead. As he pushed it home, another car passed him to win.

Perhaps Gurney pushes his cars too hard, but most other drivers and veteran observers consider him a shrewd, stylish artist who simply has been an underdog every time, with less than the best equipment, doing the best he can. He himself says, "If I abuse a car, I know it. I am not above making mistakes. If I would lie to anyone, I would not lie to myself. To the very best of my knowledge, I have not caused most of my mechanical breakdowns. If a car can't take the punishment of leading and winning, that's not my fault."

Now he builds his own cars. He admits his luck sometimes has run the other way. In two of Gurney's Grand Prix victories, Jim Clark broke down in front of him. Sometimes Gurney has made his own luck. In a Three-Hour Enduro at Daytona, Gurney was far ahead when his engine failed in the last few minutes. He coasted to within inches of the finish line, waited interminable seconds for the closing gun to fire, then burped across on battery power, barely in time to beat the next car home.

Apart from sheer frustration, Gurney's career has not been painless. He stalled in a race at Riverside, California, and was rammed from behind, suffering a concussion. The first time he drove a Grand Prix car, he was so eager that he went too fast and flipped over. Luckily, he landed right side up. "Things happen too fast for you to realize just what is happening at such times," he says with a smile, "but you figure it out and get scared later. I landed erect with grass in my hair."

In Holland, in 1960, he was coming out of a 145-miles-per-hour straightaway into a 180-degree turn when a brake hose burst; his brakes failed and he shot off the course, hit an eighteen-year-old boy who had ducked under a police line to get a better view, flipped, and crashed. Dan's arm was broken and the boy was killed. Later, he said, "This is a cruel sport," a phrase that has lingered. He says, "I do not think about it often, but I never will forget it. It was not precisely my fault, but was part of racing luck and the risks we all take, sometimes even the fans on open courses. But it is not a pleasant thing to live with."

Early in his career, Gurney said, "The essence of motor racing is to go as fast as you can without killing yourself. I think about that all the time." In 1965, he said, "After ten years in this business, I'm a realist. Anyone who thinks he can take chances forever is a fool, and only fooling himself. I will not take chances much longer." He was in his garage in Santa Ana, surrounded by racing equipment and posters and pictures. He thought back to his boyhood in Long Island, when he had made a banner to wave at a favored driver. Then he recalled how he felt when he first saw a "Gurney for President" banner—the wheel had come full turn.

Gurney's wife came into the garage with two of their four children. One of his sons came bounding up to him, calling "Papa, pa-pa." Dan wrestled with him gently, tousling his hair. The author asked his wife about his racing. She said, "It is hard to be married to a race driver, but a woman can't stop a man from doing what he feels he must do."

Later, when his family had left, Gurney laughed about the "glamour" of racing and spoke about the beginning of his career, when a prospective Grand Prix sponsor had suggested that he sleep in a sleeping bag to save hotel expenses. He spoke about traveling around the world to race, living out of suitcases, going without sleep to meet commitments. He spoke about leaving his family behind to meet all sorts of problems alone, and always worrying about his wife and children. He spoke about driving in pain in uncomfortable cars.

He said, "In Grand Prix racing, you drive sometimes in rain and fog, but all racing otherwise is all the same, each different, yet somehow all the same. You have a car and a course and you get around as quick and as sure as you can. You have to be as hard as a killer, yet as sensitive as a safe-cracker. You scratch to keep going. You make big money, yet somehow you always spend more than you make. Fortunately, it is not always your own money you spend." A smile wrinkled his aging but still youthful face. "It's a job. Somehow you endure. It's a thrilling job. It never ceases to be thrilling. It's hard to leave it for ordinary things."

So he has gone on with it. When his marriage ended he made a new marriage. As the 1960s ended he was still building cars and racing them, perhaps only an impulse away from retirement. He was one of the greatest American race drivers, a versatile artist of a sport that spreads from Grand Prix racing in the forests of Belgium to Indianapolis racing in the cornfields of our Middle West, from sports car racing in France to stock car racing in Florida, and even to all-out speed racing on the Salt Flats of Utah and the drag strips of the United States.

9

THE KINGS OF SPEED

The Bonneville Salt Flats in Utah, a desolate desert, seem to extend to nowhere. There is a twelve-mile stretch of sand that has been designated for automobile speed runs. Every winter it rains, flooding the desert and breaking up the surface. Every summer the sun is intense, burning the desert dry. By late summer and fall, when the flats have restored themselves to smoothness, men come with many kinds of cars to seek speed records.

In 1964, Craig Breedlove and the Arfons brothers, Walter and Art (who were bitter rivals), arrived at Bonneville with streamlined jet-powered racers. Each of the three men was determined to break the land speed record for the mile run. The record had been raised only once in the preceding twenty-five years before Breedlove had boosted it to 407.45 miles per hour with a three-wheeled car in 1963. The two teams were prepared to embark on an orgy of speed such as the world had never before known.

These were men who seemed to be made of some sort of steel, who refused to be bent by fear as they drove their souped-up special cars in a deadly duel for supremacy. "Sometimes as I sit in the cockpit just before taking off," Breedlove admitted, "I wonder just what in the hell I am doing there." He later confessed that he had nightmares of crashing and being killed, but he would not admit that then.

The flats are rented to drivers for speed runs and United States Auto Club officials are paid to regulate and time the runs officially. To set an official record, which is the average speed of two runs, a car must go both directions through the mile course within an hour. The measured mile is exactly in the middle of the course. The course is eighty feet wide and there is a six-inch strip of tar down the middle of it by which the racers guide themselves. At the speeds they go, the world becomes a blur and the salt flats seem endless, and the drivers would not know where they were if not for that black line.

The drivers and their crews usually sleep by their cars through the ghostly, silent night. They arise before dawn to work on their cars and prepare for runs through the chill, quiet morning. Whenever the wind is still and the weather is good, whether it is cool early morning or blazing hot afternoon, they may take off. Their cars are given just enough expensive, explosive fuel to carry them through the runs, so that if they crash the danger of severe fire is minimized.

When the time comes, the drivers pull on their flameproof equipment and crash helmets, climb into their tiny reclining cockpits, in which they virtually lie on their backs, pull on their oxygen masks, fasten their shoulder harness, and signal that they are ready. Their crews close the canopies, fire up the cars, and the drivers move away. They gather speed through two or three miles of warm-up strip, hurtle through the mile in less than seven seconds in a blur of flames, then pop parachutes and apply their brakes as they slow down through five miles of afterrun.

Usually, they have more power than they can use. It is their judgment as to how much power to apply. They have their sights set on a certain speed, but they must guess how much their cars and their ability to control the cars can tolerate. At more than 400 miles per hour, the racers are strained to their limits, skipping along the flats, sometimes bouncing as high as a foot off the ground, constantly on the edge of swerving off course, constantly trying to lift into the air like an airplane.

That time in 1964, Walt Arfons had a heart problem, so his partner, Tom Green, drove his "Wingfoot Express." On October 2, Green propelled the twenty-four-foot, forty-eight-hundred-pound, Goodyear-sponsored craft at 406 miles per hour one way, 420 miles per hour the other way, for a 413-miles-per-hour mark that set a new record.

Three days later, Art Arfons drove his twenty-one-foot, six-thousand-pound, Firestone-sponsored "Green Monster" at a speed of 396 miles per hour one way, 479 miles per hour the other way, for a 434 mark that took over the record. At the conclusion of his run a tire blew, exactly as it had in an earlier practice effort, and Art tore up his car's rear end before he skidded to a safe stop.

Eight days later, Craig Breedlove drove his thirty-four-foot, eight-thousand-pound, Goodyear-and-Shell-Oil-sponsored "Spirit of America" even faster for an average speed of 468.719 miles per hour. But he was dissatisfied. He felt that he could go much faster with his car and that, if he did not, Art Arfons would. He suspected that Walt Arfons's car had reached its limits but Art's had not. Breedlove determined to try again in two days.

He and Art were friendly rivals. The night before Craig's renewed assault on the record, Art asked Craig, "What are we going to do, just keep trying to beat each other until we kill ourselves?"

Breedlove smiled wistfully, shrugged, and said, "I guess so."

The next day, Breedlove boomed his special car both ways through the mile at a new record of more than 525 miles per hour. He began to swerve. As he popped his parachutes to slow himself down, both tore away. At 500 miles per hour, his brakes were powerless and he hurtled out of control like a bullet that cannot be diverted and will not stop until it is spent. He sliced through a telephone pole at its base as if his car was a scythe and the huge pole was a blade of grass, hopped a hill, and plunged nose down into a brine pond.

"As I came out of the mile, I realized my steering wasn't working," he recalled later. "I put out my first chute and it tore off. I put out the second and it tore off. I had about three miles of road in front of me and then soft stuff, but I was veering off course. I tried the brakes, but the pedal went to the floor. I saw a telephone pole coming at me and I thought I'd had it, but my car's axle sheared right through it.

"All this time, it seemed like I was watching myself. It was strange. I was very aware of being surrounded by dials and all sorts of machinery. I was functioning, but there wasn't much I could do. I felt trapped in the cockpit. I had always wondered how I was going to die and I thought about that then. I thought about jumping out. Can you imagine that—at four or five hundred miles an hour? I thought better of it.

"I ripped my oxygen mask off. I saw the ridge coming up at me and thought I'd flip, but I didn't. As I sailed over it, I popped open the canopy. As I hit the water, I was unbuckling myself. As the car went down, I pushed out of it and swam for shore. I remember standing there and looking down at myself. I studied my arms and legs. I wanted to see if I was all in one piece, if I was really all right. I couldn't believe it. I began to laugh, and then felt tears on my cheeks."

As terrified officials and crewmen rushed across the flats to his side, Breedlove turned to them, laughing and crying, and said, almost hysterically, "For my next act, I will set myself on fire."

When he calmed down, he asked anxiously if his run had been good enough. "There is no way I am going to do it again today," he giggled. He was assured that he had the new record, even if he no longer had a car fit to run.

Less than two weeks later, Art Afrons pushed his "Green Monster" out again. His brother was beaten. Only Breedlove remained to be beaten and his car was crippled. Arfons fired up and screamed by at 515 miles per hour one way. Then he turned around, prepared again, and ripped by at 559 miles per hour the other way. His average, 536.71, surpassed Breedlove's new standard.

As Art finished his run, a tire blew out, one of his parachutes pulled out, and he hurtled helplessly for a while before he managed to bring his craft to a stop. "I was scared to death," he admitted. But the record was his. The rains came and the salt flats were shut down for the year.

Undaunted, Breedlove returned to Los Angeles to repair his wrecked racer. He altered it, too. Now it had four wheels like the others. Arfons, meanwhile, worked on his car. Late in 1965, both returned to Bonneville.

On the second day in November, Breedlove blistered the salt at 555.127 miles per hour, reclaiming the record. Arfons went out five days later and took it back at 576.553. As he completed his run, his car veered off course and struck a steel surveyor's post that had been embedded in the ground and carelessly left behind. The impact tore off the front end of the car and ripped off the right tire, and the car went careening across the flats. Smoke and fumes obscured Arfons's vision. He threw off the canopy and almost choked from the black smoke streaming back at him. Somehow, as he neared the ditch that had claimed Breedlove's car the year before, Art brought his car under control and to a stop. "I've always wondered if I could make a turn at our speeds," he sighed later. "I found out I could."

Someone said, "Your car is wrecked."

Arfons replied, "So is the record."

Now it was up to Breedlove. "You can't worry about accidents or the past," he explained. "You have to have desire or you can't do it. You have to hit an emotional pitch. You have to get up." On November 15, he felt ready. He brought his bulletlike streamliner to its mark and took off. He went one way at 593.178 miles per hour. He went the other way at 608.201 miles per hour. He was the first man to burst through the 600-miles-per-hour barrier officially, his average speed a new record of 600.601.

The record and the riches that went with it were his—appearance money, endorsement money, prize money. There was no one who could go faster. Everything had worked for him that month. He asked his wife if she would like to take his car and try for the women's record, which was just above 270 miles per hour. She had never driven competitively. With this car, there's not much you have to do, Craig said. Just be brave. She said she'd try. She went 307 miles per hour and the women's record was hers. The Breedloves were the king and queen of speed.

Men not only race each other in cars, but they race the clock, too. In competitive auto racing, the men who set qualifying records in time trials or unofficial records in test runs are primarily bidding for good starting positions in races. At the same time, they often seek greater speeds for the sheer thrill and accomplishment of it, not to say the dividends in publicity and prestige. It is natural for man to want to jump higher, jump farther, go faster than any other man has ever managed.

Those who race against the clock are not precisely race drivers. Craig Breedlove admitted this. "A real race driver like A. J. Foyt could take my car and do much better with it than I can," he once said. "We're not race drivers. But we're not stunt men, either. I don't know what we are." Significantly, when he began to think about becoming a competitive race driver, he went to a school for race drivers. The fastest driver in the world went to school to learn how to handle a race car.

Even drag racers, who compete in a series of match race eliminations, side by side, cannot be considered race drivers in the purest sense. The great drag racer Don Garlits once conceded, "We're not really race drivers because we don't have to drive in traffic, vary speeds, pass other drivers in traffic, go around corners. But," Garlits added, "we need all of the tools of the good race driver—determination and courage and quick reflexes. We become race drivers when we get in trouble, like Breedlove at Bonneville."

The fact is, drag racers cannot be disqualified entirely from the company of race drivers because they belong to that breed that builds, works on, develops, practices, and runs cars of one sort or another to their limits, at great risk. They are a kind of race driver, a strange and unique kind.

Many of the great early race drivers, such as Barney Oldfield, Bob Burman, Ralph De Palma, Tommy Milton, and Jimmy Murphy, sought the land speed records. That was an early era in automotive development, when the public was as interested in sheer speed as in competitive results. If the records these men set do not appear in the record books, except with asterisks, perhaps it is because they usually made one-way runs.

Land speed records are sanctioned internationally in hundreds of classes for different kinds of cars, for different distances, for different endurances, even for going around closed-oval courses over a period of hours.

The record that stands above all others is that for the mile—two miles, really, because it is made up of the average speed for two runs, up and back, so as to equalize the advantages or disadvantages in the course and in weather conditions. Even the mile record has come to be divided into two classes, one for piston-driven cars—that is, cars that transmit their power through the wheels—and one for jet cars, which do not. Because it is sheer speed that is sought, the faster record set by jet craft is the glamour standard and the one that is most universally recognized.

The first listed record was set in 1898 at 39.24 miles per hour by a French count, Chasseloup-Laubat, in an electric car. For five months, he exchanged the record back and forth with another Frenchman named Jenatzy, until the latter set it at 65.79 miles per hour before the turn of the century. In the early 1900s, the record was raised some ten times, once by William Vanderbilt to 76.08, another time by Henry Ford to 91.37. Then Arthur MacDonald surpassed 100 miles per hour unofficially in a one-way run, and then, in 1904, a Frenchman named Rigolly did it officially at 103.76 on a two-way run.

Henry Segrave, an Englishman, was the first man to pass through the 200-miles-per-hour barrier, at 203.79 in 1927. Ray Keech raised the record to 207.552 in 1928, and he proved to be the seventh and last American to do so for thirty-five years. Sir Malcolm Campbell, a Britisher who raised the record nine different times with different cars usually named "The Bluebird," smashed the 250-miles-per-hour wall with a run of 253.96 in 1932. Three years later he passed through the 300-miles-per-hour wall with a run of 301.13.

In the late 1930s, two Britishers, John Cobb and George Eyston, dueled bitterly, claiming and reclaiming and raising the record. Cobb surpassed 350 miles per hour in 1938 and set the standard at 394.20 in 1947. There the record stood for more than fifteen years, standing off occasional assaults, including one by Mickey Thompson of the United States, who became the first driver to surpass 400 miles per hour in one run. But Thompson's car broke down before he could attempt a return run at a comparable speed with which to claim the official record.

Then came Breedlove and the Arfons brothers. Along the way, Donald Campbell, the late Sir Malcolm's son, raised the record for gas turbine four-wheeled cars to 403.1 with a half-million-dollar "Bluebird." But Donald, who had set the jet-powered speedboat record at 260.3 miles per hour, was killed trying to raise that at Lake Eyre in South Australia. The Summers brothers, Bob and Bill, of the United States hiked the record for

"Little Joe" Weatherly (left) with Rodger Baldwin before a NASCAR race.　*(NASCAR Photo)*

The great Buck Baker.
(NASCAR Photo)

Fred Lorenzen (left) with Junior Johnson. *(Ford)*

David Pearson buttons up before a race. *(Ford)*

Lee Roy Yarbrough and son relax before 1969 Daytona 500, which Lee Roy won. *(Ford)*

Ned Jarrett leans to the left as he takes a turn in the 1964 Dixie Classic at Atlanta Speedway. *(Ford)*

Grand Prix champion Phil Hill.
(Phil Hill collection)

Cale Yarborough talks with Glen Wood of the famous Wood brothers pit crew before the start of the 1968 Daytona 500. *(NASCAR Photo)*

Cale Yarborough (21) slingshots past rival Lee Roy Yarbrough during 1968 Daytona 500. Cale won.

(Ford)

Hill driving his Ferrari at a breakneck pace around a slippery turn at Le Mans in 1958. This was the first of his three victories at Le Mans.

Hill with Richie Ginther, another of the four U.S. Grand Prix winners. *(Phil Hill collection)*

Phil Hill (in a Ferrari) leads the great Jim Clark (in a Lotus) through a turn at Zandvoort, Holland, in the 1961 Dutch Grand Prix. Hill came in second behind Ferrari teammate Count Wolfgang von Trips. *(Julius Weitmann, Los Angeles Times—Phil Hill collection)*

Sports car master Jim Hall in a winged Chaparral with automatic transmission gets by Parnelli Jones at the Stardust Raceway in Las Vegas. Later in the race, Hall crashed and was seriously injured.

(Las Vegas News Bureau)

Dan Gurney, a truly great American race driver.

(John W. Posey)

Dan Gurney in one of his wedge-shaped Eagles at Indianapolis in 1969. He finished
second.
(Bob Tronolone)

At the Daytona Speedway Dan Gurney (21), in a Cobra, leads A. J. Foyt (35), in a Scarab.

Gurney is pulled out from under his British BRM after a crash in the 1960 Dutch Grand Prix at Zandvoort. Gurney's brakes had failed and he hit and killed an eighteen-year-old boy who was standing in an area forbidden to spectators.

Mickey Thompson with his Autolite Special. He was timed at an unofficial 425 miles per hour.

Mickey Thompson in the cockpit of Challenger I, with which he set an unofficial record of 406.6 miles per hour at the Bonneville Salt Flats in Utah. The car was powered by four supercharged Pontiac engines.

(Rapid Pace)

Craig Breedlove tests the soft sand at Bonneville just after his jet-powered "Spirit of America" came to a wild stop during a speed run in 1965.

Breedlove's "Spirit of America" roars through the measured mile at Bonneville in 1964 on its way to a world land speed record of 526.28 miles per hour. A moment later Breedlove lost control of his vehicle, which sliced through a telephone pole and landed in a pond (below). Miraculously, he escaped unhurt.

(Goodyear)

"Big Daddy" Don Garlits (right) stands on a rear tire of his dragster while waiting for the start of his race.

(Ross Russell)

A dragster pops its chutes.

(Ross Russell)

"Big Daddy" blasts off. He was the winner.

(Ross Russell)

Tom "The Mongoose" McEwan waits in dragster.
(Ross Russell)

John "The Zookeeper" Mulligan in spaceman gear.
(Darryl Norenberg)

Mulligan pats the engine of his car after winning his race.
(Darryl Norenberg)

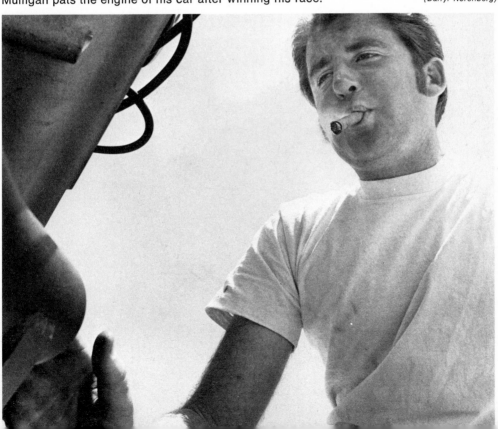

Danny Ongais works on his dragster.

(Ross Russell)

piston-driven cars to above 400 miles per hour. But it was Breedlove's magic 600 that captured the fancy of the public. It stood and was still standing as the 1960s entered their last months.

Breedlove was the son of a Hollywood special-effects man and a mother who grew African violets. An ambitious young southern Californian, he became interested in hot-rodding around the age of twelve. He bought his first car, a 1934 coupe, with $40 he had saved and $35 given him by his parents. He was permitted to buy the car on condition that he could work on it but not drive it. As he got older, he did begin to race some. However, he dreamed about setting speed records. He read and came to believe that Americans were not interested in sponsoring such costly ventures, which were attempted mainly by wealthy Europeans or Britons. It was only after he read of Mickey Thompson's obtaining support from United States firms for such projects that Craig began to take his own ambitions seriously.

But Breedlove had no money. He worked for a while for a racing-car firm and then as a fireman. He read up on jet power and aerodynamics and began to plan a car that could surpass all existing records. He quit work, lived on unemployment checks, and brashly barged into the offices of automotive companies in quest of financial help. For two years, he received rejections. He was young and seemed foolish. But, at twenty-four, he reached sympathetic ears and got guarantees from Goodyear Tire Company and Shell Oil Company that they would provide him with cash and supplies.

After that, Breedlove hired help and began to build his car. He would spend a half-million dollars on the well-financed project before he was through. After working eighteen hours a day, seven days a week, he finally realized his dream in 1963. Then, in 1964, he had to back it up, and almost lost his life in the attempt before he finally lost the rank of king of speed to Art Arfons. Bravely and determinedly, he rebuilt his car and returned to Bonneville in 1965 to battle Arfons again. When the salt dust had settled, the record had been raised for the ninth time in three years, and Breedlove held it at more than 600 miles per hour.

From this, he made perhaps $200,000. He moved into a fancy home in the plush Palos Verdes suburb of Los Angeles. He traveled around the country as a hero. He opened several businesses. He dreamed about building a new racer that would surpass the speed of sound, around 720 miles per hour, at Bonneville. Why? "It has meaning," he says. "It's an international thing. The rich Englishmen used to hold all the records, but now I hold them. I'm patriotic. That's why I named my car 'The Spirit of America.' "

But life turned sour on Breedlove. His wife left him. He got a divorce, remarried, then had the new marriage annulled. His previous wife sued him and a tire company he had opened went bankrupt. A rainstorm flooded his racing headquarters, ruining $100,000 worth of uninsured equipment. Suddenly he was broke again. He moved into his office, where he slept on a mattress on the floor. He had lost his personal cars, so he traded four tires to a friend for a beat-up ten-year-old jalopy to get around in. But he had nowhere to go.

Craig Breedlove estimates that ten thousand stories have been written about him and his record-setting achievements. He has many of these stories in scrapbooks. But after a while reporters stopped coming around. For a long time, no one came to see him. Then Joe Scalzo, a writer for *Car Life* magazine, visited him. He found Breedlove living in his office, dressed like a hippie, wearing his hair long. Loud rock-and-roll music banged around the deserted place.

"I don't care what people think," the thirty-one-year-old Breedlove said. "I used to worry because my sponsors sweated about the way I talked, dressed, and lived. I was very conscientious. They didn't want me to portray any kind of image other than the clean-cut all-American boy. That's the commodity they wanted to buy, so I sold. I really sold. But it doesn't mean that much to me now. The only person I should be interested in keeping happy is myself."

The gold and glory had gone in four years. Now he was in debt. He talked of becoming a regular race driver. He talked of taking the late Donald Campbell's "Bluebird" and surpassing Campbell's record of 409.-277 miles per hour for wheel-driven cars. He talked of building a new "Spirit of America" and seeking 1,000 miles per hour. But he could not find anyone to sponsor him. "I guess no one will be interested until someone breaks my record and there's a new mark for me to shoot at," he sighed wistfully. "You'd think if I was willing to risk my life, someone would be willing to risk their money."

Art Arfons and his older brother, Walter, were raised in Akron, Ohio. Both were interested in cars, but for years neither did much about them. Then Art built a dragster. It went just 85 miles per hour. Eventually, however, his dragsters were going much faster. In 1956, he became the first driver to drag a quarter mile at more than 150 miles per hour. The next year he rolled a car over fourteen times but survived. He set many of the lesser speed records before he went after the big one.

For a while, Art and Walt operated as a racing team. Both drove, and they divided their earnings and pooled their resources. However, they were too competitive. They risked everything they had to beat not only other drivers but each other. Finally, they split up and stopped talking to one another. When their father died, they divided their inheritance and put up a fence between them. They lived in separate houses fifty yards apart and did not even visit one another.

In quest of the mile record, Walt got Goodyear support, Art Firestone support. Then Walt had a heart attack and turned the driving over to a partner, Tom Green. They surprised everyone by getting the record once, a rare achievement in itself, but they never could get it back.

Art did better. An ingenious man, he built his streamliner out of anything he could find that was useful. The front axle came from a 1937 Lincoln, the rear axle from a 1947 Ford truck. The steering apparatus came from a 1955 Packard. The shocks, brake pedal, and instruments came from a junked airplane. Someone asked him why his car was only twenty-one feet long, much shorter than his rivals' machines. He smiled and said because that was as long a car as his old towing bus would accommodate.

He worked on the car in a garage in the yard behind his house. His engine was a used $200,000 F-104 fighter plane jet engine that he had bought from a Florida war surplus store for $5,000. When he ran it in his yard, he burned a sixty-foot-long channel through a nearby woods and blew a chicken house to eternity. His co-workers were terrified and neighbors called the police. Still, he persisted. In contrast to Breedlove's expensive operation, Art spent only $20,000 on his car, though he did receive $50,000 worth of wheels and tires from Firestone, plus additional sponsorship help for fuel and other items. Compared to Breedlove's brilliant and beautiful creation, Arfons's car looked like a locomotive. Even so, Breedlove had his hands full going faster than Arfons.

Art Arfons was thirty-eight when he first took the record from his brother in 1964. Art lost it to Breedlove, reclaimed it from Breedlove that year, lost it to him, reclaimed it, then crashed and lost it to him again the following year. In November of 1966 he went after it again.

Before he went out, he called his wife, June, who disapproves of his dangerous efforts. She said, "Don't go too fast, and come on home." He took his new "Green Monster" out on the salt flats and went 585 miles per hour on his first run. He was hitting more than 600 miles per hour as he came out of his run. Suddenly, his car veered and began to roll over and over, flames shooting from it, wheels and parts ripping off and flying high through the air. A chute popped and the car tumbled end over end, landed on its side, and slid a long way before it came to a stop.

When rescue workers got to him, he was sitting in his smoking cockpit with blood streaming down his face, half-unconscious, moaning and trying to unhook himself. He was pinned down by a piece of steel. Someone got an ax and whacked the metal apart and Arfons was pried from the twisted wreckage of his car.

He was asked how he felt. "I think I'm all right," he said. "Call June." Then he asked, "How is the car?" The wreckage of the car was strewn over two miles.

"He coulda had the record," an aide said wistfully.

They loaded Arfons on a stretcher and put him in an ambulance. "Don't drive too fast," he said to the driver. "We don't want to have an accident."

In the hospital, it was determined that he had scratches, cuts, and salt burns in and around his eyes, and bruises all over his body, but would recover all right. Lying in his hospital bed, Art said to one of his team, "Hey, maybe I'll fly home and not drive."

"Good idea," the teammate said.

Art Arfons was forty and his dream of reclaiming the record seemed out of the question now, though one never knows with these fellows. In 1970, still thirsting for speed, he turned to the quarter-mile strips and set the world drag-racing record at 276.07 miles per hour in his jet car at Rockingham, North Carolina. And he had set the old world land speed mark for the flying mile three times, anyway, which was three more times than most men who seek this elusive standard, including spectacular men like Mickey Thompson.

Mickey Thompson built a career and successful business enterprises on speed. He was born in December of 1928 in San Fernando, California, and reared in Alhambra. His grandfather had been a blacksmith and a machinist; his father was a mechanically inventive construction worker who later became a policeman. On a family vacation when he was eight years old, Mickey saw a speedster flashing across Bonneville's salt flats and was hooked. At twelve, he built a soap box derby coaster. Then he bought a junk battery for 12 cents, a junk starter motor for a quarter, and other odd parts, and built his own car. Then he bought a junked 1927 Chevy coupe for $7.50, got it running, and sold it for $125. Later he bought a Model A Ford for $9 . . . and so on. He loved building cars.

In high school, he was a good athlete and a good student, but his interests were in cars and speed. At fifteen, he began to race jalopies on dry lake beds in the Mojave Desert. Drag racing was starting to become popular in the 1940s and California highway patrolmen, anxious to get kids off the streets, helped them to organize clubs and race meetings at improvised strips. Mickey got in on the early days of drag racing. Eventually, he became one of the first men to break every one of drag racing's barriers, from 100 to 150 miles per hour in a quarter mile from a standing start. He also designed a skeletonlike racer in which the driver sits behind the engine, between and behind the rear wheels. His design came to be known as the "slingshot" dragster and revolutionized the sport.

Thompson married young and to support his wife he found work as a pressman at the *Los Angeles Times,* where he stayed ten years. But Bonneville beckoned. His early idol had been Frank Lockhart. When Lockhart was killed in quest of the mile record on the beach at Daytona, the speed kings of the day began to turn to Bonneville. "There's something about speed, about going faster than a man has ever gone, that holds some people," Mickey once said. "To drive fast, all it takes is guts. But to design a car, to build it, to work on it, to do it better than anyone else ever has, to drive it faster than anyone else ever has driven anything like it, that's accomplishment. That's a challenge worth meeting."

Thompson begged, borrowed, and saved money to build various cars, which he took to Bonneville. He broke record after record and he kept planning for the big one, the land speed record for the mile. Along the way, he kept racing. He entered the Pan-American Road Race in Mexico in 1953 with a friend, Roger Flores, in quest of the $4,000 first prize in the small-stock-car division. He set out on the 1,908-mile marathon and as he came around a corner at 60 miles per hour near the town of Tehuantepec, he came upon a crowd that had surged across the road to see another car that had crashed into a ravine. Trying to miss the people on the road, Thompson cut inside and rolled end over end into a ravine, where he landed on five people, killing them. He and Flores were not seriously hurt. They returned the next year and got through Tehuantepec this time, but just outside of San Juan del Rio their steering wheel gave way and they smashed through a stone wall at 90 miles per hour. Somehow, he and Flores survived. Afterward, Flores got married and decided to quit such foolishness.

Thompson continued, however. He built a car he called "Challenger," a small, streamlined speedster with four engines, two for the front wheels and two for the back wheels. In 1959, with Goodyear and Pontiac money behind him, he invaded Bonneville in quest of that great record and just missed it. He modified the car and returned in 1960 to become the first man to drive faster than 400 miles per hour, with a speed of 406.6 on his first run. But as he was heading into his return run, a drive shaft snapped, tearing up the inside of his machine to end his chances that year.

Thompson drove himself hard and took great risks, but the record he prized above all others eluded him. Later in 1960, he took four cars and five engines to March Air Force Base in Riverside, California, and set fourteen of the eighteen records he sought there. He went back to Bonneville in 1968 with a drag racer named Danny Ongais and set a bundle of stock car marks. Throughout his career, Mickey Thompson has set 485 speed records of one sort or another, more than any man in history, but the big one has remained beyond his grasp.

Racing of any sort can be frustrating business, though. Thompson has been injured many times in cars. He has also entered a lot of boat races, but never finished one. In 1960, he was running a drag boat on Lake Mead at 50 miles per hour when it bounced and flipped him high in the air. As he came down, the boat came up to meet him. He suffered severe spinal injuries and was temporarily paralyzed. Now the husky, handsome speedster walks with a trace of a limp. In 1970, Thompson was practicing for an unusual snowmobile race in the resort town of Mammoth Mountain, California, and suffered a broken arm and four broken ribs.

It is painful for Thompson to drive, but he does anyway. He would have liked to have driven at Indianapolis. Instead, he has designed and built cars for others to drive there. They have been radical cars, for Thompson is an innovator. "There is no point in copying what others have done," he has said. Dan Gurney drove Thompson's first car at Indianapolis. Dave MacDonald was killed while driving one of his cars at Indy, touching off the accident that killed Eddie Sachs, too. Indy frustrated Thompson. Most of the innovations he has dreamed up for the 500 have been banned. But some, such as wide wheels, have been copied and accepted. He has been a revolutionary force at Indianapolis, but he has never beat it—not yet, anyway.

As the 1960s were passing, Mickey Thompson was hustling on. He had a successful speed shop that sold specialized equipment. To seek that elusive record he had a new car—the Ford Autolite Special, built with Ford, Goodyear, Gulf, and Reynolds Metals money for $100,000. It was a monster of a car, almost thirty feet long, weighing more than five thousand pounds, only three feet wide and two to three feet high, powered by twin engines.

He had had a good marriage, but that had gone bad and he was alone now. Men driven to seek speed and records and conquests are hard on marriage and family life. These are men set apart. "We don't run with the herd," Mickey says wistfully. "But we run. We never seem to stop running."

No matter how many races such men win, there is always one coming up that they have not won. No matter how many records they set, there are always records that they have not set.

10

THE DEMON DRAGSTERS

Big Daddy said, "I used to do it for the glory of it, the glamour of it, the sheer fun of it, drag racing, blowing down the other boys. It was a ball souping down a strip. I felt brave as hell. And later when one of the guys would come by and ask, 'How'd you do, dad?' I'd say, real casual like, 'Oh, I turned two-oh-four,' and they'd shake their heads and say, 'Wowee, Big Daddy sure cranked one on.' Well, man, it was a kick. I mean, when you are the best, it is a thrill. And it's still a kick, a thrill. It's still a sporting thing. But it's a business thing more now, like any other kind of auto racing. You gotta make the bucks or you don't go on with it for five minutes—you stay home and watch TV.

"It's a dangerous thing, drag racing. You can get killed. Many have been killed. I've almost been killed. It's safer than most auto racing, but it's not safe. And it scares me. Why lie? It didn't used to, but it does now. I quit a couple of times, but came back right away. I'm not ready to quit yet. I'm making twice what I could at anything else I'm capable of doing. I'm making more than a hundred grand a year. I've been offered big money just to prepare cars and work on engines, but I like driving. I couldn't take an eight-to-five job. I'm not cut out that way. I'm cut out for this cockeyed thing I do."

"Big Daddy" is Don Garlits, a short, slim, dark, intense fellow who is in his thirties. He is the biggest name in drag racing today. If he is not exactly a pure race driver, as he himself admits, he is still a certain kind of race driver and the greatest race driver produced in this hot new American sport.

Unofficially, a person is drag racing when he takes his hot new car that mama let him buy (with only twenty-two monthly payments left hanging over his head) and tries to beat the guy in the next lane away from the stoplight when it turns green. Officially, a person can drag race in approximately one hundred classes of cars, even Volkswagens or, say, motorcycles, which are not cars at all, of course.

The major automotive firms are interested mainly in the stock car class that at least resembles the cars that are driven on highways. In the late 1960s, superlight and superfast versions of stock cars were put into a "funny-car" category of cars that went almost as fast as pure dragsters and achieved great public popularity. However, pure dragsters have remained the fastest of drag-racing vehicles.

Pure dragsters themselves run in two classes, one for those that are powered by gasoline, another for those that are powered by exotic fuel blends. Because they are the fastest of all, the fuel dragsters remain the glamour cars of the sport of drag racing.

The pure dragster is a sort of car, but it does not look or act like a car, not even an extraordinary car like an Indianapolis championship or Grand Prix racer. Stock cars and sports cars are subdued versions of those that race at Daytona and Le Mans and can travel the city streets. In a pinch, a person could drive to the market for a loaf of bread in an Indy or a Grand Prix racer. But he would not even want to try to circle his backyard in a pure dragster. Like its fancier, larger, and more powerful counterpart, the land-speed-record streamliner, it was created for and is good for only one thing— short, straightaway speed.

A pure dragster is a skeleton of a car—a frame of lightweight metal rails supported by two thin bicycle-type wheels up front and two fat airplane-type tires in the back and supporting a high-rise, high-powered engine amidships and a cockpit for the driver behind the engine and between the rear wheels. There seldom is any body cover except at the cockpit, which is brightly painted and gaudily covered by the number and name of the car, the driver, and the owner, along with decals advertising the automotive products used by the car. It is around forty-five feet long, three feet wide, one to three feet high, and weighs about fifteen hundred pounds. Most of the weight is packed in the engine and is toward the rear.

A drag strip consists of a quarter-mile-long two-lane track, plus a slowdown stretch of perhaps another quarter mile beyond the finish line. Between the two lanes is a so-called "Christmas tree" of colored lights on a pole. The lights flash on and off in descending order until green lights flash on to send the drivers on their way. If a driver crosses the starting line before the green light goes on, a red light flashes on the tree on his side and he is disqualified.

A driver wears flameproof coveralls, boots, gloves, and a face mask resembling a gas mask to prevent him from gagging on the fumes that fly at him. He wears a metal crash helmet and dark tinted goggles. Fully attired, he looks even more exotic than a spaceman. When he climbs into the cramped cockpit, he is wedged in, virtually lying on his back, with his legs hiked up around his equipment and his tail inches above the ground. The engine sits high and naked in front of him, obscuring most of his vision. He must look out the side to see guidelines. If the engine should explode, it will rain fire and hot liquids and shoot pieces of metal back at him like shrapnel. The driver is almost lost in the cockpit, like a pebble in a slingshot, and in a moment he will hurl himself 440 yards at a speed of more than 220 miles per hour in between six and seven seconds.

The drivers pull up to the starting line, rev up their engines, and take off from a standing start when the green goes on. As the enormous power of the car's engine is transmitted to the back wheels, they spin for traction, the front end raises up, and the car snakes away in a great blaze of flames and smoke and dust. Improvements in tires, fuel, equipment, and design in recent years have tended to keep the front end down and reduce the smoke and the weaving getaway, so the starts are less spectacular than they once were.

The drivers try to get their cars away from the starting line as quickly as possible, hold them as straight as possible, accelerate to top speed as quickly as possible, and hold it through the finish line, if possible. At the finish, they pop their braking chutes and hit the brakes, and try to slow down smoothly before running into a net or a wall.

Mainly, the drivers are racing against the clock. However, in the top classes, there are elimination competitions in which a series of drivers line up side by side in separate duels until two finalists remain for the final duel. The drivers' elapsed times for the quarter mile and their peak speeds through one-tenth of the distance, the sixty-six feet on each side of the finish line, are recorded and records are kept. But the man who gets to the finish line first is the winner. Sometimes a driver may get away slower, reach the finish line later, but have attained a greater peak speed at the end. Nevertheless, he has lost.

Drag racing grew up in southern California in the 1930s. The first cars were stripped-down Model T and Model A Fords. Many were raced in meets on the dry lake beds of the Mojave Desert, but they were also raced on the streets. Police officers, seeking to crack down on this illegal and dangerous practice, helped the drag racers to organize clubs that would hold meets on abandoned airfields and other such enclosed stretches of unused and paved ground, and police themselves. In the early 1950s, the National Hot Rod Association was founded, and a man named Wally Parks became its president and holds the position today. Later, the American Hot Rod Association, NASCAR, and other groups began to sanction drag racing, too. Major drag-racing stadiums began to spring up.

By the end of the 1960s, there were more than six hundred drag-strip arenas, in every section of the country, which annually held more than three thousand meets, attracted more than three hundred thousand competitors, drew more than five million spectators, and paid out more than $1.5 million in prizes, mainly money but also equipment and trophies. Most of these were small weekly events held through the summer, but some were massive contests—such as the NHRA's Nationals, Springnationals, and Winternationals—and the World Championships, some of which draw more than fifteen hundred competitors, lure around a hundred thousand fans and pay out close to $150,000 in awards.

The scene at a major meet is staggering, with cars covering acres of ground as far as the eye can see, swarms of drivers and crews working on the cars, swarms of fans walking among them, studying them, and cars formed into long lines enduring long waits for their turn to blast away from the starting line before full grandstands of excited spectators. Each race is short, but there's always another one coming up. "Hurry up and wait. The waiting is worse than in the service," a driver says. Some meets last for many hours, some for several days.

It is one of the few forms of auto racing in which fans are permitted in the pits. Most fans are hot rod enthusiasts, and the officials of the sport wish to keep them close to the creations they admire. It is one of the few forms of auto racing in which women can be found not only in the pits, but with the crews of the teams and often working on the cars. They may be boiling water for instant coffee or cooking eggs over hot plates; they may be turning wrenches or even driving. "There's a lot of amateurs in this sport," an official explains. "The only way the guys can get away to compete is if their women come with them. It's a family sport."

With all of this, the image of the typical drag racer as a long-haired, foul-mouthed character wearing a black leather jacket, tight pants, and boots, racing other toughs down public streets, making out with gumchewing babes, drinking heavily, and intimidating outsiders has almost completely disappeared. In the mood of the times, many wear long hair, and some wear beards and favor exotic dress. Doctors and lawyers are often found behind the wheel of a dragster. Most drag racers are dedicated, ambitious, and young. They reserve their racing for the track and are making valuable contributions to the automotive industry.

A multimillion-dollar business has sprung up around drag racing. There are more magazines on the newsstands devoted to this sport than there are devoted to movies and television. Books like *The Adventures of Stoker McGurk*, movies like *Hot-Rod Gang*, and records like "Jive Driver" and "Asphalt Eater" are marketed successfully. Other enterprising people sell everything from model-car kits to custom-built automobiles, from engraved dipsticks to T-shirts displaying such enduring phrases as "Thou Shalt Drag."

So far, there are perhaps only 350 full-time professional drivers in the sport. Some have climbed to prominence by dominating their classes. The most prominent is Don Garlits, who has climbed to prominence by dominating the fuel dragsters. He is the "Big Daddy" of the sport.

Don Garlits was born and reared in Tampa, Florida, in the 1940s. His father was a farmer, a dairyman, and a general handyman who died when Don was ten. His mother later became a horticulturist, a specialist in raising flowers. As a teen-ager, Don was not interested in flowers, though. Like many other boys, he had the automotive bug. He and his friends spent every minute they could spare working on hot rods in their backyards and garages. After graduation from high school, Don worked in a bookkeeping office for six months, but hated it. "I thought there must be more to life than this," he recalls. "One day, I walked in, turned around, and walked out."

He worked as a mechanic, scraped together some money, and opened his own small auto shop. After picking up a lot of speeding tickets, he turned his speed to the tracks. When he first entered the bigger meets, his cars were such makeshift creations that he was nicknamed "Don Garbage." "The first time I raced on the West Coast," he recalls, "they were used to those glittering, chrome-plated, technically perfect dragsters of wealthy guys. They took one look at my nightmare and they almost rolled over laughing. They would shout something like, 'Go home, you Florida hick.' But they never laughed long. I'd clean up on them and they'd go home shaking their heads."

Garlits had a genius for this sort of thing. He threw all the fancy stuff off the dragster and made it pure, lean, balanced, nimble. He worked on engines until he had power plants that threw enormous strength to the wheels and wouldn't run down or blow up after a few runs. He had the guts and quickness to get away fast and hold it hard to the end. He was the first drag racer to hit 170 miles per hour and the first to break through the magic 200-miles-per-hour barrier. He is the only man ever to win three Nationals, 1964, 1967, and 1968, and he has won several other major-meet titles, plus the vast majority of his match races over the years. In fact, he has won far more races than any other drag racer. He is, so far, incomparable in his profession.

Since drag racing is an exotic sport, many of the top hands bear fancy nicknames, like "the Snake" and "the Mongoose" and "the Zookeeper." Between the big meets, they tour the country giving exhibitions and engaging in match races. The best of them are paid $1,000 or more per appearance. "I get as much as fifteen hundred dollars an appearance," Big Daddy says. "I'm the fastest gun in the country. So everyone wants to knock me off."

He was in Pomona, California, the cradle of drag racing, less than an hour from Los Angeles. Thirty thousand fans sat in grandstands running the length of the drag strip. Every half minute, cars of all kinds would pull up to the starting line, warm up, *varoom, varoom, varoom,* and roar away, *aaaawhaaaa.* Flashes of fire, bursts of sound, and stabbing smells of burning fuel and rubber would envelop the screaming spectators.

Garlits was in the pits working on his car, the "Wynn's Jammer." Mickey Thompson had orginally developed this "slingshot" dragster, but others, especially Garlits, improved his design. Big Daddy says, "The driver is not nearly as important as the car in drag racing. In other forms of racing, maybe the driver is fifty-fifty. In drag racing, the driver is twenty-eighty. The engine is the most important part of the car. The car, with the engine, is eighty percent of this business. That makes the designer, the builder, and the mechanic eighty percent. I'm the designer, the builder, and the mechanic as well as the driver of my cars. That makes me, with a lot of help, one hundred percent. Some of these guys treat their cars like they were sacred. We're sacred, not the cars. The cars are only so much metal and rubber stuff until we fix them."

On the surface Garlits seems to be an ordinary country boy. There is no slick sophistication to his manner or his talk. He speaks with a soft southern accent. But he is shrewd and sharp, perhaps brilliant. A few years ago, he might have been one of the toughs, but times have changed. He was wearing a black jacket, all right, but it wasn't leather, it was cloth, and it was so short that it kept hiking up in the back, and Don was complaining to a public relations man from one of the automotive firms. "This dang jacket pulls up and my shirt pulls up when I'm bending over the car and my back is bare and it gets cold as hell. Jeez, you guys got a little longer jacket you could give me?" The PR man assured Don he would check into it.

As Garlits fiddled with his car, he paid little attention to the crowd of curious spectators hovering around him. Occasionally he exchanged a brief greeting with a friend. Mostly he worked in silence with his assistants. After a while, he got involved in conversation with two men, but he wasn't talking drag racing—he was discussing the coin shortage and the gold and silver standards, pet passions of his. He is an ardent coin collector. At other times, he will discuss politics or civil rights. Sometimes he doesn't seem particularly passionate about drag racing, but this is a mask. "Drag racing is my life, at least a big part of it," he admits. "But I hate for people to say the guys in drag racing have no interest in other things."

All the while cars were zooming away on the strip a half mile away, but the blasts of noise and the roar of the crowd and the drone of the announcer carried to Garlits's pits. Eventually, it was time for Garlits's car to be pushed to the rear of a long line. His crew waited by it. Garlits killed time, talking to people and posing for photos. He seemed almost uninterested in the whole business of racing until it was time for him to get ready. Then he underwent a swift transformation as he pulled on his fireproof gear and squeezed down into the cockpit. Suddenly his face was solemn, drawn, almost as though he was a little afraid. Someone spoke to him and he answered without looking, curtly, as though annoyed to have his concentration disturbed. Then he looked up at the man, recognized him as a friend, smiled apologetically, and returned to his somber thoughts. As he was pushed near the front of the line, he put on his mask and goggles and tightened his harness. Although his face could not be seen, he gave the impression that he was in sober concentration under his disguise.

He sat in his slingshot on rails and waited. A truck came up behind him and pushed him into motion. He moved onto the strip, made a short circle, and pulled up to the starting line. Another car pulled up alongside him They revved up their engines, *varoom, varoom, varoom.* The lights flashed, the green came on, the cars accelerated, rear tires digging in, front ends lifting off the ground. They were completely enveloped in a great cloud of smoke. Then, with a horrible roar, the cars reappeared out of the smoke and shot down the track. In the distance, the white chutes could be seen popping out. The announcer shouted out the winner's name, "Don-ald Big-Daaa-ddeee Gar-liiitzzz," and the times. In less than seven seconds, it was all over. For Garlits, his long day was over, too.

His wife waited by his truck as the crew brought his car back. Their young daughters were playing in the truck. His wife said, "Don had raced before we were married in 1953. He didn't race for a little while right after we were married, but he wanted to get back to it and he did and he's done very well and I'm proud of him. He spends a lot of his time with his cars, but he takes us with him as much as possible. It's hard traveling so much, but exciting and broadening. We have a home in Tampa, whenever we're in it. Except when he's been hurt, I've never asked him to quit. He has been hurt and it does scare me.

"I can't help watching. I just sort of hold my breath from the time he takes off until the time he stops. It's easier than in other kinds of racing. I don't know how other racing wives stand it. I can hold my breath for seven seconds, but not for an hour or two or three, could I? I remember once when he was racing Art Malone. At the end, one of the cars flipped and I wasn't sure which one. My heart stopped. It scared me to death. All sorts of things went through my mind, like how was I going to take care of my kids. They told me it was Art, not Don, who had flipped, and I just about laughed with relief. What a mean thing that was. I mean I know Art and I like him and everything and I wouldn't want anyone hurt, but it was only natural, I guess, my relief that it wasn't Don. Fortunately, Art wasn't hurt either."

She shook her head wistfully. "Don works on his own cars and I know he checks everything very carefully and he's very good, so most of the time it's all right. It's a safer sport than most realize. But Don has been hurt and some have been hurt worse. He takes a lot of risks and works hard for everything he's gotten out of this thing. Writers and others who don't like drag racing twist it around and don't give fellows like Don the credit they deserve. It's a hard sport and a good sport, a clean sport, a family sport, and it just makes me sick when people like Don don't get the credit they deserve."

Don was back, shrugging it off. "You get used to it," he said. "Some people will never learn we're not a bunch of hotheaded hot rodders anymore. The guys in this game are very smart now. There's very little drinking and very little fooling around. There's too much at stake now. It's become very big business. I've got about $20,000 sunk into my car. It costs me around $35,000 a year to travel around. I started out with nothing. I'm probably worth more than $200,000 now. It's been a hard haul, but I've done well."

He drove into town and stopped at a diner for a bite to eat. He seemed relaxed. The driving was done for the day. He said, "The secret to my success and survival is my ability to develop a car and engine to the point where it'll get away just a little quicker, go just a little faster, hold up without coming apart, stay in the groove, stop, and be ready to go again. The differences between most of the good cars can be measured in fractions. We're dealing with a very fine, very competitive sport. A lot of fellows could handle my cars well enough to do well. As a driver I just can't give away the fractions I've gained as an engineer. It takes reflexes. Reflexes and guts. And coolness. I can't red-light much despite all the pressure I face, but I have to react to the green and I can't take my foot off the accelerator. A lot of guys do, you know. The cars get to shaking and they do.

"A tenth of a second is no more than the blinking of an eye. In our game, that's thirty feet. We go more than three hundred feet a second. This isn't Indianapolis. I don't have to do all the things Indianapolis drivers do. But I have to drive my car the way it has to be driven, and if I get in trouble, my ability to handle the car may be the only thing that will keep me alive.

"The stress on these cars is fantastic. The sudden thrust of power threatens to tear them apart. And the power builds rapidly. These things are like bullets. They'd like to go on the same way even after you do lift your foot off the accelerator. If I miss my parachute release when I go for it, I'll travel six hundred or seven hundred feet before I can go for it again. If I hit my brakes too soon or too hard, I'll go right off course. If I do begin to move off course and correct too sharply, I may flip. There are a thousand things that can go wrong."

Garlits has had several accidents and been badly burned several times. He broke his back when his car crashed at the end of the runway. His supercharger exploded in his face once. "I was burned inside and out," he says calmly. "I had third-degree burns all over me and the flesh on my hands was just hanging off. I was charred up and it made people sick just to look at me. They didn't think they could save me, but they did, though I later caught pneumonia while in my weakened state. They socked a lot of morphine into me to kill the pain, which was the worst thing. By the time I went home, I was hooked. I kicked the habit, but I was in agony. When I got burned again, I wouldn't let them give me any narcotics. I was lucky my condition wasn't as painful. But I'm always scared something like that will happen again."

He wrapped his hands around his cup and let the steam from the coffee warm his face. "When I broke 170, a lot of guys thought it couldn't be done, so they started inviting me to their tracks to prove it. A guy invited me to

Texas. I told him it was a long way and I couldn't afford it unless he paid for it. So he paid me and I became a professional. The competition didn't use to be very tough, but now it is. There are plenty of hot cars and plenty of hot drivers capable of beating you any time out, and a lot of different teams have been winning all the big meets. It's hard to dominate the sport now.

"Whenever you're working, there's always guys scuffing around checking out everything you do. Some of the guys call up the manufacturers trying to find out just exactly what you're getting from them. We've got a hell of an espionage system. If I discover something, I'll try to keep it a secret, but the next day everyone will have it on their car. They all copy. Because I've been on top a long time, everyone points for me. Those hot shoes come around, revving up, trying to tell me what kind of killers they are, how they'd lick me good if they had equipment like mine. Some do. If they lose to me, they don't believe it. Deep down, they all think they're killers. Which is what makes it so dangerous.

"One time I was racing a fellow—best out of three. There were delays and it was dark by the time we got to it. You couldn't see beyond the finish line. On the first run, I drove right into the darkness. I suggested we postpone it to another day. The officials, even the fans, thought this was reasonable. But the other guy wouldn't have any of it. So I said to hell with it. I went out and we raced and halfway down the strip I shut off. So I lost. That's okay. Who needs it? I'll raise my foot sometimes now, when it's smart. I wouldn't have used to, but I'm older and wiser and more cautious now. Some of the guys in this racket are crazy. I honestly think that if you had a drag strip running up to a cliff with a two-thousand-foot drop at the end of it, the top ten would pass it up, but there'd be a hundred others almost as good who want to crack the top ten who would go out there and race right off the end of the cliff, thinking the other guy would chicken out and shut off before they would."

He sighed, shook his head, and sipped his coffee. "I don't know how much faster we can go and still stay in one piece and on the track and stop before we run out of track. I feel like I'm pushing my luck now. It's crazy to go on. But I go on," he said. "I'm not particularly interested in driving at Bonneville or Indy. I'm not capable of driving at Indy. I mean, I'm sure I would have been, but I would have had to learn some things and I didn't have the time and now it's too late. I might be interested in preparing a car for Bonneville or Indy someday. That would be an interesting challenge, if I had good support."

Big Daddy got up and walked out into the night. No one paid any attention to him. "It's funny, but to look at me, no one would think I'm worth a dime. The way me and my wife and kids have to live, apart or traveling around in a truck, the way I live, like gypsies, no one would take us for much. In drag-racing circles, I'm a big man. It's real nice, you know. The fans are unreal. They like to pull me and my cars apart. I appreciate that. The other guys in the sport respect me. They want to knock me down, but you got to expect that. But beyond the sport, I'm no one. No one knows me. It's all right," he said. "I'm not beyond the sport. I'm in it. It's me." And he walked off into the dark night to drive on to his next place.

Late in 1969, Garlits's dragster exploded in a run at Long Beach, California. The explosion ripped the car in half and sent the driver's half rolling over several times. Inside the cockpit, Garlits was machine-gunned by flying parts of metal. Five of his toes had to be amputated and he was sidelined for a long time. When he recovered, he resumed building racers, with others driving them. And talked of resuming driving himself.

Don Garlits is the best that American drag racing has produced so far, but there have been many good ones and many others are coming along every year. Some come and some go. Cal Rice, Melvin Heath, Buddy Sampson, Ted Cyr, Rod Singer, Len Harris, Pete Robinson, Jack Chrisman, and Bobby Vodnik won "top eliminator" titles in the Nationals before Garlits took over. Don Prudhomme and Mike Snively have won the Nationals since. Bennie "The Wizard" Osborn won the World title two years in a row in the late 1960s. Hank Westmoreland, Maynard Rupp, Jim Warren, Connie Kalitta, Jack Williams, Red Henslee, Emery Cook, Tommy Ivo, Art Malone, Danny Karemesines, Tom McEwan, John Mulligan, Danny Ongais, and many others, many in other classes of drag racing, most with the help of automotive masters, have also attained considerable glory.

Gordon Collett is the only driver through the 1960s ever to have scored the NHRA's "grand slam" of the four major drag-racing titles, the Nationals, Winternationals, Springnationals, and World crowns. But he does not compete in the fastest class. Collett drives a gas-powered dragster, not an exotic-fuel-powered car. Gordon's nickname is "Collecting," and the collector from Ohio may have gathered more big trophies than any other dragster. In 1969, he was driving his gas-powered rails through the quarter mile in between seven and eight seconds, just a tick more than the fuel-powered leaders. He was hitting around 190 miles per hour at his peak.

Aside from Garlits, who is a three-time Nationals champion, Don "The Snake" Prudhomme is the only driver to have won this title more than once.

Prudhomme became the first Nationals winner to hit more than 200 miles per hour when he captured the 1965 crown with a peak of 207 miles per hour. The twenty-eight-year-old star from Granada Hills, California, returned in 1969 to win the laurels with an elapsed time of 6.51 seconds and a peak speed of 223.34 miles per hour in his Plymouth-powered dragster. Prudhomme was the original driver of "The Hawaiian," perhaps the most famous dragster in history, a creation that dominated the middle 1960s. Prudhomme has won three of the "big four," missing only the World Championships crown.

Osborn, the first driver to win the World title twice, won 14,000 by beating McEwan in a single race at the Orange County, California, strip. It was the biggest single purse ever offered for a match race in drag racing. However, Tom "The Mongoose" McEwan is still a towering figure in the sport. "I've been the house fighter at Lions Drag Strip in Long Beach for a long time," he said once. "I take on the invading stars. Sometimes I go somewhere else to take on someone in their backyard. You win some, lose some. Ours are short sprints. It doesn't take much of a slip to lose one. The point is, you can't lose many. Big purse or small purse. You have to win your share or you've had it. I'm good. I have good cars. I win my share. I just don't win 'em all."

He was asked about his nickname. "We're like wrestlers, except we're legit," the Mongoose explained. "The fans dig the fancy names and we draw as much publicity as we can to build this thing up. We have heroes and villains. I'm a villain. Villains make more money than heroes. I always pop off about the other racers and the fans pay their way in to see me get beat. Only I don't get beat very often. And when we race, we're on the level."

He smiled. He said, "I'm married. I have children. We live in a nice house. I was racing when we got married and my wife is used to it. I'm a drag racer. It's my job just like some guys are mechanics and some guys are salesmen and some guys are something else. When I go to the office, I'm going to the drag strip. It's a good business. Everyone drives a car. Most people, especially men, are interested in cars. And we're closer to the average guy. A kid can't build an Indianapolis racer in his backyard and expect to make the 500, but a kid can soup up a hot rod and try his luck at a drag race. It's easier to get started in our profession.

"Some of us get sponsors. One or two make $100,000 a year. Some make $50,000 a year. Some make $20,000. The number of guys making a good living at this goes up all the time. It's dangerous, but not like Indianapolis racing. We don't have to pass cars in traffic around corners. We go in a straight line and there's only one other car on the track with us we might hit. I'll admit that in our flimsy skeletons if something does happen it's apt to turn out bad, but that's the chance you take. It's a dangerous profession, but so are some others. It's a living."

John "The Zookeeper" Mulligan was a short, chubby fellow with a round face. In the late 1960s he set the record for the fastest run ever, zipping through the quarter mile in 6.65 seconds and attaining a peak speed of 233.85 miles per hour. If the Mongoose's specialty was match racing, the Zookeeper's was speed. He used to race on the street, collecting numerous tickets. His first dragster was a roadster that ran 157 miles per hour, hopping all over the place. Then he got a fuel dragster. He'd never driven so powerful or fast a machine before. He said it seemed like an animal to him. But he took it out and beat Garlits with it. Then he kept his animal in a garage he called "The Cave" and only let it out when it was eating time. In 1968 the Zookeeper earned $80,000.

He was a very cool, quiet guy. He said, "I'm no big talker." Ask him about his accomplishments and he said, "Everything now is overrated." If Mulligan thought a man was good, he called him "bad." That's the going language in the sport. "Prudhomme is bad," he said. "There are maybe three hundred licensed fuelers. Only about fifteen are really bad. Maybe anybody could drive a fuel dragster. I don't know. I'm not sure. I kind of doubt it. One of the mechanics drove our car one time, slow, just about half throttle, and he said it scared him. You can't lift your foot off the gas. You keep charging.

"New guys are always coming up to challenge. Most of them try to beat me off the line. They know my car is stronger than theirs, so they don't worry about fouling out and getting a red light. They gamble. If they win the gamble, they have a chance. They try to leave on me. But my car comes on so strong that I usually kill them before the lights. I go for top speed and time. I like setting records."

Mulligan had several bad accidents. Once, his chute failed to open and he hit a sandbag at 170 miles per hour and his car folded around him like an accordion. "It broke my back and I was out for forty-five days. When I drove again, I was in a steel brace and they had to lift me into the car," he said. But he kept on driving.

Another time, the Zookeeper's engine flew apart at 200 miles per hour and a great chunk of metal pierced his helmet. Later, the piece was found and weighed. It weighed fifteen pounds. "When the engine blew, it made a noise deep down in its guts like I never heard before. Like the atom bomb," he explained. "Afterward, I said, 'That's all. No more. Build me a rear-engine dragster before this thing kills me.' " But nothing was changed and he went on driving his mid-engine car.

In the 1969 Nationals, the twenty-six-year-old Zookeeper from Garden Grove, California, was the fastest qualifier, but during a run at 188 his clutch exploded in his face. His car went out of control and crashed against a guardrail. He suffered burns about the head and arms and internal injuries. For a while he was listed in critical condition. Then it was said he was recovering. Then he died.

Shortly before leaving for the Nationals, the cigar-chewing, stocky bachelor had admitted, "You get tired of all the races. I get tired. Not just me. All the guys I run with, Prudhomme and McEwan, we all get tired of racing. We fool around. We look for things to do. We got interested in Figure 8 jalopy racing one time. Bought some old junkers. Hired some guys to race them. They tore them to pieces. Motorcycles, too. We all ride motorcycles. McEwan had a wild street bike, but it was too 'bad' for the street and he had to sell it. Me, I went riding up this mountain and fell off and went rolling into a cactus bed. Then the bike lit on top of me. I've still got cactus thorns sticking in me."

It is the nature of the beast, roaming restlessly through his jungle.

Danny Ongais sat on a pile of tires in the pits at a drag-strip meet and said, "You know, I know a guy, an architect, who has a boat, a yacht, actually. He sails all over the world designing houses. That's the sort of thing I'd like to do. You know, sail to the South Pacific or the Mediterranean or someplace, lying on a deck in the sun, designing houses or something."

Danny Ongais is a drag racer, one of the best. He was born in 1940 on Maui in Hawaii and is a mixture of many nationalities. His father was a minister who pioneered two churches on the islands and then retired to sell and give lessons on pianos and organs. While growing up, Danny played baseball and football and ran track and sometimes surfed in the giant waves off the beaches. After graduation from high school, he began to race boats, motorcycles, and sports cars. He says, "I wasn't one of those kids who are always fooling around with hot rods in their backyards or always hanging around garages. Even today, there are a lot of things going on in the inside of an engine that I don't know anything about. I'm more interested in driving the blasted things. I just like to race."

If Don Garlits is a specialist in engineering, Danny Ongais is a specialist in driving. He won a lot of trophies while driving motorcycles and sports cars. And, like most race drivers, he is no stranger to accidents. He suffered a broken ankle when he crashed in a sports car. He almost broke his skull and back in a boat crash. It happened while he was speeding along a canal. Ongais was rounding a bend and saw that the locks were open and the barrier down. But it was too late to stop. "I ducked down, hung on, and tried to slip underneath it," he recalls. "Forget it. It was too low. It ripped my helmet right off my head and scraped down my backbone. I hurtled into the canal and they fished me out. I was in the hospital unconscious for a few days, but when I got out, I got back on a cycle."

In 1957, he and some friends enlisted in the army parachute corps. "It just seemed like the thing to do," he said with a shrug. "After we got in, it didn't seem like the thing to do, but it was too late then. I was in two years and made thirty-five jumps. Naw, I never got hurt. I haven't kept up with it since I got out. They're not payin' me for doin' it now, you know what I mean? The skydivers go at it now, seeing how close to the ground they can get before they open their chutes and all that jazz, it's a real sport, but I'm not hung up on the thought of it. It all depends on what gives you kicks."

Ongais entered drag racing in 1961 when a team toured the islands and took him back to the states as a driver.

"This is not a big, complicated thing," he says. "You get a piece of equipment and an engine that are as good or better than the next guy's. You get into it. When the green light goes, you slam the accelerator to the floor and you hold it all the way down and you stay as straight as you can until you pass the finish line. Then you release the parachutes and you jam the brakes and you keep steering straight. That's all there is to it, man." He was asked about things going wrong. "Oh, yes, man, there are things that can go wrong. It's not good to think too much, you know what I mean?"

Ongais is frail looking but extremely handsome, with a lot of black, curly hair, dark skin, and pearl-white teeth. He is tough, cocky, and cool, and inclined to put everything down. He is married and has children, but he says that he and his wife have an agreement allowing him to do as he wants as long as he takes care of her, so he tours the country racing.

He had been sipping a soft drink while talking. He put it down and pulled on his gear and got into his car and was pushed off. He went to the line and blasted off. It was nighttime and the flames were frightening as they poured back from the engine past his head. He won and he came back as the announcer was saying, "The winner—Danny Own-guy-yus," and he picked up his unfinished soft drink and he took a big drink of it. "So tonight I'm number one," he said. "So tomorrow, who knows? So who cares?"

Later, he lay under a tree and said, "This is a nice thing, you know, and I got nothing against it. I want you to understand that, but I've done it now, and I want to do something else. You know what I mean? I want to race real racing cars now. I want to race at Indianapolis. I want to race on the Grand Prix circuit. It'd be kind of nice, you know, going from Nassau to London to Monte Carlo and so forth. I think I'd like that scene, man. But they don't welcome you with open arms. You know what I mean? I got people interested in me, though. Mickey Thompson is interested in me."

Mickey Thompson has said, "Ongais is the bravest son of a gun in the world." Thompson put him in one of his "funny cars" (very light and fast version of stock cars) and Ongais began to dominate this aspect of the sport as he had never dominated the fuel dragsters. He won the 1969 Nationals with a 7.46-second quarter time and a 195.65 peak speed. Thompson then took him to Bonneville, where together they set a series of endurance and speed records in stock cars. Next, Mickey took him to Indianapolis. But after Ongais had practiced there, the officials told him to go elsewhere to get more experience in real racing cars before returning.

Ongais was disappointed, but not discouraged. He said, "If you're good, you want to be the best. The real racers race Indy, so that's where I want to be. You got to fight to get in. The establishment makes it hard. They're afraid you'll cut into their pie. But it's worth fighting for. I want to make me a bunch of bucks so I don't have to worry about anything, then go on to something else. If you've got the bread, it's not important. It's only when you don't have it that it's important. You need it to be free. And being free is the most important thing of all.

"Racing Indy is different than driving dragsters, but no faster. You get tired of waiting, you know what I mean? It's all right if you're not good enough. But if you are, it's no good. I'm good enough now. I don't want to wait till I get a beard. Who the hell wants to drive race cars when they're old and gray? Now is the only time to drive racing cars, when I'm too young to be thinking about dying. Dying is no different at Indy than it is on a drag strip in Pomona. You take a chance, that's all. Racing is a helluva way to live, but there are a lot of ways. The important thing is to live." He sighed. "Racing doesn't scare me," he went on. "I'm not afraid of dying. I'm only afraid of not living."

11

THE BRAVEST ONES

The first time Allen Heath got behind the wheel of a midget racing car and practiced with it on a racetrack, he lost control, slid into a wall, and bounced into three new racers in the infield, wrecking them. The first time he drove a midget in a race, he crashed it. The next time, he rolled it over. When he first tried sprint cars, he landed upside down four times in five races. The first time he drove an Indianapolis car at the Speedway, he slid on an oil slick and crashed into a wall.

Once, he was rammed by a car and hit in the head by one of its wheels. Despite a bad headache, he continued in the race and won it. Coming back to race the next night, he collapsed on the track. Taken to the hospital, he was found to have a fractured skull. In another accident, he suffered broken ribs and a punctured lung. The day he got out of the hospital, he was helped into a racing car and won a race.

He remembers a race in Oregon: "I got involved in an accident in front of me. I ran over a guy's car, cracked up, and took off like a ball of fire. I wasn't burned, but I was skinned from head to toe. I didn't need a shave for a month. And I was so bandaged up, all I had was a peephole to see through." As soon as the doctor unwrapped him, he folded himself inside a race car again.

In August of 1953, Heath was driving a sprint car on a half-mile dirt track at the Illiana Speedway, which is on the Indiana side of the Illinois border. His right front wheel flew off. He recalls, "I was going down the chute and I began flipping end for end. The last thing I remember is trying to keep off the fence, but I landed on top of the railing and kept flipping."

When the car came off the fence and settled onto the track in a smashed heap, both of Heath's legs, his left arm, and his left shoulder were broken in several places. His left hand was crushed; ligaments were pulled and ripped; and he was cut, broken, and bleeding. "You name it and I had it," he says, almost proudly. "They could have used a shovel to get me on a stretcher."

Heath was rushed to a hospital, where he shortly read his obituary, which was headlined in his hometown Seattle newspaper and had been brought to his bedside by his father. For weeks, Health lay in bed wrapped in bandages, splints, and casts. There was some doubt that he would be able to walk again, but he felt confident that he would. The doctors warned him he might lose some fingers on his left hand. He was ready to accept that. He figured he was lucky to be alive. He told everyone that he would resume driving when he recovered.

However, particles of dirt left in his hand when it was repaired caused gangrene to form. Allen remembers, "The doctor came in one day and said he was sorry, but I'd never drive again. He said they were going to amputate my left hand. I asked him if he had to, and he said he did. So I said, 'Well, cut the son of a gun off, then, only I'll make a damn liar out of you. I'll drive again if it's the last thing I do.' "

The doctors amputated his left hand just above the wrist.

In May of 1954, wearing an artificial clamp at the end of his left arm, he drove in a race at Culver City, California. In August of that year, he won a race at San Bernardino. And for more than ten years after that, this little guy with only one hand, only five-feet-eight and 145 pounds, who was a grandfather several times over, drove and won races. He was almost fifty years old when he finally retired in the late 1960s. They called him "the One-Armed Bandit."

Allen Heath was never one of the greatest American race drivers. But he was one of the better ones—and one of the bravest. He is discussed in this book because he is typical of his breed, a guy who would rather have died than not race cars. To understand him is to understand them all.

Allen Heath was born in Saskatchewan and raised in Seattle, Washington. As a boy he used to hang around his father's garage, where race driver Swede Lindskog kept his car. Young Heath talked Swede into giving him his first ride in a race car. Shortly afterward, Lindskog was killed in a race. Heath was disturbed, but not discouraged. He said, as so many have, "We all know it can happen—but not to us."

Heath drove successfully up and down the Pacific Coast for several years. Successfully, but recklessly. At one time or another he has been called "the Seattle Screwball," "Knothead," "Old Splinterhead," and "the Clown Prince of the Speedways." He rattles off this list with great pride. A tough, profane man, Heath is flattered by his reputation.

"I never had any fear in a race car," he says. "If I could win a race by putting my car in a place on the track the next guy wouldn't go, fine. It's all a big con game, anyway. The more I get 'em scared of me, the better I am. I play pinochle, I bid something, maybe I got it, maybe I haven't. I start something on a racetrack, maybe I can carry through, maybe not. If the boys don't know, they're gonna back off. The good ones won't. But I'll scare all the rest off if I can."

After his accident in 1953, he was reduced to ninety pounds. As he began to build himself back up, he was fitted with a ball-and-socket setup that he could attach to the steering wheel of a race car. But he found that it shook loose and he could not reattach it while racing. So he went to UCLA Medical Center and was fitted with the type of two-part hook he now wears. It consists of two rounded pieces of metal. A plastic pin is inserted through the biceps muscles of his left arm and two small cables connect the pin to the hook. He operates the hook by flexing his biceps muscles.

Once he did not have his hook screwed on properly and he made a sharp turn and it flew off. "I had to drive back to the corner and crawl around in the dirt to find it. I put it back on and got back to driving," he said with a grin. Another time, he flipped. He wasn't hurt, but his hook was bent out of shape. "I had to find me a sledgehammer to whack it back straight so I could go on driving. I'm probably the only guy who had to straighten out his left hand with a sledgehammer before he could finish a race," he says.

With his hook, he drove more daringly and won more often than he ever had before. At Ascot Park near Los Angeles, there is a ramp inside the racetrack for use in motorcycle races. He celebrated a victory there by driving up the ramp to "give the fans a show." He misjudged his speed and the extent of the ramp. He went soaring off the end, which was as high as a two-story building, landed right side up with a horrible impact, and cracked his spine. He had to spend two months in the hospital. When he got out, he went back to driving.

Another time, in San Diego, the crowd was so large that it had to be roped off in the infield. Heath lost control coming off a turn, slid into the infield, missed the people, but caught the rope in his face, breaking his jaw. He calmly got out of the car, walked over to the rope, took a knife, cut the rope in half, then walked to the ambulance and went to the hospital. When he got out of the hospital, he resumed driving again, of course. He is a re-markable man.

"Remarkable? Hell, yes, I guess I am," Heath says. "But, hell, I haven't done anything anyone else couldn't do if they wanted to do it badly enough. Being a race driver is tough. Being a race driver with a hook for a hand is a lot tougher. But if it couldn't have been done, I couldn't have done it. I'm not made of iron. People think I'm not for real. Hell, I bruise as much as the next guy. What hurts them hurts me. It's just that hurtin' never bothered me as much and sure never stopped me from doin' what I wanted to do.

"When you get hurt like I did, if you want to lay down and cry, you can. I didn't want to. I didn't want to feel sorry for myself and give up. I had a boxful of sympathy cards, but you can't eat that sympathy. I realized I had to accept what had happened and make the best of it. I even found out I could joke about it. Things are easier to take if you can laugh about 'em. I know people look at me like I'm some sort of a freak. When they're first around me, they don't see anything but the hook. But I don't hide it. And after a while, they accept it and even forget it."

His weather-beaten face creased in a smile. He said, "I've always been wheel happy. I never made a livin' racing. I always had to work, too. I never made the big time. I never got up to the big money. I took two cracks at Indy and missed both and never got another after the accident. But I kept racing because I loved it. It's like a guy who loves to drink: he gets drunk, he has a hangover, he swears off, he swears he'll never take another drink as long as he lives. But come Saturday night he's right back at it again. That's the way it is with a real race driver. You know it's a crazy thing to do, but it's what you do."

Heath's curious pride in his accidents, his hook, his going on against all good reason and surviving, says something about the spirit of the race driver. Not all are cocky, as is Heath. Not all are as fearless. And most, like Heath, retire before they are killed. But if being killed, or losing an arm or a leg, is the price they have to pay, so be it, they say. Heath sometimes used to drive against Cal Niday, who drove with only one leg. Once, before a race, Niday limped over to Heath, shook his hook, and said, "Allen, we'd make a great team. If we get in a fight, I can punch 'em, and if we lose you can outrun 'em."

Bill Schindler was another who drove with one leg. There have been a few others besides Heath who drove with one hand. There have been some who drove against heavy odds. One such is Jim Hurtubise.

Jim Hurtubise was born in California and raised in upstate New York. Like many other drivers, he became interested in cars and mechanics around his father's gas station. After two years in the Coast Guard, he began to race. He was a daredevil charger who first attracted attention on the dirt tracks of the Far West. He really enjoyed racing. Other drivers would remark about how much fun it seemed to be for "Herk." (His nickname was "Hercules.") For a while, nothing in racing seemed beyond Hurtubise.

He was a charger. Most drivers can press the accelerator to the floorboard on the straights. But the extra speed is gained on the corners, and races are won by passing cars in traffic. In the corners, Hurtubise had a style that few drivers dared copy. He went in harder and deeper than others and slowed down later. Even as he was braking, he kept his foot on the accelerator. When he took his foot off the brakes, his car would lurch forward into swift acceleration. He slid through even concrete turns as though they were dirt. He got out of the corners in a hurry. He was hard on equipment, but he was a young man in a hurry. Twice he was fined or suspended for reckless driving. But he survived and won races.

Hurtubise won in sprint cars and midget cars (smaller or more erect versions of front-engine championship cars, which are driven on shorter tracks). He hit the championship trail and won the second big race he ever drove, the Sacramento 100 in 1959. The next year, he went to Indianapolis. He had an old car that had carried another driver, Ed Elisian, to a fiery death at Milwaukee the year before. For most of the month of preparation for the race it was hampered by mechanical problems. On the fourth and last day of qualifying, Hurtubise sat in the car, hunched over the steering wheel, wearing a straw hat, waiting for gusting winds and spurts of rain to pass. There was little time left when the weather cleared. Hurtubise tossed aside his straw hat and strapped on a crash helmet. Then he roared off.

He threw his car around the track as if there was no tomorrow. He slammed it in and out of turns on the hairy edge of disaster and boomed it down the straightaways as if they went on forever. When the announcer gasped the first-lap time, a new record of more than 148 miles per hour, the fans came to their feet roaring. The second lap was faster yet, an average of more than 149 miles per hour, and now hysteria reigned. The third lap came within a fraction of a second of 150 miles per hour, a barrier that had not yet been broken at Indy. As Hurtubise roared into his fourth and final lap, madness gripped the great oval. He had the 150, and then he lost it. On the last turn he tried to go just a little harder and he lost control for just a moment and before he had wrestled his brute back into the groove, the record had slipped through his fingers. Life is like this for Jim Hurtubise.

Still, as he rolled into the pits, a rookie with a new speed record, the fans stood and cheered him and a fat smile creased his round face. Off to one side, the great Mauri Rose, now retired, said, "Once in a while, a fellow comes along with no worries. He doesn't feel like he's strapped in an electric chair. He's relaxed. He enjoys it. He loves it. It's fun for him. He doesn't know it's supposed to be so tough."

And Herk, happy in his cockpit as his joyful crew surrounded him, said, "It's not so tough."

But it was tougher than he ever thought it could be. Despite his record run that first year, he had to start far back in the field because he had qualified on the last day. He drove like a madman, but he still was behind when he broke down with only forty miles to go. The next year at Indy, he qualified third fastest and led for part of the race, but broke down just past the halfway point. The year after that, during a prerace run he slid out of control for nearly one thousand feet, smashed the wall twice, demolished his car, and was lucky to escape with his life. On the last day of qualifying he piled blocks of wood and chunks of foam rubber in the oversized compartment of an old car he had never driven. With all this insulation, he could just see above the hood. He went out and made the race. He started twenty-ninth and although he drove hard all the way—the only time he went the distance at Indy—he still finished only thirteenth. That year his buddy Parnelli Jones got the record 150 Herk had come so close to getting.

It was almost inevitable that he would eventually turn up with a Novi car, a jinxed guy in a jinxed car. Cars powered by Novi engines were the most powerful, the most publicized, the most popular, and some of the least successful of the decade. Novi cars carried many great drivers to the brink of glory, but none beyond, and some to their death. Driving a Novi in 1963, Herk qualified second fastest, getting his 150 a year too late. He outran pole-sitter Parnelli through the first lap to win a $5 bet. He outran almost everyone for half the race. Then he was waved in for leaking oil on the track. But later he found out that he hadn't been the one leaking the oil. That was the year Parnelli won the 500—leaking oil.

Herk won championship races at Langhorne and Springfield, but he couldn't win the big one at Indy. He was married by now, and he had three children at home in North Tonawanda, New York, and it wasn't easy for him. Some of his friends—fellows who had come up with him and seemed to have no more ability than he had—were getting rich and famous while he was still struggling. But he loved racing. And he went on with it. In

1964, he drove through the fiery crash that killed Eddie Sachs and Dave MacDonald and was running second in the 500 when his car failed him at 350 miles. A week later he went to Milwaukee to drive in a 100-miler.

He was driving a front-engine roadster he had built himself. He was running third right behind Rodger Ward and A. J. Foyt at more than 100 miles per hour midway in the race. Under the savage strain that racing imposes on cars, the rear end of Ward's car gave way. The car swayed and Ward slowed down suddenly. Reacting instantly, Foyt cut his car hard to the right, narrowly avoiding Ward's car. At that instant, Hurtubise also cut his car hard to the right to avoid Foyt's car. However, he was last in line and had farther to go. He didn't make it.

It took less than three seconds. The anatomy of an accident: The left front wheel of Hurtubise's car rode up over the axle of the right rear wheel of Foyt's car, and Herk's gaudy racer sailed into the air over Foyt's head. Hurtubise fought the wheel and the brakes, but suddenly he was a passenger, a prisoner in a car out of control. His car took off to the left, twisted in the air, and nosed down to the right into an outer wall. The right front of the car exploded like a bomb with a shriek of tearing metal as it hit the barrier and bounced off. A wheel came off and bounced high in the air. Pieces of broken metal shot through the air. As Herk's body strained against the seat belt and shoulder harness that were keeping him in the car, three of his ribs were cracked, puncturing and collapsing his right lung and filling his insides with blood. He began to lose consciousness. A front axle had been driven through an auxiliary fuel tank and, as the crippled car came clanking back across the track on its belly, fuel was pouring out. The loose tire bounded back into the cockpit, striking Hurtubise on the head and shoulders. A piece of scalding hot brake line landed on his back, searing it. The fuel sparked into flame. Suddenly, as the twisted car came to a stop with the driver slumped over the steering wheel, it became an inferno of invisible alcohol fire. One, two, three, and it was all over.

Firemen rushed in, poured foam on the fire, hurriedly extinguished it, and gently raised the unconscious driver from it. He was placed on a stretcher and hurried to a hospital in an ambulance. "I remember hitting the wall. I remember hearing that horrible noise. I remember being jolted terribly," Hurtubise said later. "Then I don't remember anything else until I began to come to again in the ambulance. I could hear the siren. I began to hurt. I guessed I was burned. I knew I was alive."

Meanwhile, back at the track, the race continued, with Foyt going on to win. In upstate New York, Jane Hurtubise, who had taken her children to an amusement park, heard her name called over the loudspeaker. She rushed in fear to a telephone and began to cry as she was told of her husband's accident. She took the children to their grandparents' home, then flew to Milwaukee to be with Jim. When she first saw him, she fainted.

Aside from his severe internal injuries, he had second- and third-degree burns over 42 percent of his body. He had a chance to live, but a slim one. Doctors pumped fluids into him and put tubes into his chest to fight dehydration, infection, and strangulation. They determined that his best chance to live lay in specialized treatment at the Brooke Army Medical Center in San Antonio, Texas, a service facility that concentrates on the care of burns. A team of doctors from Brooke flew with him back to the medical center in the middle of the night, treating him all the way. His wife flew to Brooke to be with him. His lung was reinflated. His ribs began to mend. Soon, it seemed he would live, but no one knew in what condition he would survive.

Twice, surgeons grafted skin from human and animal corpses onto his body to serve as temporary protective covering. Then they began to graft skin taken from other parts of his body onto the burned areas. His face had been badly burned, but his hands had been burned worst of all. His flameproof coveralls had given him some protection over his body, but there was little left of his fingers. His left little finger had to be amputated entirely. The doctors told Jim that his hands would never be flexible again. They could be set any way he wished, but that was the way they would stay. He had them set, with wires, the way he gripped a steering wheel. He said he would drive again. They expected that. But they didn't think he could. About one month after he was interned, he was permitted to hold a news conference. He lay on his bed covered to the neck by bandages and blankets. His arms extended to each side on pillows and were covered with towels. He could not move. "I'll race again," he said.

Probably no one who has not lived through it could understand the agony he suffered. He sang so he wouldn't scream as they washed him off with a pressure hose periodically to cleanse him of dead skin. Slowly, he began to heal. He was allowed to begin walking again, but it was an ordeal. Gradually he recovered. After three months, he was discharged from the main medical center, but for six more months he had to remain as an outpatient, continuing the delicate and painful treatment.

When he was permitted to take a trip, he flew to Indianapolis to visit a race at the Indiana State Fairgrounds. As he crossed into the infield, fans recognized him and began to cheer. He grinned wistfully. Drivers, mechanics, and sponsors spotted him and called to him, "Herk, old boy . . . Howareyadoing, boy . . . Hey, goodtoseeya, guy." They looked at his scarred face, but they were used to this sort of thing. They reached out to shake his hand and he reached out to shake theirs, but his hands were still bandaged and sore, so they drew back awkwardly. They didn't ask him if he was going to drive again. But he kept saying he would.

That winter, after nine months, Hurtubise went home. He rowed boats, chopped wood, and kept squeezing a little rubber ball to strengthen his sore, frozen hands. And he worked on race cars, rebuilding his charred wreck, among others. Spring came. In March, he turned up at Phoenix for a 100-mile race with a car that he had been given to drive, the Tombstone Life Special. He made the starting field and drove well until his brakes gave out, and then drove even better after that, without brakes, more carefully than usual. He got very sore and tired, but he finished the race in fourth place. "I'm really satisfied," he said later, struck with wonder by his own accomplishment. Everyone was awed by it. More people crowded around him than around the winner. Still, most suspected it was a special effort that he would never be able to repeat.

In April, he showed up at the Atlanta Raceway in Georgia, hoping to find a car to drive in the 500-mile race there. He begged for one from John Holman, a powerful sponsor. Holman stood in the sun looking at Hurtubise's scarred face and stumpy, twisted hands as the big cars boomed around the track and said, "I'm sorry, Jim, but I don't have anything for you."

Scuffing his toe in the dirt, Hurtubise said, "Anything, John. I don't care what it is. I want to show these guys I can still drive."

Holman looked away from him, as though he was studying the cars practicing on the track. "We know you can, Jim," he said. "Honest to God, if I had anything, I'd give it to you. But it wouldn't be fair to give you something that's not right. I'll tell you what—we'll get something fixed up for you and you can run the next race, next month."

"I'll be running Indy then," Hurtubise said.

"I'm sorry," Holman said.

"All right," Hurtubise said. "But maybe I'll hang around awhile just in case something breaks."

"Sure, Jim," Holman said.

Herk went off then, his head lowered. He was asked why he still wanted to race, after all that had happened to him. "Now, after it's happened, why not?" he said. He watched the drivers practicing for a few days and talked to a number of car owners, but he could not get a ride. Finally, he went home to wait for Indy. At Indy, he was asked again why he was still driving. "Racing is my profession," he said. "I've been a race driver thirteen years. It took me eight years just to get here, to Indy. I'm not going to give it up now. What else can I do? What else do I want to do? Nothing. Not even now. Not even after the accident. I got through it. I'm okay now." He held out his hands. "My hands are okay. You use your grip and your wrists in steering. You don't use your fingers."

He worked hard all month. On the first qualifying day, he lost control of his own car in practice when the throttle stuck. He smashed into an outside wall. The front end of the car was bashed and torn apart. Both front wheels were torn off. The fuel tank split. There was no fire, however. Still, it was a horrible-looking accident, especially under the circumstances, and all who saw it rushed over, sure that Hurtubise had been killed. Instead, he got out of his car and walked away from it. He did not even seem shaken. He was disappointed, of course, but undisturbed.

The car was towed to the garage and Hurtubise and his crew worked for many days and nights to try to repair it sufficiently for qualification. But they could not. Now Hurtubise did not have a car.

One of Andy Granatelli's cars had been wrecked and he had pulled an old car off a truck and given it to another driver to try to qualify, but the driver had failed. On the last day of trials, Granatelli offered the car to Hurtubise. Jim got into it and drove it brilliantly, qualifying for the race as the crowd cheered. It was a very dramatic scene as Hurtubise rolled happily into his pits. His wife wept. Granatelli said of him, "He is a superhuman being."

Hurtubise started on race day full of high hopes. On the second lap, his transmission failed and his car came to a stop. He climbed slowly out of the car and stood there with his hands in his pockets while the crowd around him applauded sympathetically. Finally he walked off, dejected.

But he did not give up. For the rest of the 1965 season he drove whenever and wherever he could get a ride. In a 150-mile race at Trenton, he started sixteenth. After thirty miles, he was second. At the forty-five-mile mark, he lost control and spun out. But he regained control and resumed running, now far back again. He moved up steadily and at the finish he was second again, closing in on the winner. In the Yankee 300 stock car race, he wrestled his heavy car over a tough, twisting road course for more than four hours and took third place. "I got very tired," he said afterward. "I kept thinking of stopping and getting out and letting someone else finish. But I didn't do it. I'm glad I didn't. I think I proved something—to myself as well as everyone else."

After finishing second in a stock car race at Milwaukee, where he had nearly been burned to death, he returned for another stock car race. He drove furiously to take the lead and held it determinedly to win. At the end, he climbed awkwardly out of his car, sweating in the bright, hot sunshine, and said, "This was the one I wanted."

In April, he returned to Atlanta for the 500, the race in which he had been denied a car the year before. But now he was given a car, and he dueled Petty, Pearson, Turner, Jarrett, Yarbrough, and Lorenzen, the greatest stock car drivers in the world, and beat them at their own game. He drove 334 laps in three hours and forty-nine minutes at an average speed of more than 131 miles per hour. He was in and out of the lead all day and scored one of the most dramatic victories in auto-racing history. He drove into victory lane with a broad smile on his scarred face, waving his scarred hands to the cheering crowd, and he said, "Hell, I never even gave a thought to quitting." He was asked if he was surprised he had won. He said, "Hell, no. Why should I be?"

This was the peak of his career thus far. He has not won many races since, but he has continued to drive. Indy has continued to haunt him, but he has not given up there. In 1966, he qualified late and broke down early. In 1967, he qualified early, but was bumped out of the starting field by a faster car. Then he made the field in a slower car in which he qualified late, but was bumped again.

The next year, Hurtubise took his own car, an old-fashioned front-engine car that he had built himself, and managed to qualify. He started in thirtieth and last place and finished thirtieth, breaking down in less than twenty-five miles. In 1969, he again took his own car, but failed to make the field. He said, "If I'm not in it, I don't even want to see it." He hung up a sign on his garage that said he had "gone fishin' " and he went off to wait for another time. In 1970, he tried with a front-engine car and failed to qualify again.

Still, he goes on. And he is not the only one. In recent years, Norm Hall drove against him with only one leg. Mel Kenyon drove against him with a fingerless hand. When Kenyon was injured in a five-car crack-up at Langhorne, Hurtubise pulled over and helped pull Kenyon out of his burning car. Kenyon mended and resumed driving, and he finished third at Indianapolis in 1968. It is the nature of these fellows to go on in spite of injuries and handicaps. But this is not to say that there are drivers who don't feel frightened. Some will admit their fear and some will not. Some seem most afraid of being thought afraid. When J. C. Agajanian asked his successful and rich driver, Parnelli Jones, why he did not retire, Jones replied, "The guys would think I'm chicken." It is incredible to think that, after all he has won, he would worry about such a thing. But this is the sort of worry some race drivers have. They are proud of their bravery, and that is understandable. Racing may frustrate drivers like Allen Heath and Jim Hurtubise and deny them greatness, but the most horrible injuries cannot stop them. In fact, the opportunity to overcome such injuries has given them a special form of greatness.

12

THE FRUSTRATED ONES

The Indianapolis 500 is the world's most spectacular annual sporting event. It draws more persons and a greater field of competitors than any other yearly contest. Most of the outstanding racing men of this country prepare eleven months of the year for May at Indy. They race elsewhere, often in important events, but there is nothing for them even remotely comparable to Indy.

In 1970, the Ontario Motor Speedway opened in southern California. This is a new version of old Indy. The track is faster and fans are able to see all of it, whereas they can see only a part of the course at Indy. There is a 500-mile championship car classic every Labor Day weekend as there is every Memorial Day at Indy. The track and especially its main event are a most valuable addition to the American racing circuit. As time goes on other major racing events will be staged there that are not staged at Indy. Some controversial 500s at Indy may be resolved at Ontario. The crowds may someday approach those at Indy and the purse may come close, too. Until now, only Indy has offered even a reasonable return. Few men get rich in racing—a few drivers, a few sponsors perhaps. But men do not race to get rich unless they are fools. They race because it is what they want to do. There is certainly not enough money at stake to repay the heavy investments they make and the risks they must run. It is good that men who invest so heavily and risk so much will have a second chance for a reasonable return at Ontario.

But great as it may be, Ontario cannot surpass Indianapolis. The Ontario 500 did not begin in 1911 as did the Indianapolis 500. There is simply no way that the new southern California citadel of racing can gain the colorful history and rich tradition of the Hoosier classic.

Racing teams with investments of $100,000 or more in racing cars, spare engines and parts, contracted drivers and mechanics begin to pour into Indianapolis the first of May each year. All month they practice with new and improved cars. Perhaps seventy-five or eighty-five are entered each year. Perhaps forty-five or fifty drivers are on hand each year, some already assigned rides, some seeking rides. Rookies must take tough, intensive tests under the careful observation of veteran drivers and officials.

By Indianapolis standards, a rookie is one who has not qualified for the 500 before, no matter what he has done elsewhere. Grand Prix champions have been considered rookies and have had to take tests at Indy. Good drivers have been sent away to improve their skills. Qualifying trial runs of four laps each are conducted for four days over the two weekends prior to Memorial Day, to cut the field to the thirty-three fastest cars. The drivers who qualify on the first day get the highest starting positions among the thirty-three fastest, no matter how fast other drivers go on the following qualifying days. The two-and-a-half-mile oval track has been paved over with asphalt, with only a symbolic strip of bricks remaining at the start-finish line, but otherwise the track is still only mildly banked and much the same as it was in 1911, when it was built for cars with top speeds of less than 100 miles per hour. Today, cars exceed 170 miles per hour there. And if those same cars ran the steep banks of Daytona, they'd exceed 200 miles per hour. Because conditions remain standard at Indy, the yearly improvements in equipment and speed, if not in drivers, are very meaningful.

If men braved a greater unknown in racing cars in the early 1900s, they did not then challenge the limitations they seem to face today. How much faster can human beings push cars and retain control over them and keep them in one piece? Who knows? At 170 miles per hour for an average qualifying lap, the difference between the car that wins the coveted pole position and those that do not even make the race is often less than three seconds. It is not much, but it is the difference between victory and defeat, joy and despair.

It is almost impossible to win the 500 without a high starting position. By the fourth and final day of the time trials, the desire to achieve a high qualifying speed and make the starting field, even in a position from which it may be almost impossible to win, is incredibly intense. Parnelli Jones has observed that "in the last minutes of qualifying, I've walked down the row of drivers sitting in their cars waiting for one more chance they probably won't get and I know I could pass among them with guns then and they'd swap their cars for the chance to shoot themselves dead."

More than a million persons pay to attend the practice, trials, and race at Indy during the month of May. On May 30, more than 300,000 persons attend the race itself. Days ahead of time an incredible crowd begins to form on the streets outside the track. They arrive by plane, helicopter, train, bus, car, and on foot, and pour into the great arena and swarm over the vast grounds in penthouse and grandstand seats, lined up along the fences, sitting in their cars and lying on blankets, in mud if it has rained, eating, drinking, dancing, necking, sleeping, making a circus of this cruel contest of speed. Some never see the race. They just want to be there. Others watch intently from the first gaudy preliminaries of marching bands, bursting bombs, and released balloons to that stirring moment when the president of the track says, "Gentlemen, start your engines." As the crowd hushes, thirty-three powerful cars roar to life, move away, and fall into position. Then they are sent on their way in that awesome tangle of traffic, earsplitting noise, and stinking smells through the long three hours of dizzying, blurring, round-and-round racing, with crashes here and changes of the lead there. It is a spectacle that dazzles racing fans and some begin to think of the next one as soon as a fortunate driver eases his car wearily into the madness of victory lane.

In 1970, a million dollars was paid out to the 500's contestants. More than $200,000 was paid to the winning team alone. But there is more at stake than that. Former winner Jimmy Bryan once said, "If you never win another dollar in racing the rest of your life, you will still be someone if you have won the Indianapolis 500. You will always be known for that. You will always be famous. Men will envy you. Women will chase you. Wherever you go, people will look at you and point you out to others. People will buy your name. When you're old and tired and scared and ready to die, you will still be someone who once won the 500."

So they seek it. Seventeen men have been killed practicing or qualifying for the race. Seventeen have been killed driving in the race. Of the thirty-two men who have won it, thirteen have been killed in other races, two in subsequent 500s. Many great drivers have never won it. It is a hard race to win. It must be won in the workshop and the garage, in practicing and qualifying, in the pits and on the track, and it can be lost in any one of these places. It has been lost because a piece of metal worth pennies failed. It has been lost because someone made a mistake or lost his courage.

Of seventeen different men who won the national title, ten never won the 500, including Earl Cooper and Ted Horn, both of whom won the United States crown three times, and Ralph Mulford, Rex Mays, and Tony

Bettenhausen, who each won the title twice. Cliff Bergere and Chet Miller drove this race the most times, sixteen, and never won it. Russ Snowberger, Paul Russo, and Eddie Johnson, who drove it fifteen times, also never won it. Twenty men who won the pole position never won the race. Such are the frustrations of the 500. And even some who won it have shared in its fierce frustrations.

One does not have to have won the 500 to be considered a great driver, but even so it is the race that contributes the most toward an image of greatness. Mays and Horn must be considered among the great American race drivers, but because they did not win the greatest American race it is difficult to rate them above Wilbur Shaw and Mauri Rose, who drove into victory lane at Indianapolis three times, even though they seldom achieved on the rest of the circuit what some others did.

The Indianapolis 500 is a race unto itself. Greatness can be attained there, even if attained nowhere else. Bill Vukovich is one who attained greatness there and there alone.

Both former winners who were killed at Indy were killed the year following their victories. One was Floyd Roberts, who beat Wilbur Shaw in 1938 to receive the winner's plaudits. He returned in 1939, cartwheeled over a wall and into a fence just past the midway point, was thrown out, and died of his injuries as Shaw went on to score the second of his three victories in four years. The other was Bill Vukovich. Like Shaw, Vukovich almost won this race four times.

Bill Vukovich was born in 1919 in Alameda, California, as one of eight children. His family moved to a farm outside Fresno when he was a boy. His father died when Bill was thirteen. He and his brothers picked cotton, pruned trees, and drove trucks to help their mother make ends meet. She died when Bill was sixteen. He was eighteen and ambitious when he persuaded a friend to let him drive in a stock car race in 1937. After that he began to race for a living, and when he was nineteen he crashed in a midget car race and broke his collarbone and three ribs. But after he recovered he went on with it. Sometimes he raced fifteen times a week in small events on bush tracks, and there were weeks in which he won some races and wound up with $40. He'd had a hard time all his life and racing didn't change that for a number of years.

He sat out World War II in a repair shop. When the war ended, he resumed racing and swiftly began to move up. Small and gaunt, he was an almost humorless man and drove with a deadly determination. Once he drove in the 2,000-mile Pan American Road Race with Vern Houle, a fine mechanic, as his navigator. He drove so recklessly around the corners of steep cliffs that Houle was terrified and kept asking Vukovich to take it easy. For a long time, Vukovich did not say anything. Then he missed a curve and went sailing off the side of the thirty-foot embankment. The moment the car was airborne, Vukovich took his hands off the steering wheel and said to Houle, "All right, you drive." The car crashed. Somehow, both escaped critical injuries.

Although Vukovich was of Yugoslavian descent, he was nicknamed "the Mad Russian." He got along well enough with most of his fellow drivers, but he was uncomfortable beyond the bounds of the racing fraternity. Even within it, he insulted many. He would often refuse to join his own crew in victory celebrations. He'd go out of his way to avoid fans or writers, and he'd seldom sign autographs or give interviews. Vukovich had married by then and was a father and a good husband who was devoted to his family. He'd virtually flee from the racetracks to hide out at home between races.

He arrived at Indianapolis in 1951. When asked how he drove, he said curtly, "All you do is press down on the accelerator and steer left. It's just that damn simple." He hated being a hero and once said, "All these people want a villain, so I'll be one." He didn't seem to mind being hated by many people. He went his own way, giving little of himself to anyone and holding his own secrets. Even after he broke down after only twenty-nine laps of his first 500, he said, "It's a cinch."

Vukovich returned in 1952 in a good car, and he blew everyone down most of the way. He drove fast and almost perfectly from eighth starting position to first by a mile and a half, with a hundred miles to go. Then his steering began to come apart and he had to struggle to keep his car on the course. Others might have quit, but he kept on. However, he was slowing and Troy Ruttman began to close in on him. With twenty-five miles to go, Vukovich still led by a half mile. Then a pivot pin on the steering assembly broke through and his car swerved and he scraped to a stop along the wall. He climbed out cursing and disgusted. The twenty-two-year-old Ruttman drove past to become the youngest winner of the 500 and the first winner for longtime Speedway car sponsor J. C. Agajanian. "You can be damn sure it won't happen again," Vukovich griped to his crew.

He returned in 1953 with a stronger car, won the pole position in the rain with a speed of better than 138 miles per hour, and in the race he simply ran away from everyone else. It was an incredibly hot day and drivers were wilting and many gave their cars to relief drivers. One who was still running at the finish, Carl Scarborough, died later of heat exhaustion. But the lean, tough Vukovich pressed on relentlessly and led by four miles at the halfway point and eight miles at the finish. Even after his victory, he refused the pleasantries. He just went home. He was one of the least popular champions in racing history. But he worked hard at his profession. He ran a mile every morning and he squeezed a rubber ball in his hands all the time. He was called "the Indianapolis Iron Man."

In 1954, he had the same car and it was wearing out from the strain of racing. He had trouble qualifying it, but made the race far back in nineteenth starting position. Still, he remained cockily confident. He said, "I'll show these dummies my tailpipe." The day before the race he passed a group of drivers and asked them if they were figuring out who was going to finish second. On the day of the race he carried in his pocket a note from his son, Bill, Jr., that read, "Dear Daddy . . . Smoke those hot dogs off the track." He did just that. He had to run even faster than his qualifying time to do it, but one by one he cut down those in front of him. He led for the last 125 miles and won by 3 miles over runner-up Jimmy Bryan.

He returned in 1955 saying, "I want to be the first slob to win it three in a row." However, the strain of sustaining his pace as the iron man who dominated this hard place seemed to be wearing on him. He wanted to win, but he had never seemed to enjoy racing, and the brighter the spotlight on him, the more he seemed to loathe it. Most great drivers seem most at home in the cockpit of a racing car. Vukovich seemed strangely lonely there. Seeking an unprecedented third straight 500 triumph, he was more on edge than ever. The night before the race, he said to his wife, "Esther, this is crazy. Let's go home." But he did not. On race morning, he stood near another driver, looked at the fans, and said, "They think we're freaks. And you know something—they're right."

He drove with his usual cold fury. He had qualified fifth, and he swiftly raced to the front of the pack, cutting down Jack McGrath, who had set new time trial records of better than 140 miles per hour the year before and better than 142 miles per hour this year. After 125 miles, Vukovich was a half mile in front. As he moved onto the backstretch, he prepared to lap three tailenders in front of him. At that moment, Rodger Ward's car broke an axle, lurched out of control, and overturned. Al Keller swerved to avoid him and sideswiped Johnny Boyd's car, knocking it into the path of Vukovich's car. The left front wheel of Vukovich's car rode over the right wheel of Boyd's car, sending it rolling off. Vukovich's car went sailing over the wall, rolled over in the air, hit the ground nose first, bounced high in the air twice, spinning wildly, and crashed upside down and in flames. Bill Vukovich was already dead inside of a skull fracture.

Bob Sweikert went on to win the 500. Thirteen months later, Sweikert was killed in another race. After Vukovich's death the AAA quit sanctioning auto racing and USAC—the United States Auto Club—was formed to govern the circuit. Sweikert was the first national champion under USAC direction. Jimmy Bryan won the next two titles. Then Tony Bettenhausen won his second.

As in the past—with rivalries like those of Oldfield and De Palma, Murphy and Milton, Meyer and Shaw, Horn and Mays—two drivers, Jimmy Bryan and Tony Bettenhausen, came along at the same time to dominate a prolonged period of American auto racing through the 1950s. And, as it had been for Bill Vukovich, Indy was a hard place for them. Bettenhausen couldn't beat it even once, although he tried fourteen times.

Melvin Eugene "Tony" Bettenhausen was born and raised on a farm in Illinois. After his father died, the farm was sold to provide for the family. Years later, Tony bought the farm back so he could raise his own family where he had been raised. He loved quiet, hardworking farm life, but not quite as much as he loved noisy, glamorous auto racing. He kept talking about retiring to his farm and his family, but he drove race cars for twenty-three years, until he was forty-four years old, and he could never quit. He once said, "I think our Maker cuts everyone out for something different in life. It so happens some of us want to be automobile race drivers."

Bettenhausen won the national driving title in 1951 and again in 1958, and he came close several other years. He was a hard driver who drove every race as if he had a chance to win, even though his situation might be hopeless. He once won the United States crown in a season in which he consistently placed high, but did not win a single championship race. He won his other crown when he won nine championship races during the season, which was the record until A. J. Foyt bettered it years later. He survived so many accidents that he came to be considered indestructible. Bettenhausen was as tough as Bill Vukovich, but much friendlier. He was a genial, outgoing guy who enjoyed being with people and really enjoyed racing. He was one of the most enthusiastic spokesmen for auto racing the sport has ever had.

Bettenhausen spent sixty days in hospitals from twenty-eight accidents, some of them severe, but he insisted that racing was safer than generally believed. "I'm only too well aware that many drivers have been killed, many of them my friends, but driving cars is dangerous, period," he once observed. "I don't have any figures to support it, but I believe that mile for mile driven, more people are killed in passenger cars on public highways than race drivers in race cars on racetracks. A lot of years can go by without a single fatal accident in a given race, then let one driver get killed in one race and people start yakking about abolishing the sport. It's not fair."

When critics made light of the use of auto racing as a proving ground for passenger car equipment, he got upset. He would point to the many pieces of equipment in general use in ordinary cars that were first proved in racers. He noted that the Army Air Force had not found a tire to stand up to the stress of landing its new P-38s until it turned to the tires Firestone had developed at Indianapolis. He said it was not equipment or speed or racing that produced fatalities, but human error. As drivers and mechanics got smarter, and stronger racing organizations enforced tighter rules, his sport would soon be as safe as such hard-contact sports as football.

Bettenhausen once said, "I've been getting a worm's-eye view from behind the steering wheel of a go-fast bus for seventeen years. I've driven all kinds of racing cars as many as six nights a week, and I've never been afraid. I have absolutely no fear in a race car. It may seem terrifically dangerous to you, but it doesn't seem so to me. On the other hand," he said laughingly, "it makes me terribly nervous to climb a ten-foot ladder. I could never be a house painter."

Like most drivers, Bettenhausen was a fatalist. He would mention a friend's young cousin who had slipped on her kitchen floor, hit her head, and died. He would point out his own father, who had died when he was kicked in the head by a horse he was leading to the stable. "So why shouldn't I be a fatalist?" he'd ask. "My father worked hard all his life for very little and when he died, when I was nine, he left very little to his family. I had only eight years of schooling before I quit school, but racing has earned me a lot, and when I go, I'll leave something to my family. If I have to take some risks for that, it's all right. There'll always be guys like me who like to race. And there'll always be people who want to watch us."

He said he didn't worry as long as he could count his accidents. He never counted his twenty-ninth.

Bettenhausen never had much luck at Indy. He started racing there in the first race after World War II and drove nine 500s before he finished a race or placed among the leaders. His cars stalled or broke down, or he spun out or crashed. Finally, in 1955, the year Vukovich was killed and most of the other fast cars crashed or broke down, Bettenhausen finished second behind Bob Sweikert, but far behind. After that, it was the same old story again, though he finished fourth in 1958 and again in 1959. In all this time at Indy, he led only one race and for only twenty-four laps. No outstanding driver ever did less in this classic race. Still, Bettenhausen never gave up hope that he would someday conquer Indianapolis.

In 1961, the veteran got a hot car and outran everyone during practice at Indy for two weeks, coming very close to the then still elusive 150-miles-per-hour mark. He went around smiling and said, "I'm sure I'll get the record, the 150, and the checker. I'm sure this is my year." He was the most popular driver in racing at the time and everyone was happy for him, and even many of his rivals were rooting for him. He was always good to other drivers, and they loved him for it.

On the day before the opening of the time trials, he was relaxing in the pits when one of his old friends, Paul Russo, who had been having trouble with his car, asked Tony to test-drive it for him. This is an old practice, though a dangerous one. Sometimes one driver can feel something that is slowing a car down when another can't, but it is risky to jump into a strange car and take it right to its peak speed. Still, drivers don't mind risks and do it all the time. Tony went to his sponsor, Lindsey Hopkins, to ask permission. Hopkins didn't like the idea, but he didn't want to turn Tony down. "If you want to, go ahead, but be careful," he said.

Tony took Russo's car and turned several fast laps in it. He slowed down as he neared the pits and seemed about to go in, when he suddenly sped up and moved around the track again, possibly not yet having found anything wrong with the car and deciding to go one more lap. The car seemed to sway and then swerved into the main-stretch wall. It vaulted onto the three-foot-high concrete ledge and ripped down five iron posts and three hundred feet of steel wire as it flipped along the barrier until it came to a stop. Tony was dead. A ten-cent bolt holding the front support had fallen off, causing the car to sway. When Tony applied his brakes, the car had swerved into the wall. Eddie Sachs said, "I saw Tony heading for the wall. I watched until it was over. Then I sat down and cried like a baby."

A friend called Tony's wife.

"There's been an accident," he said.

"Tony?" she asked.

"Yes, Tony."

"All the way?" she asked.

"All the way," she was told.

The wives and families of race drivers lead a nervous existence. Yet even those who have lost men in the cruelest of sports often remain strikingly sympathetic to it. Bill Vukovich's widow married another race driver. Vukovich's son, Bill, Jr., a tough, hard person like his father, became a race driver, too, and with some success. Tony Bettenhausen's sons, Gary and Merle, also became successful race drivers. The sons of 500 winners Johnny Parsons, Troy Ruttman, and Rodger Ward became race drivers. Sadly, Ruttman's son was killed in 1969 when he was just beginning. Still, it is striking that, despite deaths, the families of men who love this sport often come to share their devotion to it.

During Tony Bettenhausen's life, his strongest rival was Jimmy Bryan, who won national honors in 1954, 1956, and 1957, becoming the fourth driver in history to win this coveted crown three times. And he did it in these years without winning the 500, which, because it is the longest race, has the most championship points at stake and often boosts its winner to the United States crown. However, fifteen American champions never won the 500. Bryan did win it once, in 1958, but it was his only victory in nine tries.

Bryan was a big, genial, fun-loving, cigar-smoking cowboy from Phoenix, Arizona. He packed 220 pounds on his six-foot frame and was as wide as a pro football lineman. He almost had to be shoehorned into cramped racing-car cockpits. He used to say that cars got so hot in action that it would burn the skin off a driver just to touch a metal part, but once he was wedged into a cockpit there was no way he could avoid touching metal.

Bryan was a strong, roughhouse driver who was at his best on dirt tracks, wrestling bulky racers over rutty courses. He won twice on the dirt tracks at both Langhorne and Du Quoin. At Sacramento and the Indianapolis Fairgrounds he won three times each. He was probably second only to Foyt as the greatest dirt track race driver who ever lived, which is no small honor.

While Tony Bettenhausen was winning twenty-one championship races in his career, Jimmy Byran was winning nineteen, but while Tony won on all kinds of tracks, Bryan won mostly on dirt tracks. Bryan was not a smooth driver with a delicate touch, so he was not at his best on paved tracks. However, he was hard to beat under any circumstances. In 1957 and 1958 many of the greatest drivers in the world were assembled at the paved, banked course in Monza, Italy, for 500-mile races. The first year Bryan won at more than 160 miles per hour, and the second year he finished second to Jim Rathmann at nearly 175 miles per hour. Bryan also battled Indy bitterly, and it took him awhile to conquer it even briefly.

In 1952, the first year he drove at Indy, Bryan went the distance and finished sixth. Two years later he dueled Vukovich for nearly half the race until his springs and shock absorbers broke down. Yet he continued to drive hard, though he was almost shaken apart, and finished second. In 1957, Bryan finished third. Finally, in 1958, he outlasted everyone else and won, after driving right through a seventeen-car wreck on the first turn of the first lap that demolished eight machines and took the life of one driver, Pat O'Connor. It was a cheerless triumph, though. In a subdued victory lane, Bryan could not speak right away. Finally he said, "It was awful. I never saw anything like it. I lived with it for two hundred laps."

He wanted to retire after that, but he could not stay away. When drivers have lost their carefree enthusiasm and want to retire, they should retire. The least safe thing in racing is to try to play it safe. Bryan returned to Indianapolis in 1959 with caution on his mind. He qualified late to take a place far back, and his car did not even start when the others did. When it finally did start, it broke down on the very first lap. Bryan returned in 1960, but he was not in contention for the lead and his car broke down again.

The following month, he drove on his beloved dirt at Langhorne. He was cut off in traffic and turned too sharply. His wheel was caught sideways in a rut and bucked the car into the air. The car nosed up high, then came down heavily, first the front end, then the rear end. In the cockpit, Bryan's harness came apart and he was flung back and forth like a rag doll. He met his death at the age of thirty-three. It was the sort of accident that is seldom fatal. Men have walked away from much worse. But the circumstances are different each time.

Bryan had beaten most tracks many times, but Indy only once, and it seemed to frustrate him and goad him on. Another driver who won many races on many tracks, but won at Indy only once, though he brought it to its knees several times, is Parnelli Jones. He goes on driving today, though no longer on the championship trail or at Indy. Like Bryan, Jones came out of the Southwest. He was born in Texarkana, Arkansas, though he was raised around Los Angeles.

Parnelli, whose brother, Paul, also became a race driver, was a tough kid who grew up in a tough area where there are a lot of racetracks. He says, "I don't exactly know why I became a race driver. It just sort of happened. As a kid, I used to flip buggies in the fields for kicks. I thought I was the bravest bastard in the whole world. I always figured I had more guts than anyone. I always figured race drivers had the most guts, so I started wanting to be one. It's dangerous, but without that it would be something anyone could do. I never wanted to do just what anyone could do."

After his parents were divorced Parnelli lived with his mother, who later remarried. He used to race her car secretly, or do stunts with it, and when he wrecked it, he lied about how it happened. He used to sneak into the nearby racetracks. Parnelli had difficulty staying out of fights and trouble. He quit school and went to work, first in automotive repair shops, then as a cement finisher. He raced for a little while, but he was always wrecking his cars. "I didn't have any respect for cars in the beginning," he recalls. "I figured the more dents you had in a car, the better it looked. I figured why shouldn't I win more races than anybody else—hell, nobody had any more guts than me." He decided to quit racing, but he did not like the laboring work he was doing. "I want to tell you, there's better ways to go," he says. So he went back to racing.

At first, most owners were afraid to risk their cars with him, but he soon found out he couldn't win if his car didn't finish in one piece. So he asked questions, worked at his profession, and swiftly improved. He had a great talent for driving a race car. He was tough and determined and soon he was moving up through the classes rapidly. He went from jalopies to midgets and sprinters and stock cars. Soon he was in championship cars. He won two national sprint car titles in a row and later a national stock car title. He won a lot of stock car races, too, including the rugged Riverside 500. He also won the first sports car race he ever drove, the Riverside Grand Prix, against a powerful field of international stars, even though he lost clutching power early in the event. In his career, he has won only six races on the championship trail, including Indy, but his cars were often not as well prepared as others.

There are those in racing who say the skilled, versatile Jones could always get more out of a given car than any other driver and that he really has been the most brilliant race driver of all time, but his record does not bear this out. He is one of those who might have become the greatest had they been more fortunate. There does seem to be such a thing as luck in racing, and racing luck has often run against him, especially at Indy. There was never a driver who drove that merciless Indianapolis oval better, but there have been many who wound up farther ahead.

Indy is a complicated challenge, especially for newcomers. In 1961 Parnelli was one of the brightest rookies ever to make a debut there. He qualified as the fifth fastest, then startled everyone by hurtling into an early lead and holding it for a long time. He seemed on his way to victory until a piece of metal was sucked off the track to strike and cut him severely over his right eye. Then his car lost a cylinder and began to slow down. But even though his goggles kept filling up with blood that had to be emptied out periodically and he was nursing a sick car, he kept going. He gave ground grudgingly and was still running at the finish, though far behind by then.

In his second year at Indy, he became the first driver to break through the 150-miles-per-hour barrier, and took the pole with his new speed records. During the race he took the lead and was running away from the other cars when his brakes gave out. Even then, he did not quit. A driver who can win a sports car race on a road course without clutching power can keep driving a championship car at Indy at more than 145 miles per hour without brakes. He did, but it put him back in eighth place.

The next year, Parnelli became the fourth driver to win the pole position two years in a row at Indianapolis, with new speed records of more. than 151 miles per hour. This time he did run away from everyone else to win the race, even though his oil tank split, dumping oil on the track, and some thought he should have been disqualified.

Parnelli was hurt by the arguments that followed his controversial victory and even punched fellow driver Eddie Sachs in a brief rhubarb. He remembers most vividly waking up the night after he had won the great race and being unable to believe he had really done it. He tells about getting up and looking at himself in the mirror and looking at the newspaper headlines that heralded his triumph: "I turned out the light and I lay back down on the bed and I lay there most of the rest of the night without even wanting to fall back asleep, thinking how far I'd come and how hard it had been and how unbelievable it all was, but now here I was, the champion of Indy. And so nothing else really mattered right then, and no matter what might matter later on, they couldn't take this away from me now. No matter what."

He returned to Indy in 1964 to qualify fourth fastest and drove through the second-lap crash that killed Sachs and Dave MacDonald. He led the race until his car exploded in the pits and he dove out of it severely burned. The next year, he almost crashed in practice when a wheel flew off his new rear-engine car. Even with a broken bone in his neck he managed to qualify as fifth fastest. During the race his engine went sour early, and it was the first 500 that he did not lead. Yet he nursed his sick car home in second place, which some consider the greatest feat of his career.

He built his own car for 1966 and qualified as fourth fastest, but his car broke down early. Then, in 1967, he made history of a sort. He was tempted by Andy Granatelli to try a new turbine-powered racer and fell in love with it. Parnelli parted on friendly terms with his longtime sponsor and continuing partner, J. C. Agajanian, and took the revolutionary STP Special to Indy. It was an entirely new kind of car that made unique demands of the driver, but Parnelli was able to alter his style and adjust to his new machine. He qualified it only sixth fastest, but smoothly pulled away from the piston-engine cars in the race until he led by two miles with only eight miles to go. Then a ball bearing gave way in the car's gearbox—the great machine coughed and sputtered and died.

It was a cruelly dramatic moment as Parnelli coasted to a stop and A. J. Foyt came on to sweep past him to his third victory. Jones got out of the cockpit, took off his helmet, and, without saying a word to anyone, sat down at the base of the pit wall. Andy Granatelli and his brothers, the car's "parents," who had been trying without success to beat Indy for twenty years, slumped beside him, gazing sightlessly at the pavement. Finally they got up and began to walk back to their garage. There was a wreck on the track and everyone turned to it excitedly. Everyone except the STP crew, who continued on without breaking stride, without expression.

After that, USAC officials reduced permissible power in turbine engines and Parnelli refused to return, though he began to sponsor his own cars with other drivers at Indy. Granatelli returned in 1968 with new turbine cars, and one driven by Joe Leonard led by a half mile with twenty miles to go when it, too, failed. Bobby Unser drove past Leonard to win the classic and go on his way to the national title. The next year, USAC hit the turbines with new restrictions and Granatelli bitterly turned away from them to more conventional cars, finally winning the big one with Mario Andretti as his driver.

In 1970, Jones presided over the building of the car that he and Vel Miletich sponsored in the 500. Al Unser drove it to the pole position in qualifying and to victory in the race, and dominated the season.

Jones had by now become a wealthy businessman through racing. He had married late in life and had a new baby. Yet at the end of the 1960s, though he had dropped out of the championship trail as a driver, he continued to race various events and refused to retire. He explained, "I'm a race driver. I've been one a long time. When a man's a carpenter or something, he doesn't just stop doing it when he gets to be thirty-five. I always knew I could die doing this thing. I've lived with it a long time. I think living close to death makes us like living more.

"The thing is, most people work hard every day of their lives and yet they never have anything. Maybe they don't risk anything, but they never have anything to risk. Racing has brought me everything I could want out of life. And I really enjoy racing. I used to think nothing could scare me. I know better now. And I've had some disappointments. But I've had some big moments, too. And when I do give it up, I know I'll miss it. It's been one helluva ride."

Probably no one ever enjoyed racing or loved Indianapolis more than Eddie Sachs. He was born in Pennsylvania. His parents were divorced when he was five and he went with his father, who remarried, to live in North Carolina. His father was a traveling salesman. Long before Eddie was old enough to get a driver's license, his father let him sit on his lap to steer the family car, and later took him on trips and let him drive through part of the night. After a stint in the navy, Eddie went back to Pennsylvania and saw his first auto race and was fascinated by it. He talked a car owner into giving him his first chance in a jalopy and crashed it in his first race.

He took lessons at a small school for race drivers, but he was not very good at it. He was considered a "leadfoot," a "fencebuster" who ruined his cars, and he had trouble getting rides. What little money he made, he spent foolishly. He was a happy-go-lucky guy and rarely had a dime in his pockets. Once his car was repossessed. He even opened a bar, but it was unsuccessful.

Sachs did not become serious about racing until he saw his first 500. After that, he wanted to become a champion. In 1952 he tried to get into the track in hopes of finding a ride, but he had no credentials and was thrown out by guards. Embarrassed and defiant, he shouted at them, "I'll be back. Remember the name—Eddie Sachs."

He was back the next year, but when he took his driver's test for the first time he failed it and was told to go away and get more experience. He stayed all month anyhow, working as a lackey in the pits by day and as a dishwasher in a nearby restaurant by night, just so he could stay close to the race. The next year, he flunked his test again. He finally passed in 1956, but qualified only thirty-fourth, missing the starting field by one position. Afterward he stood on the back of his car and watched the race with a wistful expression on his face.

Sachs did not have the natural ability of some drivers, but he became outstanding by working at racing determinedly. Other drivers used to say, "He learned to race before he learned to drive."

Sachs himself said, "I was ab-so-lutely the worst race driver ever to come to Indianapolis." But he insisted that he would win the 500 someday.

He did win other races on the championship trail, six in all. He finally made
the 500 in 1957 by qualifying brilliantly, second fastest, and drove well
until his engine quit. In 1958, he led for a lap and was in contention until
his engine gave out again. In 1959, he almost finished for the first time, but
broke down with only forty-five miles to go. Stubbornly optimistic, he said,
"If you can lead the 500, you can win it. All you have to do is finish."

Sachs was a colorful and controversial character who enjoyed life in
general and racing in particular. He once brought a jazz band to play for
the fans at Langhorne. He stood up in his car before the race, grinning
broadly, and led the musicians in a rousing Dixieland number. He once
paraded behind the marching band at Indy, strutting and smiling while
flipping an imaginary baton. He talked a lot and sometimes he got in trouble. One example is the time he was punched by Parnelli Jones, but even
Parnelli said later he knew that Sachs had meant no harm.

No one ever interviewed Eddie Sachs—he interviewed them. When a
microphone was handed to Eddie, it might never be returned. After winning
one race, he took an interviewer's microphone and talked until it was getting dark and the fans had left. He was less than modest, but more than fair.
If a writer criticized him, Eddie shrugged it off, ordered extra copies of the
newspaper, thanked the writer for the publicity, and sent him an auto-
graphed photo.

Someone once said, "If you stood on his scrapbooks, you could touch
the stars." That's what Sachs was trying to do—touch the stars. He was
called "the Clown Prince of Racing," but he was very serious about winning
at Indy. He said, "I think of Indianapolis every day of the year, every hour
of the day, and when I sleep, too. Everything I ever wanted in my life, I
found inside the walls of the Indianapolis Motor Speedway. I love it all,
from the first to the last day in May. On the morning of the race, if you told
me my house had burned down, I'd say, 'So what?' The moment that race
starts is always the greatest moment of my life, and the day I win that race,
it will be as if my life has ended. There is nothing more I could want out of
life."

Sachs used to cry in his cockpit when the music played just before the
start of each 500. Although he crashed and was severely injured or burned
in races, he went on because he wanted to win the 500.

In 1960, he won the pole position with record speeds of more than
146 miles per hour. When Jim Hurtubise took the records away from him
later in the trials, Eddie grabbed the microphone and congratulated him
grandly. In the race, Eddie led, but was sidelined at 330 miles. The next

year he became the third driver ever to win the pole twice in a row, and then almost won the race. When Foyt ran out of fuel with less than forty miles to go, Sachs sped into a large lead. Sachs was smiling and waving to the crowd with fifteen miles to go when a tire began to wear out. He had to decide whether to try for the victory and risk a blowout that might send him crashing or go into the pits and settle for second place. With eight miles to go, he went into the pits to replace the tire and finished eight seconds behind Foyt.

He must have been crushed with disappointment, for even his wife asked him why he hadn't gone on. He smiled wistfully and said he would get it yet. He and his wife had a son. Eddie said, "I used to want it for myself. Now I want it for my family. Someday, my son will stand in a school playground somewhere and he'll be able to say to the other kids, 'My daddy won the 500.' "

The next year, Eddie crashed in practice, returned to qualify late, started far back in twenty-seventh spot, drove the fastest race of all, but still finished only third. In 1963, he threw a wheel and crashed, but walked away from the accident. Going back to the pits, he was smiling and waving and rolling the wheel ahead of him like a child with a hoop.

In 1964, he crashed twice in practice and qualified late again, back in seventeenth place, directly behind a rookie, Dave MacDonald. On the second lap, MacDonald lost control of his car while coming off the turn into the main stretch, scraped the wall, split a side tank, and slid back across the track as his car exploded into a smoking, flaming inferno that obscured the entire area. Coming up right behind him, almost certainly unable to see him, Sachs slammed his car into MacDonald's car and was engulfed in a ball of fire. Both drivers are believed to have been rendered unconscious almost immediately. Other drivers steered blindly through the inferno, and some crashed or got burned. It was some time before the fires could be put out. When others got to them, Sachs was already dead and MacDonald was dying.

Eddie Sachs's son will never be able to say his father won Indy. But he is not the only one.

13

THE ONES WHO WIN

In 1959, three hungry veterans fought one another for 500 grueling miles at Indianapolis. Rodger Ward, a short, stocky, curly-haired, thirty-eight-year-old veteran of a dozen years of racing, had failed dismally in eight previous classics. Jim Rathmann, a slender, balding thirty-year-old veteran of another dozen years on racetracks, had once placed fifth and twice second, but never first in nine tries at Indy. Johnny Thomson, a small, tousle-haired fellow of thirty-seven, had been driving twenty years with success, but six years at Indy without success. All had done well elsewhere. None had done well enough here. All had good cars this year, however. Thomson had put his shocking-pink bullet on the pole with record qualifying speeds in excess of 145 miles per hour. Rathmann had landed his blue and orange speedster on the outside of the front row. Ward had settled into the second row with his white, red, and blue machine.

From the start, this was a three-car contest. At the green flag, Thomson thrust his gaudy speedster into the first corner in front, with Ward right behind him. At the fifteen-mile mark, Ward passed Thomson, Rathmann drove into third place, and the three began to pull away from the rest of the field. At fifty miles, Rathmann passed Thomson and Ward, and surged to the front. Lap after lap, the three battled for the lead, while the huge crowd cheered them on and the other drivers struggled desperately to remain within range. Eddie Sachs spun his car into the grass, but maintained control and continued on. Red Amick, Mike Magill, Jud Larson, and Chuck Weyant locked in a four-car crack-up that put them all out of the race. Jack Turner's car burst into flames and he fled from it. Cars were dropping out steadily while Rathmann, Ward, and Thomson poured it on.

At 100 miles, a former Indy champion, Pat Flaherty, surged into the fight for the front. As the cars of many of the stragglers broke down and fell out, the leaders moved in and out of the pits for fuel and fresh tires. Some were in and out in less than half a minute. Their crews waited for them anxiously, worked on them feverishly, and pushed them on their way eagerly. At 150 miles, even with periods at slower speeds under yellow flags because of accidents, Thomson had taken the lead and was averaging better than 135 miles per hour. Ward passed him. Then Thomson passed Ward. Then Rathmann passed Ward. The lead was traded back and forth spectacularly. At the halfway point, Ward had moved back in front with Thomson second and Rathmann third, and Flaherty was falling farther and farther back.

Round and round the cars went, engines whining, tires screaming, metal bodies straining, the drivers hot and sweaty and covered with grime and tiring under the pressure. The fans got dizzy and some sought relief, but most held fast, eyes scanning the track for the three leaders who would not release their grips on one another. Usually, by this time one or possibly two would have pulled away from the others, but in this race three cars remained together, strung like gaudy ornaments on a short rope. At 150 laps, with just 50 laps of the two-and-one-half-mile course left, Ward began to push his car harder, opening up the first real margin of the race. But his rivals refused to crumble and remained within reach. The car of Jim Rathmann's brother, Dick, caught fire in the pits. Then Flaherty crashed. Sachs spun out for good. At 400 miles, Ward was first, Thomson second, and Rathmann third, and the three pacemakers were turned toward home.

The final grueling miles slipped away. Rathmann cut down Thomson and took off after Ward in a final, desperate bid for the front. Sixteen cars sat in the pits broken down, broken up, or burned. Fourteen cars remained running with no hope of winning. As the afternoon wore on, clouds moved overhead, cool breezes blew across the sagging and sunburned fans, and the leaders hurtled on toward their destinies. In the final laps, Rathmann crept closer and closer, but Ward hung on determinedly. At 2:46 in the afternoon, Ward slammed across the finish line first for the first time as the checkered flag fluttered at him. Then Rathmann rolled across, second for a third time. Then Thomson.

As Ward coasted into victory lane, a wide smile splitting his wide, dirty face, his wife rushed at him and his dog leaped out of her arms at him and kissed him before a beauty queen could get to him. Ward was surrounded by his crew, by officials, by writers and photographers wishing him well. A huge trophy was thrust at him and a check for more than $100,000 was prepared for him.

A year later, the three men resumed their rivalry with increased intensity. It was cloudy and cool at Indy, but competition on the track was heated from the start. From the pole, Sachs sped through the first lap in front, closely followed by Ward and Rathmann. Thomson, who had started far back this year, had to work his way up through the field. At twenty-five miles, Ward had whipped into first place at faster than 140 miles per hour, with Sachs, Rathmann, and former winner Troy Ruttman on his tail. Then Ruttman, running nearly 145 miles per hour, barreled past Ward. Next, Rathmann got past Ward. But Rodger ran right back at them. At one hundred miles, Ward had spurted back into lead. Most of the cars were already far back and the weak ones began to give way. Sachs's steering failed and he turned out of the battle into the pits just about the time Thomson was joining the leaders. At the halfway point, it was Rathmann, Ward, and Thomson in a near carbon copy of the previous year's classic.

Eddie Russo had crashed. Then Wayne Weiler crashed. Others broke down. The three leaders again were far ahead of the field. As the race progressed, the wind began to whip up heavily, blowing the cars dangerously around the track. Thomson fell back, and Ward and Rathmann went at it. For 200 miles, Ward and Rathmann battled at 145 miles per hour, wheel to wheel, first one leading, then the other, as the crowd stood and roared. At 300 miles, Ward led. At 400 miles, Rathmann led. Seldom had two cars been as close to one another as these two so late in the classic. At 450 miles, Ward led. They were headed for home now, nerves frayed by the tension of their dramatic and deadly high-speed duel.

With twenty-five miles to go, Rathmann led by the length of a front wheel as the two cars burst down the main stretch. With fifteen miles to go, Ward ducked underneath Rathmann on a turn and passed him on the low side. With eight miles to go, Rathmann cut below Ward and took the lead back. Everyone in the sprawling arena was standing and screaming at the drivers. Both had badly worn tires, but neither could afford to stop. Rathmann would not stop. He had never won this great race, while Ward had won the year before. It was as though somehow Rathmann wanted it more than Ward. Inch by inch, Rathmann opened up on Ward. Suddenly it was all over. Rathmann came roaring around the final turn and sped down the homestretch and took the checkered flag, and then Ward came across.

After having come close so many times before, Rathmann finally found his way to victory lane, where the bedlam seemed to burst over him. And the winner's check, $110,000, went to him. And Ward settled for second this time—to win again another time.

In September, on the dirt track at the Allentown, Pennsylvania, Fairgrounds, Johnny Thomson crashed to his death. Born in Lowell, Massachusetts, settled in Boyertown, Pennsylvania, he had driven more than twenty years and was thirty-eight years old when he died. He died on the dirt, which he loved. He was one of the greatest American dirt track drivers and an outstanding paved track driver, though he was continually frustrated at Indianapolis. However, race drivers do not all crash and die. Thomson did, as so many had before him. But most retire, safe from the wars, to contemplate the triumphs and defeats of their exciting careers. As had Oldfield and De Palma and Cooper and Meyer and Shaw and Rose before them, Rathmann retired in 1964 to manufacture "go-karts" in Florida, and Ward retired in 1966 to move into business and accept an executive position with the new Ontario, California, track.

Rathmann, born in 1928, now lives in Miami. He was a shy, quiet fellow, but addicted to racing. His brother, Dick, was also a fine driver and once won the pole position at Indy, an honor that eluded Jim. The two brothers fought their way to the Speedway over the small, tough tracks of southern California. Once Rathmann attained gold and glory at Indy, he grew conservative about racing, seldom competed elsewhere, and did not seek national laurels. However, he amassed one of the greatest records in Indianapolis history. He drove in fourteen 500s, led six times, and ranks third on the all-time list with 5,737 miles endured. He won once, was second three times and fifth once, and earned a total of $174,000 at Indy.

Ward did even better. After he finished first in 1959 and second in 1960, he was third in 1961, first again in 1962, fourth in 1963, and second again in 1964—a six-year record of consistency that has seldom been surpassed at the Speedway. He drove in fifteen 500s and led only four, but won two and was second twice, third once and fourth once, and earned $274,000. Parnelli Jones, another Speedway star of the sixties, drove seven 500s and led six of them for 492 laps. Only Shaw and Rose, who led seven races each, led more races. Only De Palma, who led 613 laps, and Shaw, who led 508 laps, led for more laps at Indy. But Jones won only once and placed second only once. However, he did earn $189,000 at Indy. By the end of the 1960s, A. J. Foyt had led six races for 322 laps, won three, placed third once, and earned an unsurpassed $405,000 at the "goldyards."

By the 1960s American auto racing had entered an age of affluence.

Throughout its history, the sport has been supported largely by automotive concerns, but never so splendidly as in the 1960s, when the shape of the sport altered severely.

First, the shape of the cars changed. George Salih and then A. J. Watson lightened and streamlined the heavy front-engine cars that had dominated Indianapolis and the championship trail into the 1950s. Salih built a small car for $20,000 and won Indy with it on consecutive years with Sam Hanks and Jimmy Bryan as drivers. By then, A. J. Watson had developed clean, neat roadsters about fifteen feet long, three feet wide, and three feet high, weighing about sixteen hundred pounds, powered by Offenhauser engines, and worth about $35,000 each. He built cars under contract for a man named Bob Wilke. He also built and sold cars for other sponsors and usually wound up competing with himself. Some years Watson built or plotted half the cars that made the starting field at Indy, and some years he built the cars that won the pole, won the race, and finished second in the race.

As mentioned earlier, Dan Gurney brought Colin Chapman from England to the Speedway in the 1960s, and Chapman later returned with Grand Prix-styled cars—lighter and lower than the front-engine heavyweights, twelve and one-half feet long, two and one-half feet high, two and one-half feet wide, weighing about fourteen hundred pounds, and powered by Ford engines from the rear. Scotland's Jim Clark came close to winning before he finally did win in 1965, and after that foreign entries dominated the Speedway until Dan Gurney deserted the Grand Prix circuit to build his Grand Prix-styled Eagles for the American championship trail. By the end of the 1960s, all cars starting in the Indianapolis 500 were rear-engine lightweights, low and frail and nimble.

Chapman brought Ford with him, and that company had millions to pour into racing to publicize itself, forcing radical modernization of the Offenhauser engine before it could keep up. Goodyear came in to challenge Firestone for supremacy among tire manufacturers on the Speedway battleground. It is estimated that Ford spent $5 million one year and Goodyear $2 million to gain racing prestige. Other automotive product manufacturers joined in the battle. Granatelli brought a turbine to Indy and, win or lose, spent a fortune promoting STP, a fluid additive. One year he spent $6 million. It paid off. In 1963 STP sales amounted to $8 million. In 1968, STP sales were $45 million.

The drivers benefited, too. The best ones were paid handsomely to drive, use, or promote products. Young Chuck Barnes formed Sports Headliners, Inc., to manage such race drivers as Ward, Jones, Foyt, and Mario Andretti. By the end of the 1960s Barnes's active champs were being guaranteed $250,000 a year before they even turned a wheel.

Over the years, purses have risen in all USAC divisions. Specialists who have dominated various USAC divisions include Parnelli Jones, Roger McCluskey, and Don Branson in sprint car racing, Shorty Templeman, Jimmy Davies, Bob Wente, Mike McGreevey, and Mel Kenyon in midget car racing, and Fred Lorenzen, Paul Goldsmith, Norm Nelson, and Don White in stock car racing. Even those who did not venture onto the championship trail were able to make good livings. However, it was the championship car drivers who benefited most from the bonanza.

No driver keeps all he earns in races. He wins for his team. Usually, he gets 40 percent; the car owner, who bears the burden of all expenses, 60 percent. In some cases, it is fifty-fifty. Product sponsors sweeten the pot. The top drivers also get base salaries. Parnelli Jones reportedly received $100,000 just to drive Granatelli's STP turbine, win or lose. Had he won, he also would have shared in the jackpot. Ward was probably the first of the great American race drivers of the 1960s to cash in on the bonanza.

Ward was born in 1921 in Beloit, Kansas. He later moved to southern California, where he began to drive race cars, and finally to Indianapolis. He was attracted to dangerous, exciting pursuits as a boy. All he can remember of his childhood is wanting to grow up to be an airplane pilot or a race car driver. He learned to fly fighter planes during World War II, thought he did not see any action. After the war, he began to race cars. He was good at driving right from the start, but he seemed uninspired. For many years, he was just another driver. A good-looking fellow, he was a carefree soul who loved the ladies, liked to party, and swiftly spent most of the money he made.

Ward came into his own only when he teamed with A. J. Watson under the sponsorship of Bob Wilke. For years, the three W's dominated racing. A conservative driver, but smooth and shrewd, Ward took Watson's incomparable cars, got the most out of them, and consistently placed high. He won the 1959 and 1962 500s and national titles, and would have won two or three other national titles had A. J. Foyt not come along to outdo him. In his career, Ward won twenty-six national championship races, which was unsurpassed until first Foyt and then Andretti passed him.

Along the way, he survived many crashes. In the 1955 Indianapolis classic, his wreck touched off the accident that proved fatal to Bill Vukovich. In 1963, while Ward was driving a Chevrolet-powered Chaparral in a sports car race at Riverside, his front end came apart at more than 100 miles per hour in heavy traffic, and he gunned the car off the track and crashed into a ditch. He wound up in the hospital with fractures of his lower spine.

Shortly after he recovered, he spoke of why he was resuming his racing career. "I was pinned beneath my car, not seriously hurt, but helpless, when Vukie crashed to his death," he said. "I've seen many of my friends killed driving. I came very close to being killed many times, including this last time at Riverside. You have to believe death can't happen to you, however. This comes from having confidence in yourself. All good drivers have great egos. They have to believe they can do this difficult and dangerous thing better and safer than anyone else or they'd never go near a racing car. We all get afraid sometimes. I do. Not before a race. Not during a race. Not even during an accident. But when an accident is over, when you think about it. You wonder how you survived. But it passes. It's something you learn to live with."

A wistful smile spread over Ward's round face and he looked down at his strong hands. "No one ever made anyone drive," he said. "We've all gone into this thing of our own free wills. Of course it's depressing when a friend dies. I was close to Bettenhausen. I thought of quitting when he died. But Tony wouldn't have wanted me to quit, I don't think. I wouldn't have wanted him to quit if I had died. Most of us love every moment we have in racing. I wouldn't trade the thrills and satisfaction I've had in my racing career for any longer, safer life that I might have led.

"We're set apart from other people, racing drivers, so we're more sympathetic to one another than most men in most professions. We'll do anything to win on a racetrack, but we're very close off the track. It's a very exclusive fraternity. It's a very special thing being a race driver. I'll be one until I'm no longer a winner."

Ward still felt like a winner then. He was no longer young, but still sure of himself. He said, "In racing, just as in any sport, it's the fellow who makes the fewest mistakes who usually wins. In racing, you usually can't afford too many mistakes and still survive. I made a lot of mistakes while I was learning to race, as many as anyone ever made, until I realized that if you can't finish, you can't win. I used to think speed alone won races, that it was important to lead every lap you could. I used to think that if a driver rode you rough, you had to get back at him. I know better now. I know fate will take care of the wild driver. And I know that the only lead that counts is the one at the end of the last lap. I let the hot dogs burn themselves out. I run my car only as hard as I have to run it to win. No one ever wins the 500. Thirty-two drivers lose it. Give me a hundred dollars for every driver who ever broke down in front of me and I could retire comfortably."

By then, Ward had become the most outstanding spokesman for auto racing since Bettenhausen. He drove only major races and toured the country speaking fondly of his sport. "I don't recommend auto racing to everyone," he said, "but it has brought me success, money, prestige, and thrills enough to last several lifetimes. A person couldn't go through his life and have enjoyed it more than I've enjoyed mine. Why, everyone in the world ought to envy Rodger Ward."

Still something of a playboy, Ward had just suffered a broken marriage, but had soon been remarried, to a beautiful young beauty queen. He was asked, frankly, if one of the reasons he was going on was that his pretty new wife had not enjoyed his earlier successes and he wanted to show her there was plenty of fight left in the old dog. Rodger grinned broadly and said, "You've seen my wife. What do you think?"

He did not win the 500 that year. Nor did he ever win it again, though he came close. He was on the way out, though he did not know it then. The new cars were coming in and the old establishment was giving way. Mechanics like George Bignotti and Clint Brawner and A. J. Watson were having to build and prepare new kinds of cars, and drivers like Foyt and Jones and Ward were having to learn how to drive them, and it did not come quickly or easily to them, if it came at all.

In 1965, Ward took a new rear-engine lightweight built by Watson onto the Speedway and he could not get it up to competitive speed. Each driver is allowed three chances to qualify each car, and Ward took two of his chances on the opening day of qualifications and was waved off as too slow both times. In Ward's first 500, when he was twenty-nine, it took only a little more than 130 miles per hour to make the race. Now he was forty-three and the cars were going 25 to 30 miles per hour faster.

As qualifying and practice continued, and Watson and Ward worked desperately, others looked with sympathy at these falling heroes who had dominated this hard place for so long. During the week, someone asked Ward what was wrong. "Everyone's asking me what's wrong. If I knew, I'd do something about it, wouldn't I?" the usually pleasant veteran snapped harshly. Then he felt bad. Guiltily, he smiled and put his arm around the person who had asked the question and sighed, "I wish I knew."

On the third of the four qualifying days, while warming up before attempting his final trial, Ward brushed an outside wall, spun, slid five

hundred feet and smacked the inside wall, flattening the car's nose and ripping off a wheel, then slid two hundred feet back into the infield. He was
not hurt and he walked slowly back to his garage. Watson patted him on
the back. "Ward, you're fired," he said jokingly, with a thin smile. Then
Ward went to see if the car could be repaired in time to try with it again
the next day. He and his crew worked on it all night.

With one hour to go on the final day of qualifying, Ward sat in the repaired car waiting to go on the track and talking about the baby daughter
who had just been born to him and his young wife. One of his two almost-
adult sons stood by his side. When it was Rodger's time, the son shook his
hand and he pulled out. He needed something close to 154 to make the
race. He got a high 153. He missed by a tenth of a second.

Now, after fourteen consecutive years in the race and two victories, he
was out. He parked in the pits and sat there with his head down for a long
time as photographers popped flashbulbs at him. Then he got out of his car
and sat on a pit wall, slumped over, his elbows on his knees, his hands rubbing together, staring at the ground through his sunglasses.

One photographer asked him to get back in his car for more pictures.
Shrugging, Ward did so. Then, when he began to get out again, a photographer asked him to hold it for "just one more." Ward said, "Aw, come
on, what the hell," and got out. Watson and others tried to console him.
Ward said, "Maybe I shouldn't be in this thing anymore." He shrugged
his shoulders, turned, and walked away. Watson stood quietly watching
him go.

The next year, Ward returned with a new Watson car. He was first
out in time trials and he averaged 159 miles per hour, which he knew would
not be good enough to win the pole but would probably be enough to get
him in the race. "I'll settle for it," he said. "I'm just glad to be back in it."

Some feel that that's all he wanted to do, make the race one more time
and not retire from the outside.

In the race, he drove 185 miles well back, then pulled into the pits,
parked, and shut his engine off. His crew seemed stunned. "What's wrong?"
Watson asked. "Everything's wrong," Ward said. He got out of the car,
took off his helmet, put it in the cockpit, and walked away, head lowered.
No one said anything to him, but some patted him on the back as he passed.

At the victory banquet, Rodger Ward stepped forward, took the microphone, and said, "Years ago, I told myself if it ever stopped being fun, I'd
quit." He paused as the gathering hushed. He began to cry and as he resumed his voice choked in his throat. "Yesterday, it wasn't fun anymore,"

he said. He paused again. With great effort, he added simply, "Thank you." Then he waved and stumbled back to his chair, where he sat and wept unashamedly. The crowd stood and gave him an ovation. Some wept with him.

Ward had several businesses going for him when he retired, but within a few years most of them were doing poorly. Not as careful with his money as a Foyt or a Jones, subjected to costly broken marriages, Ward had begun to get hungry again when the new Ontario Speedway offered him a position as its traveling spokesman. Handsome and articulate, he became a splendid one. Although he was nearing fifty, he sometimes spoke wistfully of resuming his racing career. "When I see the mistakes some of these young drivers make and the sort of money they make, well, I'm tempted," he said.

Reluctantly, Ward had walked away from racing. Jones had walked partway away from it. Foyt was still in it, still fast enough to win the pole position at Indy in 1969 with an average speed of more than 170 miles per hour. But he broke down in that race and he did not win many races that year. As the 1960s faded into history, Mario Andretti had become the dominant figure in American auto racing, the latest in the line of the greatest.

Like the great Ralph De Palma, who drove more than a half century before him, Mario Andretti was born in Italy, moved to the United States, and became a citizen. Since he has done most of his racing here, he is considered an American driver. Certainly he has proved himself a great one, though he seemed to be reaching his peak at the end of the 1960s.

Mario was born near Trieste in northern Italy in 1940 as one of twins. Their father was a farm administrator, an important person in his province, but World War II took everything from him. He moved his family to Florence, where he found work in a toy factory. Growing up, Mario and Aldo worshiped racing drivers and frequented garages where racing cars were prepared.

At thirteen, without telling their parents, who would have disapproved, Mario and Aldo joined a sort of Little League auto-racing program for youngsters. When Aldo got injured in a race, they told their parents he'd fallen off a truck. When he got burned, they said a box of matches had exploded in his hands. When Mario broke a kneecap, they said he'd fallen off the church steps. They confided in their uncle, and he had to keep their secret because he was a priest.

So many boys got hurt or killed that the program was discontinued.

Still, Mario and Aldo dreamed of becoming Grand Prix drivers when they were old enough. Then the family moved to the United States in 1958. They went to live near relatives in Nazareth, Pennsylvania, where the senior Andretti found work in a textile mill. Mario and Aldo were discouraged until they found racing all around them, a different form of racing, but still racing.

As soon as they could, both boys began racing in jalopies on the bush-league tracks of their area. They did not tell their parents, who could not read English and so did not read United States newspapers. Their secret came out when Aldo was almost killed in a race. He hooked a fence, went end over end, and was rushed to a hospital unconscious. Mario slept in the hospital corridor overnight and called in his parents only when authorities insisted. The distraught parents rushed to their son's bedside. Mr. Andretti was furious. "Did I raise my sons to have them brought home in a basket?" he yelled at Mario.

When Aldo revived, he said to Mario, "I'm glad it was you, not me, who had to tell them." While Aldo was being nursed back to health, Mario resumed driving on his own. When his father refused permission and even refused to talk to him, Mario moved out of the house. Aldo was unable to drive for a long time, though. After he did resume, he did poorly. He'd retire, then try again. When Mario tried to talk him out of driving, Aldo got furious and suggested that Mario wanted all the glory for himself. But Aldo continued to get nowhere. Both he and Mario had married and had begun to raise families, and racing was hard for them.

Mario was wild and erratic at first, but Clint Brawner, a racing mechanic, thought he had a chance and offered him the car he had prepared for owner Al Dean. Mario talked it over with his wife and they decided to give racing a full-time gamble. Prepared by Brawner, Dean's cars had done well on the championship circuit with A. J. Foyt, Jimmy Bryan, Eddie Sachs, and others driving them, but they had never won Indianapolis. Drivers like Foyt and Bryan had won Indy, but only after they had left Dean and Brawner for others. The closest Dean and Brawner ever came was in 1961, when Sachs dropped out of the lead late and settled for second. They were like many great owners and mechanics who were frustrated by the 500.

Mario is a tiny person, only five-feet-five and 135 pounds, extremely neat, clean and meticulous, very good-looking, and very serious about racing. He says, "No one taught me how to drive. I've been driving all of my life. When I got to the big time, I asked guys things, but no one would help me much. So I watched guys like Parnelli drive. And I drove. I learned by doing."

More daring than smooth, Andretti is a charger who moves his cars around on the track and takes chances to win. And he is a winner. Before long, his parents were proud of him and his father was bragging about him.

Mario is the first great driver of the modern generation of racing drivers. Although he learned by driving jalopies, midgets, and sprinters on dirt tracks, he came into the big time in the recent era of sports car and foreign-racing influence. The Grand Prix-styled rear-engine lightweights now dominate Indy and most of the championship trail, and road races have replaced most of the dirt races on that title tour. He is versatile and more at home in the new cars and on the new courses than the older Foyt. And, like Foyt, he has won many kinds of races, though not yet as many. For example, Mario has won the Daytona 500, most prestigious of the stock car classics, and the 12 Hours of Sebring sports car endurance test. He returns to Europe occasionally to seek a Grand Prix triumph.

Mario moved onto the championship trail in 1964 and had one high finish, a third in the Milwaukee 200. The next year, he broke in brilliantly at Indy by qualifying fourth fastest at more than 158 miles per hour, and, though his chassis came somewhat unglued, he nursed his sick car home in an impressive third-place finish. Then he went on to win the national title. Although he won only one of the seventeen races he contested on the championship trail, he placed high so consistently that he accumulated sufficient points to prevail.

In 1966, he won eight races and successfully defended his national laurels. In 1967, he won eight races, tops in victories on the tour for the second straight year, but was narrowly nosed out for the title by Foyt. A. J. won only five races that year, but one was the point-rich 500, and, after dropping out of the final race of the season, he picked up extra points by driving relief for another driver. The next year, Andretti won only four races, but placed consistently high and was again nosed out for the United States crown, this time by Bobby Unser, who had won the 500 jackpot. Like Foyt, Andretti tried to pick up extra points by driving relief in the final race, but he fell just short. Sometimes it seems that Andretti is better than he is lucky.

Certainly Indianapolis frustrated him, and his failures there cost him two national championships. In his second 500, in 1966, he won the pole position with a record run of more than 165 miles per hour, but his engine

One-legged Bill Schindler hands his crutches to a friend before the start of a 1947 midget race.

(Acme—Bob Shafer collection)

One-handed Allen Heath (97), hook on left arm, drives his midget racer at Ascot Park.

(Walter Mahoney)

Jim Hurtubise, with scars from his 1964 accident visible on hands and face, stands by his Plymouth before the start of the Daytona 500.

Bill Vukovich with his wife after second Indy victory in 1954.

(John W. Posey)

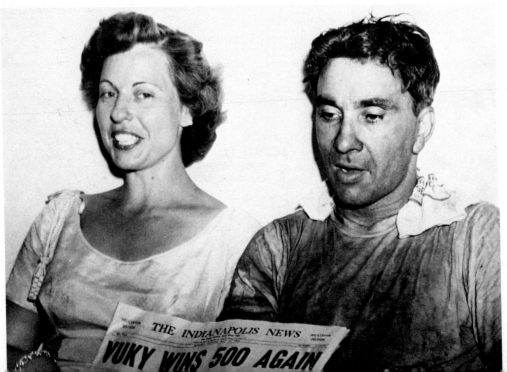

THE INDIANAPOLIS NEWS

VUKY WINS 500 AGAIN

The crash scene in the first lap of the 1958 Indianapolis 500. Seventeen cars were involved in the crash and driver Pat O'Connor was killed. *(Indianapolis Speedway)*

The late Tony Bettenhausen. *(John W. Posey)*

The late Jimmy Bryan. *(John W. Posey)*

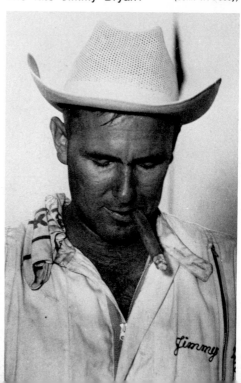

The irrepressible Eddie Sachs sags in contented weariness after a race. He died at Indy in 1964. *(John W. Posey)*

The great Rodger Ward.
(John W. Posey)

At Indy in 1964 Ward's car is speedily serviced by his pit crew. Ward placed second.

Parnelli Jones (66) puts his dirt-track jalopy through a turn early in his racing career.

Parnelli Jones and J. C. Agajanian. All is not well.   *(George Stewart—J. C. Agajanian collection)*

Parnelli bails out of "invisibly" burning car at Indy in 1964. He was hospitalized with minor burns.

Start of race at Indianapolis Speedway in 1969. In front, left to right, Bobby Unser, Mario Andretti, and A. J. Foyt.
(Indianapolis Speedway)

Bobby Unser, winner of Indianapolis 500 in 1968.   *(John W. Posey)*

His face blistered from a crash in practice, Mario Andretti waves to the crowd after winning the 500 in 1969.
(Indianapolis Speedway)

Al Unser streaks down the straightaway during the 1970 Indianapolis classic. Driving from the pole position, he won his first 500 victory by a wide margin.
(UPI)

failed him before the race had gone 70 miles. In 1967, he captured the coveted pole spot for the second year in a row with a new record of more than 168 miles per hour. But his engine went sour at the start, and then he lost a wheel and was sidelined within 150 miles. The next year, when Joe Leonard put a turbine on the pole at more than 171 miles per hour, Mario qualified as fourth fastest, but his engine threw a piston within two laps. He immediately jumped into teammate Larry Dickson's sister car, but it broke down at 60 miles.

Car owner Al Dean died before the 1968 race without ever having won the 500, but Brawner and Andretti bought the equipment from his estate and carried on alone with sponsorship help. Prior to the 1969 race, they signed for exclusive sponsorship by Granatelli, who still had not won the 500 after twenty years as driver, mechanic, and car owner, with standard cars, experimental cars, Novis, and turbines. Andretti had his own car, a Hawk built by Brawner, but he aimed at the 500 in a Lotus built by Colin Chapman.

On the Wednesday before qualifications began, Andretti's Lotus was turning laps of close to 172 miles per hour when a right rear wheel flew off. The car skidded into and along a wall, tearing off tires and sheet metal and bursting into flames, severely burning Mario's face and hands before he could free himself.

They always say that it is impossible to tell exactly how good a driver is until he has had his first really serious accident and attempts to come back from it. Now, Andretti faced this test. His original car was demolished. So he and Brawner unpacked the Hawk. Mario qualified it at just under 170 miles per hour. The only driver to go faster was Foyt, who turned just over 170 in a Coyote he had built himself. In the race, Foyt, Leonard, and Lloyd Ruby broke down and Andretti charged to an easy victory.

For Mario, for Brawner, and for Granatelli it was a first conquest of the Speedway. Granatelli got to Mario first, planting a big kiss on the embarrassed Andretti's cheeks and STP stickers on everything in sight, including the big Borg-Warner Trophy that goes to the winning team. A check for $205,727 (out of a record purse of more than $800,000) went to the winning team, too. Plus a full measure of long overdue glory. As he climbed wearily from his car, his face and hands still raw and sore from burns, still stinging from the sweat and grime and rubbing of racing, the gallant little Andretti grinned wistfully and said, "It was a long time coming." And his pregnant wife kissed him.

Later in the season, before a championship race in his hometown of

Nazareth, Pennsylvania, a parade was given for Mario. That afternoon, his wife went to the hospital and gave birth a week ahead of schedule to their third child and first daughter. That night, he won the race. He won other races that season, too, including a 200-miler on a paved oval track at Trenton, New Jersey, a 100-miler on a dirt oval track at Springfield, Illinois, and the Pikes Peak Hill Climb in Colorado. He finished the season with thirty championship trail triumphs and his third national title, second only to Foyt's forty-two trail victories and five national crowns.

For much of 1970, he was struggling, however. Andy Granatelli provided him with new cars, "McNamaras," built by an American living in Germany, and they arrived at Indy late. In his first full day of practice in one, a part snapped and he skidded six hundred feet, slamming off the walls a couple of times. The car was rebuilt but did not handle properly, and he had to wrestle it into eighth place in time trials and sixth place in the race.

Later in the season, returning to his old Hawk, Mario smashed it into a barrier in practice for a race in Michigan. His car was rebuilt and Mario wrecked it in the race.

The accidents were coming very often now. As the California 500 at Ontario and the end of the 1970 season approached, Andretti was seriously considering offers to leave Granatelli and join Ferrari or Colin Chapman's Lotus team for a full-scale assault on the Grand Prix circuit. "Perhaps it's time to take another road," he sighed.

Years ago, when Mario Andretti was just breaking into the big time, he sat on a wall, his eyes hidden behind dark sunglasses, and he said in his slight Italian accent, "Before I'm done, I'll be the best." As he looked forward to the 1970s, Mario Andretti was the successor to his Italian-born predecessor of more than a half century earlier, Ralph De Palma, and all the great drivers who had come along since then. In 1969 Aldo Andretti had begun to race again and had been critically injured, and had finally retired. Seldom have the varying fortunes of this hard sport been more dramatically drawn than in the case of these twin brothers of auto racing.

14

AND SOME RACES THAT WERE WON

Daytona Beach, Florida, 1966, the Daytona 500, the prestige race of the southern stock car circuit. It comes early in the season, in February, and sets the pace for the rest of the season. Nearly ninety thousand fans were on hand, the largest crowd ever to see a sporting event in the South. They came from all over the country, pouring into the small, sandy, salty town and the great racing arena to soak up the bright sunshine and eat fried chicken and drink beer and soda pop and watch the great cars race.

There was no sun now, for dark storm clouds had blown over the arena and cool breezes blew across the track as the big, bright cars waited to race on the two-and-one-half-mile, steeply banked, paved oval. They looked like regular passenger cars—new Fords, Plymouths, Dodges, Chevrolets, and Mercuries—but they were not. They had been stripped to the essentials, doors wired shut, insides beefed up, and engines souped up, their high-powered engines capable of hurling them 185 miles per hour down the straightaways, 165 miles per hour through the steep corners—175 miles per hour all the way around.

The cars were painted gaudy, candy-apple reds and electric blues and virgin-pure whites with bold numbers inscribed on their flanks and sponsors' names strewn all over them. The drivers waited, too, including Richard Petty, who had won the pole position by qualifying fastest at more than 175 miles per hour. He had won this race two years earlier, and his father, Lee, had won it when it was run for the first time seven years earlier and now watched over his son's pit crew. At 12:30 P.M. the crowd came to its feet, and the drivers climbed through windowless doors and strapped themselves in, and the cars went rolling away toward the green flag. As it was unfurled and waved, the metal monsters roared into the race.

Petty pressed his Plymouth to the front and held it there for six laps as the others began to string out behind him, still close together—big cars incredibly close, accelerating and slowing down and passing within inches of each other, yet seldom touching, some pressing their noses up to others' tail ends to "draft" behind them, sucked along by the front-runners. But Petty's tires began to shred much too early, causing his car to wobble, and Paul Goldsmith shot his Plymouth past Petty into the lead. Petty clung to him, passed him to regain the lead, then surrendered it to him again. After only forty miles, far sooner than planned, Petty had to dive into the pits for new tires before resuming the chase. By the time he got out, he was two laps behind, apparently hopelessly beaten.

Goldsmith led for 35 miles, then Dick Hutcherson for 50 miles, then Marvin Panch for 12 miles, then Cale Yarborough for 65 miles, then Goldsmith again for 15 miles, then Yarborough again for 5 miles, then Jim Hurtubise for 10 miles, then Goldsmith again for 15 miles. For more than 250 miles, the leaders passed first place back and forth among them as the crowd screamed for its favorites. Every time a leader had to make a pit stop, and pit stops were frequent, a new leader took over.

The cars were wearing down under the brutal pace as they sped around the saucer. Parts broke inside the bellies of these mighty machines. The car of Indianapolis champion A. J. Foyt came apart under him. The car of gallant Indianapolis contender Jim Hurtubise was wobbling all the way, the tires wearing and throwing off chunks of hot, heavy rubber that shattered the windshields of cars driven by old Curtis Turner and young Dick Hutcherson and forced them out of the chase.

The drivers were also wearing down as they chased the contenders. Slick Setzer spun his car out. Bobby Isaac spun his car out, skidded along the backstretch guardrail, and mashed his metal sides against it before he ground to a halt. Hurtubise's car brushed Earl Balmer's car, slid, and began to hurtle sideways down the main stretch as the fans came up in horror. Hurtubise, wrestling the wheel desperately, brought the big machine back under control, got it pointed in the right direction, and sped along again.

All the while Petty was driving his Plymouth daringly through tight traffic, passing on the high sides of curves and on the low making up ground, closing in on the leaders. The fans stood and began to wave white handkerchiefs at the popular twenty-nine-year-old star, encouraging him on his mad dash. Periodically, Petty had to go back into the pits, surrendering some of the precious ground he had gained back. And then he'd roar out and set out after the front-runners again, driving far faster than anyone else in the race. Just past the 280-mile mark, Petty pulled his car abreast of Yarborough's, passed, and took the lead as the crowd cheered.

To make his incredible comeback complete, Petty still had to win the race. The skies were growing darker now and the threat of rain was increasing. It meant that the lead position would be invaluable in case the race had to be curtailed. Petty pulled a quarter mile in front of Yarborough, a half mile, a mile, two miles, lap by lap opening up his lead. Then he had to go into the pits again, giving up a mile. He came back and began to open his lead up again. Then Yarborough had to make a pit stop but, not needing new tires, he was in and out quicker than Petty had managed, and gave up less distance. David Pearson and Fred Lorenzen pressed Yarborough, who pressed Petty.

The weary but excited fans shivered as a moist breeze blew heavily across the grounds, moving the cars around on the track. Still Petty pressed on. Fifty miles to go. Forty miles. Thirty miles. Twenty miles. It began to rain. The track got wet. The big cars began to slide on the dangerously slick pavement. The officials huddled and the starter unfurled his checkered flag. Ten miles to go. Five miles. The rain was pounding down now. The checkered flag was waved in Petty's path as he slid across the finish line for the 198th time, two laps short of the planned distance. Then Yarborough came across. Then Pearson. And it was all over.

Petty had made seven pit stops, changed eight tires, come from two laps behind to win by one lap in the fastest stock car race ever run. He had averaged more than 160 miles per hour for a little less than three hours and five minutes of spectacular charging. Only seventeen cars were still running at the finish. Petty crawled wearily out of his wet and soiled car, grinned, and in his soft southern accent said, "I never woulda believed it. I never thought I had a chance till those fans started waving their white hankies at me. I figured if they thought I could make it, maybe I could."

Richard Petty was well on his way to the greatest record ever compiled by a stock car driver and one of the greatest records ever compiled by any race driver.

Looking back through the years, it seems reasonable to say that Ralph De Palma was the first truly great American race driver. And perhaps the first race that dramatized American auto racing and provided it with much of its public impact was a race that De Palma entered but did not win, and that was not even an American race. This was the French Grand Prix at Le Mans in June of 1921.

American cars and drivers seldom entered European events in those days. European cars and drivers dominated American events. Ralph De Palma, an Italian-born American, had driven French-built Ballot cars to the fastest speeds in the two previous Indianapolis 500s.

The Ballot team of Jean Chassagne, Louis Wagner, and former Indianapolis winners De Palma and Jules Goux was heavily favored to dominate the 1921 French Grand Prix. The race was to cover a distance of more than 320 miles over a sand-covered stone course, 10.7 miles around, which was ordinarily used as a public road.

The Talbot team of H. O. Segrave and K. Lee Guiness and a Sunbeam driven by Rene Thomas were considered formidable contenders. At the last minute, a four-car team was entered by Fred Duesenberg. In fact, the entry arrived late, forcing the team to pay a double fee, and the money arrived only minutes before the field was closed.

Americans Jimmy Murphy and Joe Boyer and Frenchman Albert Guyot were assigned to three of the Duesenberg cars, and a wealthy French sportsman, Louis Inghibert, purchased permission to drive the fourth car, which had been scheduled for use as a spare. Boyer was three years away from his Indianapolis triumph, Murphy a year away. Murphy had been driving only two years and had crashed and severely burned his hand at Indianapolis just a month earlier. He had been only a riding mechanic until recently. The team was given little chance.

In practice, the Duesenberg team's chances diminished greatly. Murphy and Inghibert took a car out to test its braking system, the brakes locked while going into a turn, and the car skidded sideways and toppled over in a pit, trapping Murphy underneath with cracked ribs and Inghibert with severe internal injuries. They were lucky. The road was rough and wreaked havoc on those high, clumsy cars. One Ballot crashed, killing a test driver, Louis Renard.

With the permission of the Duesenberg team's manager, George Robertson, winner of the 1908 Vanderbilt Cup, mechanic Ernie Olsen revamped the car's braking system, putting smaller brakes in the front. Boyer tested the new system and it worked perfectly. He expected to take over the number-one car, but Murphy insisted that it had been assigned to him and in spite of his injuries he would be able to drive. Inghibert could not drive and Guyot replaced him.

The great De Palma started up front in his powerful Ballot. The then unknown Murphy started far back in his white Duesenberg with an American flag on the side. He had left the hospital only two hours before the race and had been lifted out of a wheelchair into the cockpit of his car. His burned and still sore hand was bandaged. Beneath his coveralls, he was heavily taped from his waist to his chest to protect his broken ribs. Olsen climbed into the seat alongside him as his riding mechanic.

There were thirteen starters, paired in rows of two, with one at the tail end. They were sent off under gray skies at half-minute intervals. De Palma took off first and surged through the first lap at greater than 78 miles per hour, with Boyer close behind him. Chassagne was third, and Murphy had passed car after car and rolled into fourth place within ten miles.

On the second lap, De Palma's engine began to falter and, as he slowed slightly, first Boyer's Duesenberg and then Murphy's slipped past him. On the third lap, Murphy skidded around Boyer to take the lead and Chassagne got around De Palma to take third place.

Pine trees and formally attired Frenchmen and their ladies lined the course as the cars thundered and rattled through the curves, round and round. Some crashed. The sand covering was swept aside by the careering racers and the rock surface underneath began to break up and send stones as big as baseballs banging up against the cars and drivers. Some drivers and some mechanics were struck and knocked out.

Murphy, in front, tore through the shrapnel until one of his tires began to come apart and he had to go into the pits. While he was in, Chassagne surged into the lead and Boyer took second place. The Sunbeams fell out of the race completely after their tires disintegrated. Boyer began to fall out, too, his car crippled. Murphy took off after the leaders, cut down Boyer, and closed in on Chassagne. On the seventeenth lap, Chassagne's fuel tank fell apart from the pounding, his fuel poured out, and he rolled to a stop as Murphy reclaimed the lead.

Boyer's car folded and Guyot moved into the runner-up position, with the determined De Palma in third, pushing his sick car to its limits. Guyot stopped in the pits to change tires and found his riding mechanic unconscious beside him, bleeding from a rock wound at his temple. There was no one to crank up the car to restart it until a veteran driver named Arthur Duray, who was at the race as a spectator, stepped out of the crowd, cranked the car, pulled out the mechanic, and jumped in alongside Guyot as he pulled away. However, Guyot was hopelessly out of it by then.

De Palma now was in relentless pursuit of Murphy. A stone punctured his fuel tank and a thin trickle of fuel began to flow steadily from it, but De Palma continued on. A rock ripped through Murphy's radiator, water gushed out, and the car began to overheat severely. "As the stones and rocks hit all around us, it sounded like we were being strafed by machine gun fire," Olsen recalled later.

Murphy said, "It was an unnerving experience. And I was hurting badly from my injuries." All the drivers by now were weary and coated with grime and blood.

With twelve miles to go, a tire blew out on Murphy's car. He was the only driver in the race not carrying a spare tire, because he felt that it took more time to stop and change on the road than to work his way into his pit on a rim. Now he worked his way in, wobbling wildly as De Palma drew closer. Murphy guided his careering car into the pit and kept the engine running with his brakes on as Olsen jumped out, jacked the car up, took off one wheel, put on another, and poured water into the dry radiator. Murphy took off again, still in front of De Palma but with the fresh water gushing from his car.

With eight miles to go, another of Murphy's tires went flat. The car began to wobble dangerously. The engine, dry of water again, was overheating badly. But he did not stop and maintained speed recklessly. Meanwhile, De Palma remained in pursuit, the last of his fuel pouring out of his punctured tank. After four hours, seven minutes, and eleven seconds, having completed the course at an average of more than 70 miles per hour, a sick, sore, and exhausted Murphy steered his battered and crippled Duesenberg across the finish line well in front of De Palma, whose car finally ran out of fuel and began to cough badly as it limped home. There would not be a comparable victory by an American for another forty years.

In 1966, after six straight years of victories by Ferrari teams, Ford attacked Le Mans and won it, but with foreign drivers, and everyone figured it was a fluke. This was not a Grand Prix, but the 24 Hours of Le Mans, the great endurance test that had been run since 1923 and won three times by American Phil Hill and once each by Carroll Shelby and Masten Gregory in the late 1950s and early 1960s, but never in an American car. In 1967, Ford put together a team of some of the greatest American drivers and set out to attain world sports car supremacy in an American car.

The Le Mans course is no longer what it had been in Jimmy Murphy's day. The 8.38-mile layout wound through tricky bends, along peaceful pastures, and through straightaways on which cars could be driven more than 200 miles per hour. The race starts at 4 P.M. on a Saturday in June and winds up at 4 P.M. the next day. It is a torturous test through daylight and night and daylight again, as two-man teams of drivers alternate in the cockpits of their abused cars. It is a hard race on drivers, and few finish. Some die.

Nearly 300,000 persons turn out for the race, a number of them even expecting to see some of the race. By night, they can see only the lightning of headlights and hear the thunder of engines as the shadowy shapes struggle through the largely unlit course. So the fans stroll through the nearby carnival midway or lie in cars or in the grass to drink wine and eat bread and cheese, make love and sleep. And the drivers and cars charge on. In one accident at Le Mans, in 1955, a French driver crashed into the crowd and he and more than eighty fans were killed.

In 1967, fifty-four cars started the race. Enzo Ferrari had seven brand-new bloodred creations ready to roll with an international cast of star drivers. There were also Porsches, Alpine-Renaults, and other fine European cars with quality drivers. There were two of Jim Hall's winged Chaparrals and six Fords entered from the United States. In stark contrast to the undernourished Duesenberg bid made by Jimmy Murphy forty-six years earlier, the Ford company had entrusted an estimated $6 million to Carroll Shelby, Phil Remington, NASCAR stalwarts John Holman and Ralph Moody, and others, who commanded an army of 120 technicians and aides in preparation for this prestigious event. They had contracted for such great Indianapolis drivers as A. J. Foyt, fresh from his third 500 triumph, Dan Gurney, Mario Andretti, Lloyd Ruby, and Roger McCluskey to drive.

The skies were gray in the late afternoon as the signal was given and the drivers ran across the track to their cars, jumped in, fired up, and took off in the traditional Le Mans start. Gurney and Foyt, teamed together, squeezed into their candy-apple-red number-one Ford and joined the others as they sped from their stalls, one by one, in the nerve-tingling getaway. "There is a turn and then right away a long straight," Gurney remarked later. "I was going 195 before I buckled myself in. Then I stood on it."

Fords forged to the front as the widely varied field of cars began to string out over the winding road that ran through the picturesque countryside. Bolting at nearly 215 miles per hour down the straights, slowing to less than 60 on some tight turns, the Fords stretched out through the early hours, time enough to complete most races but only a bare beginning there.

The Ferrari drivers conserved themselves cautiously, holding back and waiting for the daredevil American Ford drivers to crash or break down.

Eventually, many did fold. The hood ripped off one, the rear end off another. The light faded and darkness crept in. Through the hours, the relentless pace began to tell on the drivers and their machines, and the field began to thin out and the roadsides and pits were littered with crippled machines. Night fell black and bitterly cold. Later, Lloyd Ruby, who was not used to this sort of racing, said, "A ride around Le Mans at night is enough to wake up a dead man."

A little after three o'clock in the morning, the brakes on Mario Andretti's Ford grabbed as he entered a turn at 150 miles per hour. He spun, bounced off the outside and inside barriers, and ground to a halt in the middle of the track. As Andretti, badly battered, scrambled out to safety atop a wall, sister Fords driven by Roger McCluskey and Jo Schlesser came around the bend and upon him in the shadowed darkness, and ploughed into barriers to avoid hitting him. All three cars were out. All of a sudden, only the Ford being driven by Gurney and Foyt remained in the running for first place—in the lead, but insecure, with a wave of trusty Ferraris pursuing it relentlessly, ready for this car, too, to give way.

Many cars and drivers did give way. Chris Amon's car popped a tire and crashed in flames. Mike Salmon's car also halted in flames. Gunter Klaus drove a car into the trees, where it came apart in pieces of junk. All the drivers escaped, but their cars died. Morning broke, and Foyt and Gurney were still taking turns, pulling away at a faster pace than any car ever had been driven at Le Mans. Ludovico Scarfiotti of Italy and Mike Parkes of England, runners-up in a Ferrari, picked up the pace and pressed on, but Foyt and Gurney kept pulling their Ford farther and farther in front. Early afternoon came and the sun shone down and it was time for caution. But the daring Americans let it all out and kept gunning their car round and round at a brutal pace, pausing for moments only in the pits from time to time. "We kept waiting for it to break down, but it never did," Gurney said later.

It was late afternoon. Foyt had the wheel for the last hour, driving the car daringly but with perfection over the by-now-familiar ground. The metal parts held together. The weary engine hummed on. There were no mistakes. At 4 P.M., the flag fell and Foyt gunned his Ford across the start-finish line and Gurney jumped on the hood for the ride to the victory circle. In the twenty-four hours, they had covered more than 3,220 miles at an average speed of more than 135 miles per hour, 10 miles faster than Le Mans had been driven before, more than 32 miles faster than Scarfiotti and Parkes had driven when they brought their stained Ferrari home. Some thirty-eight cars had broken down. Only sixteen cars remained running at the finish. "It's nice, but it's not Indianapolis," Foyt said, as he and Gurney popped open bottles of champagne and sprayed the fancily-dressed Ford family.

For Foyt and Gurney, it was a singular achievement, a dramatic conquest of the world's best in Europe's most famous racing event. Their victory had boosted the prestige of American auto racing immeasurably, just as Jimmy Murphy's triumph in this same town had done so many years earlier. But for Foyt, who has won the Indianapolis 500 three times, and for Gurney, who has never won it, Indy remained the single supreme challenge in their profession. For Foyt, the most memorable 500, and perhaps the most memorable 500 in American auto racing, occurred in 1961.

The great crowd had already filled the sprawling stadium as the marching bands paraded off the track and the powerful cars were pushed out to sit silently in their starting positions. The drivers and their crews stood by as writers, photographers, and officials swarmed over them. "This is the hard part," Parnelli Jones once said. "When people are bothering me when I don't want to be bothered, when I have waited so long for this damn race I think it will never begin, when I have to talk to people, which I don't know how to do, when all I want to do is to drive the hell away from there, when I only have to drive, which I know how to do."

He was a rookie then, in the second row. Behind him was A. J. Foyt, in the third row, entering his fourth 500. In front of them were Don Branson, Jim Hurtubise, former winner Rodger Ward, and, on the pole, Eddie Sachs, who had qualified fastest at more than 147 miles per hour. All were in front-engine heavyweight cars. It was the last great meeting of the great old cars. The winds of change would blow in the new rear-engine lightweights a year from then.

Fake bombs burst in the air at set intervals. Musicians played "On the Banks of the Wabash." All stood still as "The Star-Spangled Banner" was struck up. And all remained standing and silent as a bugler played "Taps" in memory of men killed in wars, and on racetracks, like Tony Bettenhausen, killed at Indy earlier in the month. The track was cleared of all but drivers and mechanics now. The drivers adjusted their flameproof suits, pulled on their metal crash helmets, drew on their gloves, lowered themselves into the cockpits, strapped themselves in, and waited.

A tenor sang "Back Home Again in Indiana," the notes hanging softly and sentimentally in the suddenly hushed air. Tears ran down Eddie Sachs's face, and when the song ended and the crowd cheered, he smiled and waved to his fans. It became quiet again and Tony Hulman said, "Gentlemen, start your engines." Mechanics activated artificial starters thrust into the noses of the cars, and the cars roared to life and began to move away as the mechanics scurried for the safety of the pits. The cars circled the track slowly several times, falling into position. Then they came down the main straightaway harder, the pace car accelerated and pulled away onto the apron, the starter waved the green flag, and the tangle of thirty-three cars went hurtling into the first turn with a roar of sound and a stench of burned fuel.

This was the fiftieth anniversary of the founding of the Indianapolis 500. Before the start, the Marmon Wasp of Ray Harroun (winner of the first Indy) had circled the track slowly. Now, the race was on and Hurtubise charged to the front and made his first circuit of the track at 140 miles per hour, twice as fast as Harroun's car had gone in the inaugural 500. On the second lap, Don Branson pulled into the pits with a sick engine. His race had lasted less than two minutes. He was perhaps the sport's greatest sprint car driver and one of the smoothest drivers of a championship car, but he would drive the 500 eight times without conquering it and die at forty-six in a race at Ascot Park near Los Angeles on the eve of his retirement.

Hurtubise led through thirty-six laps, but then his engine began to sputter and falter, and he had to limp into the pits. Defending champion Jim Rathmann had picked his way through the field to take the lead. But the rookie Parnelli Jones had come up hard, too, and, as Hurtubise made his pit stop, Jones passed Sachs, Ward, and Rathmann in one lap to take the top spot. The crowd rose in surprised excitement. Lap after lap, mile after mile, Jones held that lead. He held it as Rathmann turned into the pits with a sick engine and got out of his car and walked away, dethroned. He held it as Don Davis crashed his car on the main stretch and got out in a daze and began to walk across the track. A. J. Shepherd, Bill Cheesbourg, Jack Turner, Roger McCluskey, and Lloyd Ruby all crashed trying to miss him. Somehow no one was hurt seriously, and Jones picked his way through the debris and continued to lead.

He held the lead while Len Sutton spun out. He held it even after a piece of metal came off the track to gash his head and fill his cockpit with blood. He held it until his engine suddenly went sour and he began to lose power. First Troy Ruttman went past him. Then A. J. Foyt. Then Eddie Sachs. Then Rodger Ward. Then Foyt went past Ruttman and soon Ruttman limped into the pits, his car crippled with clutch problems. After that, the race was among Foyt, Sachs, and Ward. They swapped the lead back and forth as the fans jumped with excitement. The sun beat down hot and the fans were sweaty and dazed, but few could keep their eyes off the fierce action of the wearying but determined drivers on the track. Other cars fell out as the leaders hurtled toward their destinies.

With 125 miles to go, Sachs, Ward, and Foyt each made his last scheduled pit stop in turn. When these stops were done, Ward led, with Foyt second and Sachs third. The race had to be won on the track now. The pressure and pace were intense. Ward was the first to give way. The strain had cracked his chassis. His car began to wobble badly and he had to slow up sharply to keep it on the track. After that, victory lay between Foyt and Sachs. Gradually Foyt began to pull away, lengthening his lead over Sachs to six seconds, seven, eight. Then, as Foyt went past his pits with 50 miles to go, he saw a sign chalked on a blackboard and held aloft by his pit crew. It said simply, "Fuel Low." He could not believe it. He should have gotten sufficient fuel to finish the race at his last pit stop. But he had not. His fueling apparatus had malfunctioned. He was well in front, but running dry. He cursed bitterly.

Many had seen the sign, and the fans were standing, watching the cars closely. Sachs's crew surged to the pit wall and urged him on. For a few laps, Foyt's crew signaled him, "Keep Going." Furiously they calculated his mileage. Finally they signaled him, "Come In." As the fans roared, Foyt resignedly turned into the pits with only 25 miles to go. Hurriedly, some fuel was pumped into his tank and he was sent back on his way. Before he could get out, however, Sachs had roared past into the lead. By the time Foyt regained top speed, Sachs had a fifteen-second advantage. Foyt seemed beaten. The race had undergone a startling reversal. In Foyt's pit, chief mechanic George Bignotti stood at the pit well in despair. In Sachs's pit, Eddie's mechanic, Clint Brawner, and his sponsor, Al Dean, stood on the wall in delight, seeing their dream of an Indianapolis triumph taking shape. Sachs, who wanted it so much, was smiling broadly and waving at the crowd as he sped comfortably around the track. In the stands, his wife, Nance, was crying happily and counting off the laps—nine, eight, seven. An attendant came to escort her to victory lane. Superstitiously, she refused to budge until Eddie was finished. Tears were streaming down her face as she watched Eddie come by each time—six, five . . .

At that moment, Eddie Sachs felt his car lurch. Shocked, he looked back to see rubber peeling off his right rear tire. As he rolled past his pit, there was a sudden commotion as his crew saw it, too. The announcer screamed, "Something's going on in Sachs's pit! Something may be wrong with Sachs's car!" Nance Sachs grew taut and the color drained from her face. Her hands fluttered helplessly. George Bignotti leaped up and down and began to wave Foyt on harder. A. J. saw the signal, took heart, and pressed on the accelerator as though he wanted to drive it through the floor of his car. The crowd was standing in shock. No one really believed the race could turn upside down again, but it could.

Sachs had seconds to make the most critical decision of his life. If he went on, his tire might hold up and he would win what he had dedicated his life to winning. But if his tire did not hold up, he would not finish and might even crack up and be killed. If he stopped in the pits for a new tire, he could still finish second safely and be sure of living to try another time. He kept looking back at the tire, agonizing over his choice. Suddenly, hurtling down the main stretch with three laps left, he swerved and sped into the pits. In the stands, his wife cried, "Oh, no, Eddie, no." His crew frantically fell on the car, yanking off the bad tire, shoving on a new one, and sending him back on his way. As he was pushed away, a member of the pit crew fell to his knees and in frustration hurled a hammer at Eddie's departing car.

As Sachs reached the exit from the pits, a startled Foyt flew past and back into the lead. Sachs gunned onto the track, accelerated to top speed, and set out in pursuit. But it was hopeless, unless Foyt broke down or ran out of fuel. Even Foyt did not know how much fuel he had gotten in his last, hurried stop. Very little. This was the only hope Sachs had left with two laps to go. One lap. No laps. Foyt flew under the waving checkered flag as his fuel tank ran dry. Eight seconds later, Sachs came across. In victory lane, Foyt was enveloped in a great crush of excited fans, congratulated, kissed, slapped happily. "Racing luck," he said. Sachs pulled to a stop and walked toward this ring of joy. He stood alone on the perimeter of madness, smiling sadly, looking down wistfully, and scuffing his foot in the dirt.

And so it was for these two—symbolic of race drivers. Sachs never again came close to winning the precious prize. Frustrated, he was killed at Indy three years later in pursuit of his passion. Foyt had won his first 500. He was to win two more over the next decade and continue on in quest of an unprecedented fourth. And he was to win many other races, more perhaps than any driver who ever lived. Rich, but reluctant to retire, he drove on, recognized as the greatest American race driver, possibly the greatest race driver of any country in the world—heir to immortality.

15

RECORDS AND RANKINGS

The following pages contain results and records over the years for the most important drivers of the United States and the most important races of this country and the rest of the world. Some rankings are also included. These are strictly one man's opinion, the author's, in an attempt to put the greatest drivers in perspective. They are based on accomplishment in the driver's era, not on "what might have been" had a driver had more opportunity. Most of the rankings are based on accomplishment in a given area of competition. However, in the all-time United States rankings immediately following and the all-time world rankings at the conclusion of this section, versatility has been a prime consideration. A. J. Foyt, for example, has not only dominated his prime area of racing as no other man ever has, but has won stock car races in NASCAR competition and sports car races in major world wide competition. Phil Hill has been the United States' greatest sports car driver and ranks with Dan Gurney as a Grand Prix driver, but did not attempt other areas of competition as Gurney has. Richard Petty has been the greatest American stock car driver, but has not tried other circuits.

ALL-TIME U.S. DRIVER RANKINGS

1. A. J. Foyt
2. Dan Gurney
3. Mario Andretti
4. Rodger Ward
5. Phil Hill
6. Richard Petty
7. Ralph De Palma
8. Tommy Milton
9. Lou Meyer
10. Wilbur Shaw

Honorable Mention

Earl Cooper, Fireball Roberts, Jimmy Bryan, Ted Horn, Rex Mays, Jimmy Murphy, Mauri Rose, Tony Bettenhausen, David Pearson, Lee Petty, Junior Johnson, Parnelli Jones, Don Garlits, and Mickey Thompson.

CHAMPIONSHIP TRAIL RECORDS

CHAMPIONS OF THE CHAMPIONSHIP TRAIL
Through 1969

Driver	Titles	Years				
A. J. Foyt	5	1960,	1961,	1963,	1964,	1967
Mario Andretti	3	1965,	1966,	1969		
Jimmy Bryan	3	1954,	1956,	1957		
Ted Horn	3	1946,	1947,	1948		
Lou Meyer	3	1928,	1929,	1933		
Earl Cooper	3	1913,	1915,	1917		
Rodger Ward	2	1959,	1962			
Tony Bettenhausen	2	1951,	1958			
Rex Mays	2	1940,	1941			
Wilbur Shaw	2	1937,	1939			
Pete De Paolo	2	1925,	1927			
Jimmy Murphy	2	1922,	1924			
Tommy Milton	2	1920,	1921			
Ralph Mulford	2	1911,	1918			
Ralph De Palma	2	1912,	1914			

By the Years

Year	Driver	Year	Driver	Year	Driver
1902	Harry Harkness	1923	Eddie Hearne	1949	Johnnie Parsons
1903	Barney Oldfield	1924	Jimmy Murphy	1950	Henry Banks
1904	George Heath	1925	Pete De Paolo	1951	Tony Bettenhausen
1905	Victor Hemery	1926	Harry Hartz	1952	Chuck Stevenson
1906	Joe Tracy	1927	Pete De Paolo	1953	Sam Hanks
1907	Eddie Bald	1928	Lou Meyer	1954	Jimmy Bryan
1908	Louis Strang	1929	Lou Meyer	1955	Bob Sweikert
1909	George Robertson	1930	Billy Arnold	1956	Jimmy Bryan
	Bert Dingley	1931	Louis Schneider	1957	Jimmy Bryan
1910	Ray Harroun	1932	Bob Carey	1958	Tony Bettenhausen
1911	Ralph Mulford	1933	Lou Meyer	1959	Rodger Ward
1912	Ralph De Palma	1934	Bill Cummings	1960	A. J. Foyt
1913	Earl Cooper	1935	Kelly Petillo	1961	A. J. Foyt
1914	Ralph De Palma	1936	Mauri Rose	1962	Rodger Ward
1915	Earl Cooper	1937	Wilbur Shaw	1963	A. J. Foyt
1916	Dario Resta	1938	Floyd Roberts	1964	A. J. Foyt
1917	Earl Cooper	1939	Wilbur Shaw	1965	Mario Andretti
1918	Ralph Mulford	1940	Rex Mays	1966	Mario Andretti
1919	Howard Wilcox	1941	Rex Mays	1967	A. J. Foyt
1920	Tommy Milton	1946	Ted Horn	1968	Bobby Unser
1921	Tommy Milton	1947	Ted Horn	1969	Mario Andretti
1922	Jimmy Murphy	1948	Ted Horn		

INDIANAPOLIS 500 HISTORY

Year	Pole Winner (Fastest qualifier)	MPH	Race Winner (2nd named drove relief)	Start Pos.	MPH	Margin (Min:Sec)
1911	Louis Strang	——	RAY HARROUN Cyril Patschke	28	74.59	1:43
1912	Gil Anderson (D. Bruce-Brown)	81.00 86.50	JOE DAWSON Don Herr	7	78.72	10:23
1913	Caleb Bragg (Jack Tower)	87.50 88.50	JULES GOUX	7	75.93	13:08
1914	Jean Chassagne (George Boillot)	88.30 99.85	RENE THOMAS	15	82.47	6:39
1915	Howard Wilcox	98.90	RALPH DE PALMA Spence Wishart	2	89.84	3:29
1916	John Witken	96.75	DARIO RESTA (300 miles)	4	84.00	1:58
1919	Rene Thomas	104.70	HOWDY WILCOX	2	88.05	3:47
1920	Ralph De Palma	99.15	GASTON CHEVROLET	6	88.62	6:19
1921	Ralph De Palma	100.75	TOMMY MILTON	20	89.62	3:50
1922	Jimmy Murphy	100.50	JIMMY MURPHY	1	94.48	3:14
1923	Tommy Milton	108.17	TOMMY MILTON Howdy Wilcox	1	90.95	3:15
1924	Jimmy Murphy	108.03	L. L. CORUM Joe Boyer	21	98.23	1:24
1925	Leon Duray	113.19	PETE DE PAOLO Norm Batten	2	101.13	0:44
1926	Earl Cooper	111.73	FRANK LOCKHART (400 miles, rain)	20	95.90	0:36
1927	Frank Lockhart	120.10	GEORGE SOUDERS	22	97.54	12:02
1928	Leon Duray	122.39	LOU MEYER	13	99.48	0:44
1929	Cliff Woodbury	120.59	RAY KEECH	6	97.58	6:24
1930	Billy Arnold	113.26	BILLY ARNOLD	1	100.44	7:18
1931	Russ Snowberger (Billy Arnold)	112.79 116.08	LOUIS SCHNEIDER	13	96.62	0:44
1932	Lou Moore	117.36	FRED FRAME	27	104.14	0:44
1933	Bill Cummings	118.52	LOU MEYER	6	116.97	6:42
1934	Kelly Petillo	119.32	BILL CUMMINGS	10	104.86	0:27
1935	Rex Mays	120.73	KELLY PETILLO	22	106.24	0:40
1936	Rex Mays	119.64	LOU MEYER	28	109.06	2:17
1937	Bill Cummings (Jimmy Snyder)	123.45 125.28	WILBUR SHAW	2	113.58	0:02
1938	Floyd Roberts (R. Householder)	125.68 125.76	FLOYD ROBERTS (497½ miles, rain)	1	117.20	3:35
1939	Jimmy Snyder	130.13	WILBUR SHAW	3	115.03	1:48
1940	Rex Mays	127.85	WILBUR SHAW	2	114.27	1:14

Year	Pole Winner (Fastest qualifier)	MPH	Race Winner (2nd named drove relief)	Start Pos.	MPH	Margin (Min:Sec)
1941	Mauri Rose	128.69	FLOYD DAVIS Mauri Rose	17	115.11	1:30
1946	Cliff Bergere (Ralph Hepburn)	126.47 133.94	GEORGE ROBSON	15	114.82	0:34
1947	Ted Horn (Bill Holland)	126.56 128.75	MAURI ROSE	3	116.33	0:32
1948	Rex Mays	130.57	MAURI ROSE	3	119.81	1:44
1949	Duke Nalon	132.93	BILL HOLLAND	4	121.32	3:11
1950	Walt Faulkner	134.34	Johnny Parsons (345 miles, rain)	5	124.00	0:38
1951	Duke Nalon (Walt Faulkner)	136.49 136.87	LEE WALLARD	2	126.24	1:47
1952	Fred Agabashian (Chet Miller)	138.01 139.03	TROY RUTTMAN	7	128.92	4:03
1953	Bill Vukovich	138.39	BILL VUKOVICH	1	128.74	3:31
1954	Jack McGrath	141.03	BILL VUKOVICH	19	130.84	1:10
1955	Jerry Hoyt	140.04	BOB SWEIKERT	14	128.20	2:44
1956	Pat Flaherty	145.59	PAT FLAHERTY	1	128.49	0:21
1957	Pat O'Connor (Paul Russo)	143.94 144.81	SAM HANKS	13	135.69	0:21
1958	Dick Rathmann	145.97	JIMMY BRYAN	7	133.79	0:27
1959	Johnny Thomson	145.90	RODGER WARD	6	135.85	0:23
1960	Eddie Sachs (Jim Hurtubise)	146.59 149.05	JIM RATHMANN	2	138.76	0:13
1961	Eddie Sachs	147.48	A. J. FOYT	7	139.13	0:08
1962	Parnelli Jones	150.37	RODGER WARD	2	140.29	0:11
1963	Parnelli Jones	151.15	PARNELLI JONES	1	143.13	0:34
1964	Jim Clark	158.82	A. J. FOYT	5	147.35	1:25
1965	A. J. Foyt	161.23	JIM CLARK	2	150.68	1:59
1966	Mario Andretti	165.89	GRAHAM HILL	15	144.31	0:51
1967	Mario Andretti	168.98	A. J. FOYT	4	151.20	—
1968	Joe Leonard	171.55	BOBBY UNSER	3	152.88	0:54
1969	A. J. Foyt	170.56	MARIO ANDRETTI	2	156.86	1:54
1970	Al Unser	170.22	AL UNSER	1	155.74	0:32

INDIANAPOLIS 500 RECORDS
Through 1969

Number of Races			Races Won	
1. Cliff Bergere	16		1. Wilbur Shaw	3
Chet Miller	16		Lou Meyer	3
3. Ralph Hepburn	15		A. J. Foyt	3
Russ Snowberger	15		4. Mauri Rose	2½
Mauri Rose	15		5. Tommy Milton	2
Paul Russo	15		Bill Vukovich	2
Rodger Ward	15		Rodger Ward	2
Eddie Johnson	15			

Miles Run			Laps Led	
1. Cliff Bergere	6142½		1. Ralph De Palma	613
2. Mauri Rose	6050		2. Wilbur Shaw	508
3. Jim Rathmann	5737½		3. Parnelli Jones	492
4. Wilbur Shaw	5392½		4. Bill Vukovich	485
5. Lou Meyer	5312½		5. Billy Arnold	410
6. Eddie Johnson	5215		6. Lou Meyer	332
7. Rodger Ward	5132½		7. A. J. Foyt	324
8. Ted Horn	4860		8. Jim Clark	298

INDIANAPOLIS 500 MILESTONES

One-Lap Record			Money Awards		
				Total	Winner
1914	Rene Thomas	94.53	1911	$ 27,550	$ 14,000
1919	Rene Thomas	104.78	1920	93,550	36,300
1925	Earl Cooper	110.728	1946	115,450	42,550
1927	Pete De Paola	120.54	1950	201,035	57,458
1937	Jimmy Snyder	130.49	1957	300,252	103,844
1954	Jack McGrath	141.28	1961	400,000	117,975
1962	Parnelli Jones	150.72	1964	506,575	153,650
1965	Jim Clark	160.97	1965	628,399	166,621
1968	Graham Hill	171.88	1967	734,846	171,227
			1969	804,627	205,727
			1970	1,000,000	271,697

INDIANAPOLIS 500 RANKINGS
Through 1969

Emphasis is given to the men who won this race. However, a few who never won, but whose overall record, including number of races driven and led, laps led, high finishes attained, and pole positions won, is as good as the winners', qualify for high ranking.

Driver	Races	Pole	Races Led	Laps Led	Miles Run	Finished 1	2	3	4	5
1. Wilbur Shaw	14	0	7	508	5392	3	3	1	0	0
2. Lou Meyer	12	0	6	324	4769	3	1	0	2	0
3. A. J. Foyt	12	2	6	332	5314	3	0	1	0	0
4. Mauri Rose	15	1	7	256	6050	2½	1	2	1	0
5. Rodger Ward	15	0	4	261	4947	2	2	1	1	0
6. Jim Rathmann	14	0	6	153	5737	1	3	0	0	1
7. Tommy Milton	8	1	2	233	2090*	2	0	1	0	1
8. Ralph De Palma	10	2	6	613	4125*	1	0	0	1	1
9. Bill Vukovich	5	1	4	485	1690	2	0	0	0	0
10. Parnelli Jones	7	2	6	492	2825	1	1	0	0	0
Ted Horn	10	1	3	94	4860	0	1	4	4	0
Rex Mays	12	4	9	266	3857	0	2	0	0	0
Bill Holland	5	0	3	297	2695	1	3	0	0	0
Sam Hanks	12	0	3	140	4010	1	1	2	0	0

Honorable Mention

Driver	Races	Pole	Races Led	Laps Led	Miles Run	1	2	3	4	5
Harry Hartz	6	0	4	58	2602	0	3	0	2	0
Cliff Bergere	16	1	3	35	6130	0	0	2	0	2
Ralph Hepburn	15	0	3	66	4452	0	1	1	1	1

* Incomplete.

EARLY U.S. RACE WINNERS
1915 through 1920s
NOTE: All distances approximate.

Site	Miles	Winner	Speed
		1915	
San Francisco	300	Dario Resta	67.5
San Francisco	400	Dario Resta	56.1
San Diego	300	Earl Cooper	65.0
Venice, Calif.	300	Barney Oldfield	68.8
Chicago	500	Dario Resta	97.5
Sioux City	300	Ed Rickenbacker	74.7
Omaha	300	Ed Rickenbacker	91.7
Minneapolis	500	Earl Cooper	86.3
Sheepshead Bay	350	Gil Anderson	102.6

Site	Miles	Winner	Speed
		1916	
Santa Monica	400	Howdy Wilcox	85.5
Los Angeles	150	Ed Rickenbacker	65.0
Chicago	300	Dario Resta	98.7
Des Moines	150	Ralph De Palma	92.6
Omaha	150	Dario Resta	99.0
Minneapolis	150	Dario Resta	90.0
Tacoma	300	Ed Rickenbacker	89.3
Cincinnati	300	John Aitken	97.0
Sheepshead Bay	250	John Aitken	104.8
		1917	
Cincinnati	250	Louis Chevrolet	102.1
Chicago	250	Earl Cooper	103.1
Omaha	150	Ralph Mulford	101.4
Sheepshead Bay	100	Louis Chevrolet	110.4
		1918	
Chicago	100	Louis Chevrolet	108.1
Sheepshead Bay	100	Ralph De Palma	102.0
		1919	
Santa Monica	250	Cliff Durant	81.6
Los Angeles	150	Roscoe Sarles	71.0
Elgin, Ill.	300	Tommy Milton	73.9
Sheepshead Bay	150	Gaston Chevrolet	109.5
		1920	
Beverly Hills	250	Jimmy Murphy	103.0
Fresno	250	Jimmy Murphy	95.0
Uniontown	225	Tommy Milton	94.9
		1921	
Tacoma	250	Tommy Milton	96.9
Beverly Hills	250	Ed Hearne	109.7
		1922	
Beverly Hills	250	Tommy Milton	110.8
Beverly Hills	250	Jimmy Murphy	114.6
Kansas City	300	Tommy Milton	107.0

Site	Miles	Winner	Speed
		1923	
Beverly Hills	250	Jimmy Murphy	115.8
Beverly Hills	250	Ben Hill	112.0
Fresno	150	Jimmy Murphy	103.0
Kansas City	250	Ed Hearne	105.8
Kansas City	250	Harlan Fengler	113.4
Altoona	200	Ed Hearne	111.5
Syracuse	100	Tommy Milton	80.0
		1924	
Beverly Hills	250	Harlan Fengler	116.6
Culver City	250	Ben Hill	126.9
Fresno	150	Earl Cooper	105.0
Kansas City	150	Jimmy Murphy	114.4
Altoona	250	Jimmy Murphy	114.7
Charlotte	250	Tommy Milton	118.2
Syracuse	150	Phil Shafer	70.1
		1925	
Culver City	250	Tommy Milton	126.9
Fresno	150	Pete De Paolo	105.0
Altoona	250	Pete De Paolo	115.9
Charlotte	250	Earl Cooper	121.6
Laurel, Md.	250	Pete De Paolo	123.3
Laurel	250	Bob McDonogh	126.3
Salem, N.H.	250	Pete De Paolo	125.2
		1926	
Culver City	250	Ben Hill	131.3
Atlantic City	300	Harry Hartz	135.2
Miami	300	Pete De Paolo	129.3
Altoona	250	Dave Lewis	112.4
Altoona	250	Frank Lockhart	117.0
Charlotte	150	Frank Lockhart	117.0
Laurel	100	Jimmy Gleason	105.0
Salem	200	Earl Cooper	125.0
		1927	
Culver City	250	Leon Duray	124.7
Atlantic City	200	Dave Lewis	130.6
Altoona	200	Pete De Paolo	116.6
Altoona	250	Frank Lockhart	117.5
Salem	200	Pete De Paolo	124.3

Site	Miles	Winner	Speed
1928			
Atlantic City	100	Fred Winnai	101.0
Atlantic City	100	Ray Keech	131.6
Detroit	100	Ray Keech	77.9
Altoona	200	Lou Meyer	118.0
Salem	185	Ray Keech	125.0
1929			
Detroit	100	Cliff Woodbury	76.2
Toledo	100	Wilbur Shaw	76.4
Toledo	100	Wilbur Shaw	78.9
Woodbridge, N.J.	100	Lou Moore	74.2
Woodbridge	100	Lou Moore	73.0
Syracuse	100	Wilbur Shaw	81.0
Altoona	200	Lou Meyer	112.0
Bridgeville	100	Wilbur Shaw	71.3

CHAMPIONSHIP TRAIL CLASSIC EVENTS

Langhorne, Pa., Speedway
(Dirt, paved)

Year	Distance	Winner	Year	Distance	Winner
1926	100	Russ Snowberger	1958	100	Eddie Sachs
1927	100	Ray Keech	1959	100	Van Johnson
1929	100	Frank Farmer	1960	100	Jim Hurtubise
1930	100	Bill Cummings	1961	100	A. J. Foyt
	100	Fred Frame	1962	100	A. J. Foyt
1931	100	Billy Arnold		100	Don Branson
1935	100	Kelly Petillo	1963	100	A. J. Foyt
1936	100	Floyd Davis	1964	100	A. J. Foyt
1940	100	Duke Nalon	1965*	100	Jim McElreath
1941	100	Duke Nalon		125	Jim McElreath
1946	100	Rex Mays	1966	100	Mario Andretti
1947	100	Bill Holland		150	Roger McCluskey
1948	100	Walt Brown	1967	100	Lloyd Ruby
1949	100	Johnny Parsons		150	Mario Andretti
1950	100	Jack McGrath	1968	150	Gordon Johncock
1951	100	Tony Bettenhausen		100	Al Unser
1954	100	Jimmy Bryan		100	Al Unser
1955	100	Jimmy Bryan	1969	150	Bobby Unser
1956	100	George Amick	1970	150	Bobby Unser
1957	100	Johnny Thomson			

* Dirt track paved over.

Milwaukee, Wis., Park
(Dirt, paved)

Year	Distance	Winner	Year	Distance	Winner
1933	100	Wilbur Shaw	1958	100	Art Bisch
1937	100	Rex Mays		200	Rodger Ward
1938	100	Chet Gardner	1959	100	Johnny Thomson
1939	100	Babe Stapp		200	Rodger Ward
1941	100	Rex Mays	1960	100	Rodger Ward
1946	100	Rex Mays		200	Len Sutton
1947	100	Bill Holland	1961	100	Rodger Ward
	100	C. Van Acker		200	Lloyd Ruby
1948	100	Emil Andres	1962	100	A. J. Foyt
	100	John Mantz		200	Rodger Ward
	200	Myron Fohr	1963	100	Rodger Ward
1949	100	Myron Fohr		200	Jim Clark
	200	Johnny Parsons	1964	100	A. J. Foyt
1950	100	Tony Bettenhausen		200	Parnelli Jones
	200	Walt Faulkner	1965	100	Parnelli Jones
1951	100	Tony Bettenhausen		150	Joe Leonard
	200	Walt Faulkner		200	Gordon Johncock
1952	100	Mike Nazaruk	1966	100	Mario Andretti
	200	Chuck Stevenson		200	Mario Andretti
1953	100	Jack McGrath	1967	150	Gordon Johncock
	200	Chuck Stevenson		200	Mario Andretti
1954*	100	Chuck Stevenson	1968	150	Lloyd Ruby
	200	Manuel Ayulo		200	Lloyd Ruby
1955	100	Johnny Thomson	1969	150	Art Pollard
	250	Pat Flaherty		200	Al Unser
1956	100	Pat Flaherty	1970	150	Joe Leonard
	250	Jimmy Bryan		200	Al Unser
1957	100	Rodger Ward			
	200	Jim Rathmann			

* Dirt track paved over.

Trenton, N.J., Fairgrounds
(Dirt, paved)

Year	Distance	Winner	Year	Distance	Winner
1949	100	Myron Fohr	1964	100	A. J. Foyt
1957*	100	Pat O'Connor		150	A. J. Foyt
1958	100	Len Sutton		200	Parnelli Jones
	100	Rodger Ward	1965	100	Jim McElreath
1959	100	Tony Bettenhausen		150	A. J. Foyt
	100	Eddie Sachs		200	A. J. Foyt
1960	100	Rodger Ward	1966	100	Rodger Ward
	100	Eddie Sachs		200	Mario Andretti
1961	100	Eddie Sachs	1967	150	Mario Andretti
	100	Eddie Sachs		200	A. J. Foyt
1962	100	A. J. Foyt	1968	150	Bobby Unser
	150	Rodger Ward		200	Mario Andretti
	200	Don Branson	1969	200	Mario Andretti
1963	100	A. J. Foyt		300	Mario Andretti
	150	A. J. Foyt	1970	200	Lloyd Ruby
	200	A. J. Foyt			

* Dirt paved over.

Springfield, Ill., Fairgrounds
(Dirt) (All 100)

Year	Winner	Year	Winner
1934	Billy Winn	1954	Jimmy Davies
1935	Billy Winn	1955	Jimmy Bryan
1936	Wilbur Shaw	1956	Jimmy Bryan
1937	Mauri Rose	1957	Rodger Ward
1938	Tony Wilman	1958	Johnny Thomson
1939	Emil Andres	1959	Len Sutton
1940	Rex Mays	1960	Jim Packard
1947	Tony Bettenhausen	1961	Jim Hurtubise
1948	Ted Horn	1962	Jim Hurtubise
	Myron Fohr	1963	Rodger Ward
1949	Mel Hansen	1964	A. J. Foyt
	Johnny Parsons	1965	A. J. Foyt
1950	Paul Russo	1966	Don Branson
	Tony Bettenhausen	1967	A. J. Foyt
1951	Tony Bettenhausen	1968	Roger McCluskey
1952	Bill Schindler	1969	Mario Andretti
1953	Rodger Ward	1970	Al Unser
	Sam Hanks		

Indianapolis Fairgrounds
(Dirt) (All 100)

1946	Rex Mays	1961	A. J. Foyt
1953	Bob Sweikert	1962	Parnelli Jones
1954	Jimmy Bryan	1963	Rodger Ward
1955	Jimmy Bryan	1964	A. J. Foyt
1956	Jimmy Bryan	1965	A. J. Foyt
1957	Jud Larson	1966	Mario Andretti
1958	Eddie Sachs	1967	Mario Andretti
1959	Rodger Ward	1968	A. J. Foyt
1960	A. J. Foyt	1969	A. J. Foyt

Du Quoin, Ill., Fairgrounds
(Dirt) (All 100)

1948	Lee Wallard	1959	Rodger Ward
1949	Tony Bettenhausen	1960	A. J. Foyt
1951	Tony Bettenhausen	1961	A. J. Foyt
	Tony Bettenhausen	1963	A. J. Foyt
1952	Chuck Stevenson	1964	A. J. Foyt
1953	Sam Hanks	1965	Don Branson
1954	Sam Hanks	1966	Bud Tingelstad
1955	Jimmy Bryan	1967	A. J. Foyt
1956	Jimmy Bryan	1968	Mario Andretti
1957	Jud Larson	1969	Al Unser
1958	Johnny Thomson		

Sacramento, Calif., Fairgrounds
(Dirt) (All 100)

1949	Fred Agabashian	1961	Rodger Ward
1950	Duke Dinsmore	1962	A. J. Foyt
1953	Jimmy Bryan	1963	Rodger Ward
1954	Jimmy Bryan	1964	A. J. Foyt
1955	Jimmy Bryan	1965	Don Branson
1956	Jud Larson	1966	Dick Atkins
1957	Rodger Ward	1967	A. J. Foyt
1958	Johnny Thomson	1968	A. J. Foyt
1959	Jim Hurtubise	1969	Al Unser
1960	A. J. Foyt		

Pikes Peak, Colo.
(Paved)

Dirt !

1965	Al Unser	1968	Bobby Unser
1966	Bobby Unser	1969	Mario Andretti
1967	Wes Vandavoort	1970	Ted Foltz

Phoenix, Ariz., Raceway
(Paved)

Year	Distance	Winner	Year	Distance	Winner
1964	100	A. J. Foyt	1967	150	Lloyd Ruby
	200	Lloyd Ruby		200	Mario Andretti
1965	150	Don Branson	1968	150	Bobby Unser
	200	A. J. Foyt		200	Gary Bettenhausen
1966	150	Jim McElreath	1969	150	George Follmer
	200	Mario Andretti		200	Al Unser
			1970	150	Al Unser

Hanford, Calif., Speedway
(Paved)

Year	Distance	Winner	Year	Distance	Winner
1967	200	Gordon Johncock	1968	200	Gordon Johncock
				250	A. J. Foyt

Riverside, Calif., Raceway
(Paved road course)

Year	Distance	Winner	Year	Distance	Winner
1967	300	Dan Gurney	1968	300	Dan Gurney

Sears Point, Calif., Raceway
(Paved)

Year	Distance	Winner
1970	150	Dan Gurney

Dover, Del., Speedway
(Paved)

Year	Distance	Winner
1969	200	Art Pollard

Brainerd, Minn., Speedway
(Paved)

Year	Distance	Winner
1969	100	Gordon Johncock
	100	Dan Gurney

Seattle Raceway
(Paved)

Year	Distance	Winner
1969	100	Al Unser
	100	Mario Andretti

Indianapolis Raceway
(Paved road course)

Year	Distance	Winner	Year	Distance	Winner
1965	150	Mario Andretti	1969	100	Dan Gurney
1966	150	Mario Andretti		100	Peter Revson
1967	150	Mario Andretti	1970	150	Al Unser
1968	100	Al Unser			
	100	Al Unser			

Castle Rock, Colo., Raceway
(Paved road course)

Year	Distance	Winner	Year	Distance	Winner
1968	150	A. J. Foyt	1970	150	Mario Andretti
1969	150	Gordon Johncock			

Nazareth, Pa., Speedway
(Paved)

Year	Distance	Winner	Year	Distance	Winner
1968	100	Al Unser	1969	100	Mario Andretti

Irish Hills, Mich., Speedway
(Paved)

Year	Distance	Winner	Year	Distance	Winner
1968	150	Ron Bucknum	1970	200	Gary Bettenhausen

Mosport, Canada, Park
(Paved road course)

Year	Distance	Winner	Year	Distance	Winner
1967	115	Bobby Unser	1968	100	Dan Gurney
				100	Dan Gurney

St. Jovite, Canada, Park

Year	Distance	Winner	Year	Distance	Winner
1967	100	Mario Andretti	1968	100	Mario Andretti
	100	Mario Andretti		100	Mario Andretti

ACTIVE DRIVERS WHO HAVE WON USAC CHAMPIONSHIP TRAIL RACES
Through 1969

		Victories			Victories
1.	A. J. Foyt	42	11.	Roger McCluskey	2
2.	Mario Andretti	30		Art Pollard	2
3.	Al Unser	11	13.	Joe Leonard	1
4.	Bobby Unser	9		Graham Hill	1
5.	Gordon Johncock	7		John Rutherford	1
6.	Dan Gurney	6		Bud Tingelstad	1
	Lloyd Ruby	6		Ron Bucknum	1
	Parnelli Jones	6		Gary Bettenhausen	1
9.	Jim Hurtubise	4		George Follmer	1
	Jim McElreath	4		Peter Revson	1

USAC LEADERS 1956–1969
(USAC took over sponsorship in 1956)

	Champ Cars			Sprint Cars	
		Victories			Victories
1.	A. J. Foyt	42	1.	Don Branson	28
2.	Mario Andretti	30	2.	A. J. Foyt	26
3.	Rodger Ward	24	3.	Parnelli Jones	25
4.	Al Unser	11	4.	Roger McCluskey	23
5.	Bobby Unser	9	5.	Larry Dickson	20

	Midget Cars			Stock Cars	
1.	Mel Kenyon	63	1.	Don White	42
2.	Bob Wente	60	2.	Norm Nelson	30
3.	Bob Tattersall	58	3.	Paul Goldsmith	26
4.	Jimmy Davies	46	4.	A. J. Foyt	21
5.	Chuck Rodee	35	5.	Parnelli Jones	13

USAC CHAMPIONS 1956–1969

	Sprint Cars	Midget Cars	Stock Cars
1956	Pat O'Connor Tommy Hinnershitz	Shorty Templeman	Johnny Mantz
1957	Elmer George Bill Randall	Shorty Templeman	Jerry Unser
1958	Eddie Sachs Johnny Thomson	Shorty Templeman	Fred Lorenzen
1959	Don Branson Tommy Hinnershitz	Gene Hartley	Fred Lorenzen
1960	Parnelli Jones A. J. Foyt	Jimmy Davies	Norm Nelson
1961	Parnelli Jones	Jimmy Davies	Paul Goldsmith
1962	Parnelli Jones	Jimmy Davies	Paul Goldsmith
1963	Roger McCluskey	Bob Wente	Don White
1964	Don Branson	Mel Kenyon	Parnelli Jones
1965	John Rutherford	Mike McGreevey	Norm Nelson
1966	Roger McCluskey	Mike McGreevey	Norm Nelson
1967	Greg Weld	Mel Kenyon	Don White
1968	Larry Dickson	Mel Kenyon	A. J. Foyt
1969	Gary Bettenhausen	Bob Tattersall	Roger McCluskey

U.S. CHAMPIONSHIP CIRCUIT RANKINGS
Through 1969 season

Emphasis is given national titles, championship races won, and Indianapolis 500 performances.

		Natl. Titles	Champ Wins	Indy 500 Wins	2d	3d
1.	A. J. Foyt	5	42	3	1	1
2.	Mario Andretti	3	30	1	0	0
3.	Rodger Ward	2	26	2	2	1
4.	Ralph De Palma	3	26*	1	0	0
5.	Tommy Milton	2	23*	2	0	1
6.	Lou Meyer	3	*	3	1	0
7.	Earl Cooper	3	21*	0	1	0
8.	Tony Bettenhausen	2	21	0	1	0
9.	Wilbur Shaw	2	*	3	3	1
10.	Jimmy Bryan	3	19	1	1	1
	Ted Horn	3	*	0	1	4
	Rex Mays	2	*	0	2	0
	Jimmy Murphy	2	16	1	0	2
	Ralph Mulford	2	15*	0	1	1
	Mauri Rose	1	6½	2½	1	2
	Pete De Paolo	2	*	1	0	0
	Parnelli Jones	0	6	1	1	0
	Jim Rathmann	0	3	1	3	0

* Totals uncertain.

NASCAR, HOT ROD, AND OTHER U.S. RECORDS

LEADING MONEY WINNERS

USAC Championship Circuit

1957	Sam Hanks	$103,844	1964	A. J. Foyt	$212,130
1958	Jimmy Bryan	118,327	1965	Jim Clark	166,621
1959	Rodger Ward	144,145	1966	Graham Hill	103,502
1960	Jim Rathmann	110,396	1967	A. J. Foyt	233,653
1961	A. J. Foyt	153,168	1968	Bobby Unser	261,124
1962	Rodger Ward	149,436	1969	Mario Andretti	363,283
1963	Parnelli Jones	157,382			

USAC Stock Car Circuit

1958	Fred Lorenzen	$16,939	1964	Parnelli Jones	$ 25,798
1959	Fred Lorenzen	13,993	1965	Norm Nelson	26,234
1960	Norm Nelson	14,899	1966	Norm Nelson	30,284
1961	Paul Goldsmith	17,516	1967	Don White	29,514
1962	Paul Goldsmith	24,176	1968	A. J. Foyt	34,464
1963	Don White	16,840	1969	Roger McCluskey	41,217

NASCAR Grand National Circuit

1959	Lee Petty	$ 45,570	1965	Ned Jarrett	$ 77,966
1960	Rex White	45,280	1966	Richard Petty	78,930
1961	David Pearson	49,580	1967	Richard Petty	130,275
1962	Fireball Roberts	59,825	1968	Cale Yarborough	136,786
1963	Fred Lorenzen	113,570	1969	Lee Roy Yarbrough	188,605
1964	Richard Petty	98,810			

NASCAR GRAND NATIONAL CHAMPIONS

Lee Petty (3)	1954, 1958, 1959	Joe Weatherly (2)	1962, 1963
David Pearson (3)	1966, 1968, 1969	Buck Baker (2)	1956, 1957
Richard Petty (2)	1964, 1967	Tim Flock (2)	1952, 1955
Ned Jarrett (2)	1961, 1965	Herb Thomas (2)	1951, 1953

By the Years

1949	Red Byron (Olds)	1960	Rex White (Chevy)
1950	Bill Rexford (Olds)	1961	Ned Jarrett (Chevy)
1951	Herb Thomas (Plym., Hudson)	1962	Joe Weatherly (Pontiac)
1952	Tim Flock (Hudson)	1963	Joe Weatherly (Pontiac, Merc.)
1953	Herb Thomas (Hudson)	1964	Richard Petty (Plymouth)
1954	Lee Petty (Chrysler)	1965	Ned Jarrett (Ford)
1955	Tim Flock (Chrysler)	1966	David Pearson (Dodge)
1956	Buck Baker (Chrys., Dodge)	1967	Richard Petty (Plymouth)
1957	Buck Baker (Chevy)	1968	David Pearson (Ford)
1958	Lee Petty (Olds)	1969	David Pearson (Ford)
1959	Lee Petty (Olds, Plym.)		

DAYTONA 500 SUMMARY

Year	Fastest Qualifier	Avg.	Winner	St. Pos.	Car	Avg.
1959	Cotton Owens	143.19	LEE PETTY	15	Olds	135.52
1960	Fireball Roberts	151.55	JUNIOR JOHNSON	9	Chevy	124.74
1961	Fireball Roberts	155.70	MARVIN PANCH	4	Pontiac	149.60
1962	Fireball Roberts	158.74	FIREBALL ROBERTS	1	Pontiac	152.52
1963	John Rutherford	165.18	TINY LUND	12	Ford	151.56
1964	Paul Goldsmith	174.91	RICHARD PETTY	2	Plym.	154.33
1965	Darel Dieringer	171.15	FRED LORENZEN	4	Ford	141.53
			(332 miles, rain)			
1966	Richard Petty	175.16	RICHARD PETTY	1	Plym.	160.62
			(495 miles, rain)			
1967	Curtis Turner	180.83	MARIO ANDRETTI	12	Ford	146.92
1968	Cale Yarborough	189.22	CALE YARBOROUGH	1	Mercury	143.25
1969	David Pearson	190.02	LEE ROY YARBROUGH	19	Ford	157.95
1970	Cale Yarborough	194.01	PETE HAMILTON	9	Plym.	149.60

Daytona 500 Rankings
Through 1970

		Fast Qual.	Win	2d	3d	4th	5th	Races	Races Led
1.	Richard Petty	1	2	1	1	0	0	11	4
2.	Fred Lorenzen	0	1	2	0	2	1	8	4
3.	Fireball Roberts	3	1	0	0	0	0	5	5
4.	Cale Yarborough	2	1	1	0	0	0	10	4
5.	Lee Roy Yarbrough	0	1	1	0	0	0	8	4

NASCAR SUPERSPEEDWAY WINNERS
DAYTONA
Beach—Road Course

1949	Red Byron	1952	Marshall Teague	1956	Tim Flock
1950	Hal Kite	1953	Bill Blair	1957	Cotton Owens
1951	Marshall Teague	1954	Lee Petty	1958	Paul Goldsmith
		1955	Tim Flock		

Speedway (Firecracker 400)

1959*	Fireball Roberts	1963	Fireball Roberts	1967	Cale Yarborough
1960*	Jack Smith	1964	A. J. Foyt	1968	Cale Yarborough
1961*	David Pearson	1965	A. J. Foyt	1969	Lee Roy Yarbrough
1962*	Fireball Roberts	1966	Sam McQuagg	1970	Donnie Allison

* 250 miles.

ATLANTA RACEWAY
Atlanta 500

1960	Bobby Johns	1963	Fred Lorenzen	1967	Cale Yarborough
1961	Bob Burdick	1964	Fred Lorenzen	1968	Cale Yarborough
1962	Fred Lorenzen*	1965	Marvin Panch	1969	Cale Yarborough
		1966	Jim Hurtubise	1970	Bobby Allison

* 328½ miles, rain.

Dixie Classic

Year	Distance	Winner	Year	Distance	Winner
1960	300	Fireball Roberts	1966	400	Richard Petty
1961	400	David Pearson	1967	500	Dick Hutcherson
1962	400	Rex White	1968	500	Lee Roy Yarbrough
1963	400	Junior Johnson	1969	500	Lee Roy Yarbrough
1964	400	Ned Jarrett	1970	500	Richard Petty
1965	400	Marvin Panch			

DARLINGTON RACEWAY
Southern 500

1950	Johnny Mantz	1957	Speedy Thompson	1963	Fireball Roberts
1951	Herb Thomas	1958	Fireball Roberts	1964	Buck Baker
1952	Fonty Flock	1959	Jim Reed	1965	Ned Jarrett
1953	Buck Baker	1960	Buck Baker	1966	Darel Dieringer
1954	Herb Thomas	1961	Nelson Stacy	1967	Richard Petty
1955	Herb Thomas	1962	Larry Frank	1968	Cale Yarborough
1956	Curtis Turner			1969	Lee Roy Yarbrough

Rebel Classic

Year	Distance	Winner	Year	Distance	Winner
1957	300	Fireball Roberts	1964	300	Fred Lorenzen
1958	300	Curtis Turner	1965	300	Junior Johnson
1959	300	Fireball Roberts	1966	400	Richard Petty
1960	300	Joe Weatherly	1967	400	Richard Petty
1961	300	Fred Lorenzen	1968	400	David Pearson
1962	300	Nelson Stacy	1969	400	Lee Roy Yarbrough
1963	300	Joe Weatherly	1970	400	David Pearson

NORTH CAROLINA SPEEDWAY
American 500

1965	Curtis Turner	1967	Bobby Allison	1968	Richard Petty
1966	Fred Lorenzen			1969	Lee Roy Yarbrough

Carolina 500

1966	Paul Goldsmith	1968	Donnie Allison	1969	David Pearson
1967	Richard Petty			1970	Richard Petty

CHARLOTTE SPEEDWAY
World 600

1960	Joe Lee Johnson	1964	Jim Paschal	1968	Buddy Baker*
1961	David Pearson	1965	Fred Lorenzen	1969	Lee Roy Yarbrough
1962	Nelson Stacy	1966	Marvin Panch	1970	D. Allison/
1963	Fred Lorenzen	1967	Jim Paschal		L. Yarbrough

* 382½ miles, rain.

National Classic

Year	Distance	Winner	Year	Distance	Winner
1960	400	Speedy Thompson	1965	400	Fred Lorenzen
1961	400	Joe Weatherly	1966	500	Lee Roy Yarbrough
1962	400	Junior Johnson	1967	500	Buddy Baker
1963	400	Junior Johnson	1968	500	Charlie Glotzbach
1964	400	Fred Lorenzen	1969	500	Donnie Allison

MICHIGAN SPEEDWAY

Motor State 500	Motor State 400
1969 Cale Yarborough	1970 Cale Yarborough

Yankee 600	Yankee 400
1969 David Pearson	1970 Charlie Glotzbach

RIVERSIDE RACEWAY
Riverside 500

1963	Dan Gurney	1966	Dan Gurney	1968	Dan Gurney
1964	Dan Gurney	1967	Parnelli Jones	1969	Richard Petty
1965	Dan Gurney			1970	A. J. Foyt

Falstaff 400

1970   Richard Petty

ALABAMA SPEEDWAY
Talladega 500

1969 Richard Brickhouse	1970 Pete Hamilton

TEXAS SPEEDWAY
Texas 500

1969   Bobby Isaac

NASCAR RANKINGS
Through 1969 Season

NOTE: Emphasis is given season championships, total Grand National victories, and superspeedway victories, especially Daytona 500 victories, in varying amounts. While "what might have been" cannot be weighted too heavily, it is recognized that fewer superspeedway races were available until recent years.

		Natl. Titles	GN Wins	Supers'way Wins	Daytona 500 Wins
1.	Richard Petty	2	101	8	2
2.	Fred Lorenzen	0	26	11	1
3.	Fireball Roberts	0	32	8	1
4.	David Pearson	3	57	6	0
5.	Junior Johnson	0	50	5	1
6.	Lee Petty	3	54	1	1
7.	Herb Thomas	2	49	3	0
8.	Ned Jarrett	2	50	2	0
9.	Lee Roy Yarbrough	0	13	9	1
	Cale Yarborough	0	11	8	1
	Buck Baker	2	46	3	0
	Tim Flock	2	40	0	0
	Joe Weatherly	2	26	3	0
	Rex White	1	26	1	0

Honorable Mention

	Natl. Titles	GN Wins	Supers'way Wins	Daytona 500 Wins
Jim Paschal	0	25	1	0
Jack Smith	0	21	1	0
Fonty Flock	0	19	1	0
Curtis Turner	0	17	3	0
Marvin Panch	0	17	4	1
Al Thompson	0	17	1	0

ACTIVE DRIVERS WHO'VE WON SUPERSPEEDWAY CLASSICS
Through 1969

	Wins		Wins		Wins
Lee Roy Yarbrough	9	Buddy Baker	2	Mario Andretti	1
Richard Petty	8	Donnie Allison	2	Jim Hurtubise	1
Cale Yarborough	8	A. J. Foyt	2	Charlie Glotzbach	1
David Pearson	6	Bobby Allison	1	Richard Brickhouse	1
Curtis Turner	3			Bobby Isaac	1

NOTE: Superspeedways are Grand National paved oval tracks of one mile or more around: Daytona, Fla. (2½ miles); Atlanta, Ga. (1½ miles); Charlotte, N.C. (1½ miles); Darlington, S.C. (1⅜ miles); Talladega, Ala. (2.66 miles); College Station, Tex. (2 miles); and Rockingham, N.C. (1 mile). Does not include Riverside, Calif., 2.7-mile road track.

LAND SPEED RECORD MILESTONES*
Flying start. One-mile course. Two-way average.

Date	Driver	MPH	Date	Driver	MPH
1898	Chasseloup-Laubat	39.24	1926	Parry-Thomas	170.62
1899	Jenatzy	49.40	1927	M. Campbell	174.22
1899	Chasseloup-Laubat	58.25	1927	Segrave	203.79
1899	Jenatzy	65.79	1928	M. Campbell	206.95
1902	Serpollet	75.06	1928	Keech	207.55
1902	W. Vanderbilt	76.08	1929	Segrave	231.44
1902	Fournier	76.60	1931	Campbell	246.08
1902	Augieres	77.13	1932	Campbell	253.96
1903	Rigolly	83.46	1935	Campbell	301.13
1903	A. Duray	84.73	1938	Eyston	345.50
1904	H. Ford	91.37	1938	Cobb	350.20
1904	De Caters	97.26	1938	Eyston	357.50
1904	Rigolly	103.76	1939	Cobb	368.90
1904	Hemery	104.53	1947	Cobb	394.20
1904	Barras	109.65	1963	Breedlove	407.45
1909	Hemery	125.91	1964	Green	413.20
1922	Guiness	129.17	1964	A. Arfons	434.02
1924	Parry-Thomas	129.73	1964	Breedlove	525.22
1925	R. Thomas	143.31	1965	A. Arfons	576.55
1924	Eldridge	145.87	1965	Breedlove	600.60
1925	M. Campbell	150.76			

* Includes every man who held it, but not each intermediate speed at which he held it.

NATIONAL HOT ROD ASSOCIATION
NATIONAL CHAMPIONSHIPS
Fuel Dragster Division — Top Eliminator Champions
(All races, 440 yards)

Year	Driver	Elapsed Time in Seconds	Peak Speed
1955	Cal Rice	10.30	143.95
1956	Melvin Heath	10.49	141.50
1957	Buddy Sampson	10.42	141.50
1958	Ted Cyr	10.04	139.75
1959	Rod Singer	9.76	152.00
1960	Len Harris	9.65	165.13
1961	Pete Robinson	8:92	169.49
1962	Jack Chrisman	8.76	171.75
1963	Bobby Vodnik	8.62	174.75
1964	Don Garlits	7.67	198.22
1965	Don Prudhomme	7.50	207.33
1966	Mike Snively	7.32	215.82
1967	Don Garlits	6.77	220.58
1968	Don Garlits	6.87	226.70
1969	Don Prudhomme	6.51	223.34

TOP FUEL ELIMINATOR CHAMPIONS
Winternationals

Year	Driver	Elapsed Time in Seconds	MPH
1961	Jack Chrisman	8.99	170.13
1962	Jim Nelson	8.71	170.13
1963	Don Garlits	8.26	186.32
1964	Jack Williams	8.16	193.12
1965	Don Prudhomme	7.76	201.34
1966	Mike Snively	7.54	209.78
1967	Connie Kalitta	7.17	218.43
1968	James Warren	—	—
1969	John Mulligan	6.95	211.38
1970	Larry Dixon	6.86	180.00

Springnationals

1965	Maynard Rupp	7.59	203.16
1966	Jimmy Nix	7.38	213.28
1967	Don Prudhomme	6.92	222.76
1968	Don Garlits	6.80	222.76
1969	Hank Westmoreland	6.84	214.79

Summernationals

1970	Pete Robinson	6.71	220.58

World Finals

1965	Maynard Rupp	7.59	203.16
1966	Jimmy Nix	7.38	213.28
1967	Don Prudhomme	6.92	222.76
1968	Don Garlits	6.80	222.76
1969	Steve Carbone	6.71	207.85

GRAND PRIX AND SPORTS CAR RECORDS

NOTE: Names of Americans who have won foreign competitions are printed in capitals.

GRAND PRIX "WORLD" DRIVING CHAMPIONS

Driver	Titles	Years
Juan Fangio	5	1951, 1954, 1955, 1956, 1957
Jack Brabham	3	1959, 1960, 1966
Jim Clark	2	1963, 1965
Graham Hill	2	1962, 1968
Alberto Ascari	2	1952, 1953

By the Years

Year	Champion	Nationality	Car
1950	Giuseppe Farina	Italy	Alfa Romeo
1951	Juan Fangio	Argentina	Alfa Romeo
1952	Alberto Ascari	Italy	Ferrari
1953	Alberto Ascari		Ferrari
1954	Juan Fangio		Maserati, Mercedes
1955	Juan Fangio		Mercedes
1956	Juan Fangio		Ferrari Lancia
1957	Juan Fangio		Maserati
1958	Mike Hawthorn	England	Ferrari
1959	Jack Brabham	Australia	Cooper-Climax
1960	Jack Brabham		Cooper-Climax
1961	PHIL HILL	United States	Ferrari
1962	Graham Hill	England	BRM
1963	Jim Clark	Scotland	Lotus
1964	John Surtees	England	Ferrari
1965	Jim Clark		Lotus-Climax
1966	Jack Brabham		Brabham-Repco
1967	Denis Hulme	New Zealand	Brabham-Repco
1968	Graham Hill		Lotus-Ford
1969	Jackie Stewart	Scotland	Matra

MAJOR GRAND PRIX WINNERS

	England	France	Italy	Germany	Belgium	Monaco
1950	Farina	Fangio	Farina	——	Fangio	Fangio
1951	Gonzales	Fagioli/Fangio	Ascari	Ascari	Farina	——
1952	Ascari	Ascari	Ascari	Ascari	Ascari	——
1953	Ascari	Hawthorn	Fangio	Farina	Ascari	——
1954	Gonzales	Fangio	Fangio	Fangio	Fangio	——
1955	Moss	——	Fangio	——	Fangio	Trintignant
1956	Fangio	Collins	Moss	Fangio	Collins	Moss
1957	Brooks/Moss	Fangio	——	Fangio	——	Fangio
1958	Collins	Hawthorn	Brooks	Brooks	Brooks	Trintignant
1959	Brabham	Brooks	Moss	Brooks	——	Brabham
1960	Brabham	Brabham	P. HILL	——	Brabham	Moss
1961	von Trips	Baghetti	P. HILL	Moss	P. HILL	Moss
1962	Clark	GURNEY	G. Hill	P. HILL	Clark	Ireland
1963	Clark	Clark	Clark	Surtees	Clark	G. Hill
1964	Clark	GURNEY	Surtees	Surtees	Clark	G. Hill
1965	Clark	Clark	Stewart	Clark	Clark	G. Hill
1966	Brabham	Brabham	Scarfiotti	Brabham	Surtees	Stewart
1967	Clark	Brabham	Surtees	Hulme	GURNEY	Hulme
1968	Siffert	Ickx	Hulme	Stewart	McLaren	G. Hill
1969	Stewart	Stewart	Stewart	Ickx	——	G. Hill
1970	Rindt	Rindt	——	Rindt	Rodriguez	Rindt

MAJOR GRAND PRIX WINNERS

U.S.

1959	Bruce McLaren	1963	Graham Hill	1966	Jim Clark
1960	Stirling Moss	1964	Graham Hill	1967	Jim Clark
1961	Innes Ireland	1965	Graham Hill	1968	Jackie Stewart
1962	Jim Clark			1969	Jochen Rindt

Netherlands

1952	Ascari	1960	Brabham	1966	Brabham
1953	Ascari	1961	von Trips	1967	Clark
1955	Fangio	1962	G. Hill	1968	Stewart
1958	Moss	1963	Clark	1969	Stewart
1959	Bonnier	1964	Clark	1970	Rindt
		1965	Clark		

Mexico

1963	Clark	1965	GINTHER	1968	Hill
1964	GURNEY	1966	Surtees	1969	Hulme
		1967	Clark		

South Africa

1962	G. Hill	1965	Clark	1969	Stewart
1963	Clark	1967	P. Rodriguez	1970	Brabham
		1968	Clark		

Canada

1967	Brabham	1968	Hulme	1969	Ickx

Switzerland

1950	Farina	1952	Taruffi	1953	Ascari
1951	Fangio			1954	Fangio

Portugal

1958	Moss	1959	Moss	1970	Stewart
		1960	Brabham		

Spain

1951	Fangio	1954	Hawthorn	1969	Stewart
		1968	Hill		

Argentina

1954	Fangio	1956	Fangio/Musso	1957	Fangio
1955	Fangio			1958	Moss

Austria

1964	Bandini

Pescara

1957	Moss

Morocco

1958	Moss

Sicily

1964	Siffert

SPORTS CAR CLASSICS

The 24 Hours of Le Mans

Year	Winners	Car	MPH
1923	Lagache-Leonard	Chenard	57.21
1924	Duff-Clement	Bentley	53.78
1925	de Courcelles-Rossignol	Lorraine	57.85
1926	Bloch-Rossignol	Lorraine	66.08
1927	Benjafield-Davis	Bentley	61.35
1928	Barnato-Rubin	Bentley	69.11
1929	Barnato-Birkin	Bentley	73.63
1930	Barnato-Kidston	Bentley	75.88
1931	Howe-Birkin	Alfa Romeo	78.13
1932	Sommer-Chinetti	Alfa Romeo	81.40
1933	Sommer-Nuvolari	Alfa Romeo	74.75
1934	Chinetti-Etancelin	Alfa Romeo	74.75
1935	Hindmarsh-Fontes	Lagonda	77.85
1937	Wimille-Benoist	Bugatti	85.13
1938	Chaboud-Tremoulet	Delahaye	82.36
1939	Wimille-Veyron	Bugatti	86.60
1949	Chinetti-Selsdon	Ferrari	82.27
1950	L. Rosier-C. Rosier	Talbot	89.73
1951	Walker-Whitehead	Jaguar C	105.85
1952	Lang-Reiss	Mercedes-Benz	96.67
1953	Rolt-Hamilton	Jaguar C	105.85
1954	Gonzales-Trintignant	Ferrari	105.15
1955	Hawthorn-Bueb	Jaguar D	107.17
1956	Flockhart-Sanderson	Jaguar D	104.46
1957	Flockhart-Bueb	Jaguar D	113.85
1958	P. HILL-Gendebien	Ferrari	106.12
1959	SHELBY-Salvadori	Aston-Martin	112.57
1960	Gendebien-Frere	Ferrari	109.12
1961	P. HILL-Gendebien	Ferrari	115.9
1962	P. HILL-Gendebien	Ferrari	126.7
1963	Scarfiotti-Bandini	Ferrari	118.1
1964	Guichet-Vaccarella	Ferrari	121.4
1965	GREGORY-Rindt	Ferrari	121.0
1966	McLaren-Amon	Ford	125.1
1967	GURNEY-FOYT	Ford	135.4
1968	P. Rodriguez-Bianchi	Ford	115.3
1969	Ickx-Oliver	Ford	129.3
1970	Herrmann-Attwood	Porsche	115.2

1,000 Kilometers of Nurburgring, Germany

Year	Winners	Car	MPH
1953	Ascari-Farina	Ferrari	74.75
1956	Moss-Behra-Taruffi-Schell	Maserati	80.59
1957	Brooks-Cunningham-Reid	Aston-Martin	——
1958	Moss-Brabham	Aston-Martin	84.26
1959	Moss-Fairman	Aston-Martin	82.52
1960	Moss-GURNEY	Maserati	82.77
1961	Gregory-Casner	Maserati	79.10
1962	P. HILL-Gendebien	Ferrari	82.39
1963	Surtees-Mairesse	Ferrari	82.72
1964	Scarfiotti-Vaccarella	Ferrari	87.30
1965	Surtees-Scarfiotti	Ferrari	90.66
1966	P. HILL-Bonnier	Chaparral	89.35
1967	Schutz-Buzzetta	Porsche	91.41
1968	Siffert-Elford	Porsche	95.04
1969	Siffert-Redman	Porsche	101.00
1970	Elford-Ahren	Porsche	——

U.S. SPORTS CAR CLASSICS

12 Hours of Sebring

Year	Winners	Car	MPH
1952	Gray-Kulok	Frazer Nash	62.83
1953	Fitch-Walters	Cunningham	74.96
1954	Moss-Lloyd	Osca	73.63
1955	Hawthorn-Walters	Jaguar D	78.86
1956	Fangio-Castelotti	Ferrari	84.07
1957	Fangio-Behra	Maserati	85.36
1958	Collins-P. Hill	Ferrari	86.6
1959	Daigh-Gendebien-Gurney-P. Hill	Ferrari	81.47
1960	Gendebien-Herrmann	Porsche	84.93
1961	Gendebien-P. Hill	Ferrari	90.7
1962	Bonnier-Bianchi	Ferrari	89.14
1963	Surtees-Scarfiotti	Ferrari	90.39
1964	Parker-Magiolo	Ferrari	92.36
1965	Hall-Sharp	Chaparral-Chevy	84.72
1966	Miles-Ruby	Ford	98.63
1967	Andretti-McLaren	Ford	102.92
1968	Herrmann-Siffert	Porsche	102.51
1969	Ickx-Oliver	Ford	103.36
1970	Vaccarella-Gionti-Andretti	Ferrari	107.29

24 Hours of Daytona

Year	Winners	Car	MPH
1964	Rodrigues-P. Hill	Ferrari	98.23
1965	Miles-Ruby	Ford	99.94
1966	Miles-Ruby	Ford	107.51
1967	Amon-Bandini	Ferrari	105.68
1968	Elford-Neerpasch-Stommelen-Siffert-Herrmann	Porsche	106.83
1969	Donohue-Parsons	Lola-Chevy	99.26
1970	Rodriguez-Kinnonen	Porsche	114.88

Los Angeles Times Grand Prix
Riverside

Year	Winners	Car	MPH
1958	Chuck Daigh	Scarab Chevy	88.76
1959	Phil Hill	Ferrari	89.09
1960	Bill Krause	Maserati	91.48
1961	Jack Brabham	Cooper Monaco	94.06
1962	Roger Penske	Zerex-Cooper	95.57
1963	Dave McDonald	Cobra-Cooper-Ford	96.23
1964	Parnelli Jones	Cobra-Cooper-Ford	96.24
1965	Hap Sharp	Chaparral-Chevy	102.98
1966	John Surtees	Lola-Chevy	106.86
1967	Bruce McLaren	McLaren-Chevy	114.23
1968	Bruce McLaren	McLaren-Chevy	114.35
1969	Denis Hulme	McLaren-Chevy	120.67

CANADIAN—AMERICAN CHALLENGE CUP

Year	Series Winner	Earnings
1966	John Surtees	$ 48,100
1967	Bruce McLaren	62,300
1968	Denis Hulme	93,060
1969	Bruce McLaren	160,950

GRAND PRIX DRIVER RANKINGS
Through 1969

Consideration is given only to the drivers' performances on the Grand Prix circuit. There is little to choose between the great Argentinian, Fangio, and the great Scot, Jim Clark, but Fangio won more "world" titles and almost as many Grand Prix races in an era when fewer were available to him than were available to Clark. The Grand Prix "world" championship dates back only to 1950; no titles were awarded and records are incomplete prior to 1950.

Rank	Driver	Country	GP Titles	GP Victories
1	Juan Fangio	Argentina	5	23†
2	Jim Clark	Scotland	2	24
3	Tazio Nuvolari	Italy	—	*
4	Rudolf Caracciola	Germany	—	*
5	Alberto Ascari	Italy	2	15*
6	Stirling Moss	England	0	16†
7	Jack Brabham	Australia	3	13
8	Graham Hill	England	2	14
9	Achille Varzi	Italy	—	*
10	Louis Chiron	France	—	*
	Robert Benoist	France	—	*
	Jean-Pierre Wimille	France	—	*

† Shared victories count one-half victory each.
* Totals incomplete.

INDIVIDUAL DRIVERS' RECORDS

A. J. FOYT
Through 1969

USAC National champion five times—1960, 1961, 1963, 1964, and 1967. Runner-up twice—1962 and 1965.

Indianapolis 500 champion three times—1961, 1964, and 1967.

Indianapolis pole winner twice—1965 and 1969.

All-time leader, championship race victories—42.

Most championship race victories one season—10.

Most championship race victories in a row—7.

Second in sprint car victories in USAC—26.

Winner 19 midget car victories, 21 stock car victories, in USAC.

All-time leader victories in all classes—108.

USAC stock car champion—1968.

24 Hours of Le Mans, co-champion—1967.

Nassau Trophy winner—1963.

Daytona 400 champion—1964 and 1965.

All-time money winner—more than $1 million.

Championship Trail Victories

1960 (4)

No.	Place	Distance	Track	No.	Place	Distance	Track
1	Du Quoin, Ill.	100	Dirt	3	Sacramento, Calif.	100	Dirt
2	Indianapolis, Ind.	100	Dirt	4	Phoenix, Ariz.	100	Dirt

1961 (4)

5	Indianapolis, Ind.	500	Paved	7	Du Quoin, Ill.	100	Dirt
6	Langhorne, Pa.	100	Dirt	8	Indianapolis, Ind.	100	Dirt

1962 (4)

9	Trenton, N.J.	100	Paved	11	Langhorne, Pa.	100	Dirt
10	Milwaukee, Wis.	100	Paved	12	Sacramento, Calif.	100	Dirt

1963 (5)

13	Trenton, N.J.	100	Paved	16	Du Quoin, Ill.	100	Dirt
14	Langhorne, Pa.	100	Dirt	17	Trenton, N.J.	200	Paved
15	Trenton, N.J.	150	Paved				

1964 (10)

18	Phoenix, Ariz.	100	Paved	23	Trenton, N.J.	150	Paved
19	Trenton, N.J.	100	Paved	24	Springfield, Ill.	100	Dirt
20	Indianapolis, Ind.	500	Paved	25	Du Quoin, Ill.	100	Dirt
21	Milwaukee, Wis.	100	Paved	26	Indianapolis, Ind.	100	Dirt
22	Langhorne, Pa.	100	Dirt	27	Sacramento, Calif.	100	Dirt

1965 (5)

No.	Place	Distance	Track	No.	Place	Distance	Track
28	Trenton, N.J.	150	Paved	31	Trenton, N.J.	200	Paved
29	Springfield, Ill.	100	Dirt	32	Phoenix, Ariz.	200	Paved
30	Indianapolis, Ind.	100	Dirt				

1966 (0)

1967 (5)

No.	Place	Distance	Track	No.	Place	Distance	Track
33	Indianapolis, Ind.	500	Paved	36	Trenton, N.J.	200	Paved
34	Springfield, Ill.	100	Dirt	37	Sacramento, Calif.	100	Dirt
35	Du Quoin, Ill.	100	Dirt				

1968 (4)

No.	Place	Distance	Track	No.	Place	Distance	Track
38	Castle Rock, Colo.	150	Paved road	40	Hanford, Calif.	150	Paved
39	Indianapolis, Ind.	100	Dirt	41	Sacramento, Calif.	100	Dirt

1969 (1)

No.	Place	Distance	Track
42	Indianapolis, Ind.	100	Dirt

Other Major Victories

Year	Comp.	Place	Miles	Track
1959	Sprint	Salem, Ind.	50	Paved
1960	Sprint	Langhorne, Pa.	50	Dirt
	Midget	Los Angeles, Calif.	60	Dirt
1961	Midget	Los Angeles, Calif.	75	Dirt
1962	Stock	Los Angeles, Calif.	50	Dirt
	Sprint	Salem, Ind.	50	Paved
	Stock	Detroit, Mich.	150	Dirt
1963	Sprint	Williams Grove, Pa.	50	Dirt
	Stock	Indianapolis, Ind.	300	Paved road
	Stock	Langhorne, Pa.	150	Dirt
	Stock	Indianapolis, Ind.	100	Dirt
	Sports	Nassau, Bahamas	252	Paved road
1964	Sprint	Phoenix, Ariz.	50	Dirt
	Stock	Daytona, Fla.	400	Paved
	Stock	Indianapolis, Ind.	100	Dirt
	Stock	Langhorne, Pa.	250	Dirt
	Stock	Hanford, Calif.	200	Paved
1965	Stock	Daytona, Fla.	400	Paved
	Stock	Indianapolis, Ind.	100	Dirt
	Midget	Terre Haute, Ind.	50	Dirt
1967	Sports	Le Mans, France	3,220	Paved road
	Stock	Milwaukee, Wis.	250	Paved
1968	Stock	Indianapolis, Ind.	250	Paved road
	Stock	Milwaukee, Wis.	200	Paved
	Stock	Indianapolis, Ind.	100	Dirt
1969	Stock	Dover, Del.	300	Paved

Indianapolis 500 Record

Yr.	Qual.	Spd.	Finish	Avg. Speed	Yr.	Qual.	Spd.	Finish	Avg. Speed
1958	12	143.1	16	Spun	1965	1	161.2	15	Eng. failure
1959	17	142.6	10	133.2	1966	18	161.3	26	Crash
1960	16	143.4	25	Car failure	1967	4	164.2	1	151.2
1961	7	145.9	1	139.1	1968	8	166.8	20	Car failure
1962	5	149.0	23	Lost wheel	1969	1	170.5	8	137.8
1963	8	150.6	3	142.2	1970	3	170.0	10	Eng. failure
1964	5	154.6	1	147.3					

TOTALS: Starts—13, finishes—6, won—3, 3rd—1, pole—2.

USAC Totals
Through 1969 season

Division	Starts	Victories	Approx. Earnings
Championship	175	42	$ 910,800
Sprints	122	26	78,012
Midgets	97	19	23,507
Stocks	74	21	146,567
TOTALS	468	108	$1,158,886

USAC Earnings

1956	$ 68	1963	$102,055
1957	9,337	1964	179,448
1958	22,776	1965	76,186
1959	24,882	1966	30,418
1960	58,558	1967	165,817
1961	132,177	1968	151,203
1962	57,851	1969	146,567

RODGER WARD

Championship Trail Victories
Ovals

No.	Place	Distance	Track	No.	Place	Distance	Track
			1953 (2)				
1	Detroit	100	Dirt	2	Springfield	100	Dirt
			1957 (3)				
3	Milwaukee	100	Paved	5	Sacramento	100	Dirt
4	Springfield	100	Dirt				
			1958 (2)				
6	Milwaukee	200	Paved	7	Trenton	100	Paved
			1959 (4)				
8	Indianapolis	500	Paved	10	Milwaukee	200	Paved
9	Du Quoin	100	Dirt	11	Indianapolis	100	Dirt
			1960 (2)				
12	Trenton	100	Paved	13	Milwaukee	100	Paved
			1961 (3)				
14	Milwaukee	100	Paved	16	Sacramento	100	Dirt
15	Syracuse	100	Dirt				
			1962 (4)				
17	Indianapolis	500	Paved	19	Milwaukee	200	Paved
18	Trenton	150	Paved	20	Syracuse	100	Dirt
			1963 (5)				
21	Milwaukee	100	Paved	24	Sacramento	100	Dirt
22	Springfield	100	Dirt	25	Phoenix	100	Dirt
23	Indianapolis	100	Dirt				
			1966 (1)				
26	Trenton	100	Paved				

Indianapolis 500 Record

Yr.	Qual.	Spd.	Finish	Avg. Speed	Yr.	Qual.	Spd.	Finish	Avg. Speed
1951	25	134.8	27	Eng. failure	1959	6	144.0	1	135.8
1952	29	134.1	23	Eng. failure	1960	3	145.5	2	138.6
1953	10	137.4	16	Stalled	1961	4	146.1	3	138.5
1954	16	139.2	22	Stalled	1962	2	149.3	1	140.2
1955	30	135.0	28	Crash	1963	4	149.8	4	141.0
1956	15	141.1	8	124.9	1964	3	154.4	2	146.3
1957	24	141.3	30	Eng. failure	1965		Did not qualify		
1958	11	143.2	20	Eng. failure	1966	3	159.4	15	Car failure

TOTALS: Starts—15, finishes—7, won—2, 2nd—2, 3rd—1, 4th—1.

MARIO ANDRETTI

Championship Cars

1965 (1)

No.	Place	Distance	Track
1	Indianapolis (Raceway Park)	150	Paved road course

1966 (8)

No.	Place	Distance	Track
2	Milwaukee	100	Paved mile oval
3	Langhorne	100	Paved mile oval
4	Atlanta	300	Paved 1½-mile oval course
5	Indianapolis (Raceway Park)	150	Paved road course
6	Milwaukee	200	Paved mile oval
7	Hoosier Hundred (Indy Fairgrounds)	100	Dirt mile oval
8	Trenton	200	Paved mile oval
9	Phoenix	200	Paved mile oval

1967 (8)

No.	Place	Distance	Track
10	Trenton	150	Paved mile oval
11	Indianapolis (Raceway Park)	150	Paved road course
12	Langhorne	150	Paved mile oval
13	St. Jovite, Canada	100	Paved road course
14	St. Jovite, Canada	100	Paved road course
15	Milwaukee	200	Paved mile oval
16	Hoosier Hundred (Indy Fairgrounds)	100	Dirt mile oval
17	Phoenix	200	Paved mile oval

1968 (4)

No.	Place	Distance	Track
18	St. Jovite, Canada	100	Paved road course
19	St. Jovite, Canada	100	Paved road course
20	Du Quoin	100	Dirt mile oval
21	Trenton	200	Paved mile oval

1969 (9)

No.	Place	Distance	Track
22	Hanford	150	Paved mile oval
23	Indianapolis	500	Paved 2½-mile oval
24	Nazareth	100	Paved mile oval
25	Trenton	200	Paved mile oval
26	Springfield	100	Dirt mile oval
27	Pikes Peak Hill Climb		Mountain course
28	Trenton	300	Paved mile oval
29	Seattle	100	Paved road course
30	Riverside	300	Paved road course

Stock Cars

1967

	Distance	Track
Daytona	500	Paved 2½-mile oval

Sports Cars

1967

	Track
12 Hours of Sebring (with Bruce McLaren)	Paved road course

1970

	Track
12 Hours of Sebring (with two others)	Paved road course

Championship Car Record

Year	Starts	Victories	Natl. Title
1964	10	0	11th
1965	16	1	1st
1966	15	8	1st
1967	19	8	2nd
1968	23	4	2nd
1969	23	9	1st
TOTALS	106	30	THREE TITLES

LOU MEYER'S INDIANAPOLIS 500 RECORD

Yr.	Qual.	Spd.	Finish	Avg. Speed	Yr.	Qual.	Spd.	Finish	Avg. Speed
1928	13	111.3	1	99.4	1934	13	112.3	18	Eng. failure
1929	8	114.7	2	95.5	1935	4	117.9	12	100.2
1930	2	111.2	4	95.2	1936	28	114.1	1	109.0
1931	25	113.9	34	Eng. failure	1937	5	119.6	4	110.7
1932	7	112.4	33	Eng. failure	1938	12	120.5	16	Eng. failure
1933	6	116.9	1	104.1	1939	2	130.0	12	Crash

TOTALS: Starts—12, finishes—8, won—3, 2nd—1, 4th—2.

WILBUR SHAW'S INDIANAPOLIS 500 RECORD

Yr.	Qual.	Spd.	Finish	Avg. Speed	Yr.	Qual.	Spd.	Finish	Avg. Speed
1927	19	104.4	4	93.1	1935	20	116.8	2	105.9
1928	29	—	25	Eng. failure	1936	9	117.5	7	104.2
1929		Did not compete			1937	2	122.7	1	113.5
1930	25	106.1	22	Eng. failure	1938	7	120.9	2	115.5
1931	—	—	30	Crash, relief	1939	3	128.9	1	115.0
1932	22	114.3	17	Car failure	1940	2	127.0	1	114.2
1933	23	115.4	2	101.7	1941	3	127.8	18	Crash
1934	2	117.6	28	Eng. failure					

TOTALS: Starts—13, finishes—8, won—3, 2nd—3, 4th—1.

MAURI ROSE'S INDIANAPOLIS 500 RECORD

Yr.	Qual.	Spd.	Finish	Avg. Speed	Yr.	Qual.	Spd.	Finish	Avg. Speed
1933	42	117.6	35	Eng. failure	1941	1	128.6	26	Eng. failure
1934	4	116.0	2	104.6		Relief—128 laps		1	115.1
1935	10	116.4	20	Eng. failure	1946	9	124.0	23	Crash
1936	30	113.8	4	107.2	1947	3	124.0	1	116.3
1937	8	118.5	18	Eng. failure	1948	3	129.1	1	119.8
1938	9	119.7	13	Eng. failure	1949	10	127.7	13	Eng. failure
1939	8	124.8	8	109.5	1950	3	132.3	3	121.7
1940	3	125.6	3	113.5	1951	5	133.4	14	Crash

TOTALS: Starts—15, finishes—8, wins—2½, 2nd—1, 3rd—2, 4th—1, pole—1.

RICHARD PETTY

Won more NASCAR Grand National races than any other driver—91 through 1968.

Won more money than any other—$580,759 through 1968.

Won more races in a row than any other driver—10.

Won more races in a single season than any driver—27 in 1967.

Won eight superspeedway races at Daytona, Darlington, Atlanta, and Rockingham. Also won at Riverside. First driver to win Daytona 500 twice, and in succession.

Won NASCAR Grand National driving championship twice—1964 and 1967.

Major Victories

Year	Race	Track	Car	Avg. Speed
1964	Daytona 500	Daytona Speedway	'64 Plymouth	154.334
1965	Daytona 500	Daytona Speedway	'66 Plymouth	160.627
1966	Dixie 400	Atlanta Raceway	'66 Plymouth	130.244
1966	Rebel 400	Darlington Raceway	'66 Plymouth	131.993
1967	Rebel 400	Darlington Raceway	'67 Plymouth	125.738
1967	Southern 500	Darlington Raceway	'67 Plymouth	130.423
1967	Carolina 500	North Carolina Speedway	'67 Plymouth	104.682
1968	American 500	North Carolina Speedway	'68 Plymouth	105.060
1969	Riverside 500	Riverside Raceway	'69 Ford	105.516

Daytona 500 Record

Year	Start	Finish	Laps Run	Money Won
1959	—	57	—	—
1960	19	3	200	$ 6,450
1962	10	2	200	10,250
1963	23	6	198	3,570
1964	2	1	200	33,300
1966	1	1	198	17,500
1967	—	8	193	2,750
1968	—	8	198	4,350
1969	—	8	192	3,750
1970	8	7	181	2,500

Grand National Career

Year	Races	Wins	Top 5	Total Miles	Money Won	Driver Standing
1958	9	0	0	410	$ 760	—
1959	21	0	6	2,699	7,830	—
1960	40	3	16	6,015	35,180	2
1961	42	2	19	5,392	22,696	8
1962	52	8	32	7,559	52,960	2
1963	54	14	30	7,879	47,765	2
1964	61	9	37	9,467	98,810	1
1965	14	4	10	1,692	16,450	—
1966	39	8	20	6,458	78,930	3
1967	48	27	38	9,337	130,275	1
1968	49	16	31	8,906	89,103	3
1969	50	10	31	10,425	109,180	2
TOTALS	479	101	270	76,239	$689,939	

LEE ROY YARBROUGH'S 1969 SEASON

Starts	Victories	Top 5	Top 10	Money Won
30	7	16	21	$190,908

Superspeedway Victories

No.	Month	Race	Track	Speed	Earnings
1	February	Daytona 500	Daytona, Fla.	157.950	$38,950
2	April	Rebel 400	Darlington, S.C.	131.571	14,700
3	May	World 600	Charlotte, N.C.	134.000	30,627
4	July	Firecracker 400	Daytona, Fla.	160.875	22,175
5	August	Dixie 500	Atlanta, Ga.	133.001	18,620
6	September	Southern 500	Darlington, S.C.	105.612	21,850
7	October	American 500	Rockingham, N.C.	119.932	17,620

PHIL HILL'S MAJOR VICTORIES

Year	Type of Car	Co-Driver	Race
1955	Sports Car	—	Nassau Trophy Race
1956	Sports Car	O. Trintignant	Grand Prix of Sweden
1956	Sports Car	—	5 Hours of Sicily
1957	Sports Car	P. Collins	Grand Prix of Venezuela
1957	Sports Car	—	Nassau Governor's Cup
1958	Sports Car	P. Collins	Grand Prix of Argentina
1958	Sports Car	P. Collins	12 Hours of Sebring, Fla.
1958	Sports Car	O. Gendebien	24 Hours of Le Mans
1959	Sports Car	O. Gendebien, Gurney, Daigh	12 Hours of Sebring
1959	Sports Car	—	Riverside Grand Prix
1960	Formula One	—	Grand Prix of Europe (Monza, Italy)
1960	Sports Car	Allison	Grand Prix of Argentina
1961	Sports Car	O. Gendebien	12 Hours of Sebring
1961	Sports Car	O. Gendebien	24 Hours of Le Mans
1961	Formula One	—	Grand Prix of Belgium (Spa)
1961	Formula One	—	Grand Prix of Italy (Monza)
1962	Sports Car	O. Gendebien	Nurburgring, Germany, Enduro
1962	Sports Car	O. Gendebien	24 Hours of Le Mans
1962	Formula One	—	Grand Prix of Germany
1964	Sports Car	P. Rodriguez	24 Hours of Daytona, Fla.
1966	Sports Car	J. Bonnier	1,000 KMs of Nurburgring, Germany
1967	Sports Car	M. Spence	BOAC 500

DAN GURNEY'S MAJOR VICTORIES
Grand Prix Formula One Cars

1962   Grand Prix of France
1964   Grand Prix of France
1964   Grand Prix of Mexico
1967   Grand Prix of Belgium

Sports Cars

1960   Nurburgring 1000 KMs (with Stirling Moss)
1967   24 Hours of Le Mans (with A. J. Foyt)
1967   Race of Champions, Brands Notch, England

U.S. Championship Cars

1967   Riverside 300 (Paved road course)
1968   Riverside 300 (Paved road course)
1968   Mosport, Canada, 100 (Paved road course)
        Mosport, Canada, 100 (Twin races)
1969   Minnesota 100 (Paved road course)
        Indianapolis 100 (Paved road course)

Stock Cars

1963, 1964,   Riverside 500 (Paved road course)
1965, 1966,
and 1968

U.S. SPORTS CAR AND GRAND PRIX RANKINGS

1. Phil Hill
2. Dan Gurney

ALL-TIME WORLD DRIVER RANKINGS

Consideration is given not only to the dominance of the driver in his own circuit, but to his versatility, his success in invading other circuits. A. J. Foyt not only dominated the United States championship trail as no man ever dominated his circuit, but won stock car races in NASCAR competition and sports car races in competition with the world's greatest sports car and Grand Prix drivers. Fangio dominated the Grand Prix circuits as no other did, but Clark did almost as well and won United States championship trail races, too, including the Indianapolis 500, the world's single most competitive racing event.

1. A. J. Foyt (U.S.)
2. Jim Clark (Scotland)
3. Juan Fangio (Argentina)
4. Tazio Nuvolari (Italy)
5. Rudolf Caracciola (Germany)

6. Alberto Ascari (Italy)
7. Dan Gurney (U.S.)
8. Mario Andretti (U.S.)
9. Rodger Ward (U.S.)
10. Ralph De Palma (U.S.)

Honorable Mention

Richard Petty (U.S.), Stirling Moss (England), Fred Lorenzen (U.S.), Tommy Milton (U.S.), Phil Hill (U.S.), Fireball Roberts (U.S.), Junior Johnson (U.S.), Lee Petty (U.S.), Parnelli Jones (U.S.), Don Garlits (U.S.), Mickey Thompson (U.S.), Earl Cooper (U.S.), Tony Bettenhausen (U.S.), Lou Meyer (U.S.), Wilbur Shaw (U.S.), Jimmy Bryan (U.S.), Ted Horn (U.S.), Rex Mays (U.S.), Jimmy Murphy (U.S.), Ralph Mulford (U.S.), Jack Brabham (Australia), Graham Hill (England), Achille Varzi (Italy), Louis Chiron (France).

INDEX

ABOUT THE AUTHOR

Bill Libby is the author of the recent and very successful *Parnelli*, the story of auto racing's Parnelli Jones, and of *Clown*, on basketball's Rod Hundley, just published by Cowles. Libby has ten additional books to his credit and has been a frequent contributor to sports anthologies, as well as to most of America's major magazines. An alumnus of Indiana University, he and his family now make their home in Los Angeles.